# HEALTH

## MIND BODY SOUL

Published in the United States by
**Insight Publishing Company**
**707 West Main Street, Suite 5**
**Sevierville, TN 37862**
800-987-7771
www.insightpublishing.com



Disclaimer: This book is a compilation of ideas from numerous experts who have each contributed a chapter. As such, the views expressed in each chapter are of those who were interviewed and not necessarily of the interviewer or Insight Publishing.

ISBN- 978-1-60013-869-0

10 9 8 7 6 5 4 3 2 1

# MESSAGE FROM THE PUBLISHER

Without good health, success in business and in personal life is difficult if not impossible to achieve. The first step in this undertaking is to understand the interactions of our mind, our body, and our soul. We need to realize that each of these components affects the other, which is a more holistic approach to realizing optimal health. And what does "holistic" mean? According to the *Merriam Webster Dictionary*, holistic means "relating to or concerned with complete systems rather than with the analysis of, treatment of, or dissection into parts." Sounds like a good idea to me.

We have gathered insights from several authors who have definitive ideas about this hot topic of health. The interviews I conducted with them will provide you with information you can use to get healthy and stay that way.

The conversations in this book will give you a new appreciation for how the human body is made and how it interacts in mind, body, and soul. The authors featured in *Health: Mind, Body, Soul* will give you trustworthy advice about how you can be healthy and stay healthy. All of us at Insight Publishing want to share with our readers the valuable tips these contributors have to offer so that you, too, can have health in your mind, body, and soul.

DAVID E. WRIGHT
ISN WORKS
& INSIGHT PUBLISHING

# TABLE OF CONTENTS

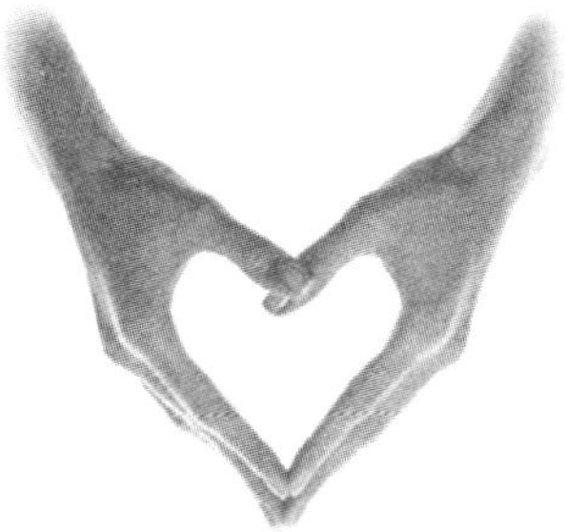

Chapter One

# Slowing the Aging Process and Living Healthier

## with Dr. Richard Bunch

THE INTERVIEW

DAVID WRIGHT (WRIGHT)

Today I am talking with Dr. Richard Bunch. Dr. Bunch, welcome to *Health: Mind Body, Soul.*

Dr. Bunch, you are well known nationally as a physical therapist and an expert in wellness and injury prevention. Aging has been a big topic lately with the graying of America's Baby Boomers. Would you tell us how we can slow the aging process and improve the quality of our health at the same time?

RICHARD BUNCH, PHD (BUNCH)

Aging is a biological process that we cannot avoid. It is becoming very important these days as we now see such a large portion of the U.S. working population aging, a phenomenon that can be referred to as the "silver tsunami." Due to a poor economy, more and more people over the age of sixty-five are staying in the workforce and delaying retirement. Consequently, it's become more of a challenge for older workers to maintain adequate physical fitness (e.g., strength and endurance) to keep up with the normal pace of work and perform more labor-intensive job tasks safely. As a response to this growing problem, it has become necessary for employers to see how they can accommodate older workers so they may benefit from their experience and intellect while helping them at the same time keep pace and be productive.

There have been a number of theories as to why aging occurs, including ones that claim it is programmed by gene expression changes and that it is the accumulative damage of biological processes. Dr. Leonard Hayflick in 1961, at the Wistar Institute, Philadelphia, demonstrated that a population of normal human fetal cells in a cell culture divide between forty and sixty times before cell division can no longer occur and cellular death occurs. This phenomenon became known as the "The Hayflick Limit." The age-limiting factor appears to deal with the progressive shortening of protective tips on the ends of our chromosomes called telomeres that occurs with each cellular replication. When the telomeres shorten to a point that makes cell division no longer possible, death occurs.

So it's not a question of stopping the aging process, as we are all going to age and of course die. However, if DNA replication can occur forty to sixty times before we die, the question becomes how long does it take for those forty to sixty replications to occur? The answer is that it varies. You can replace your entire DNA in sixty years, seventy years, eighty years, one hundred years, or one hundred and ten years. It depends on several factors that influence the speed in which your DNA replicates and how fast you age. If we can slow down the replication process, then we can theoretically live longer.

WRIGHT

So do you really believe we can slow down the aging process and avoid illnesses with age?

BUNCH

Yes I do, and research supports my opinion. The good news is that we can slow down the aging process to a significant degree and prevent a large percentage of illnesses that affect us. Some people believe that genetics dictates how long we will live. I will admit that genetics plays a role. Certainly some people have a better genetic make-up than others and faulty genetics can lead to inherited traits that develop into disease, some of which are life-shortening. For instance, there are genetic faults that can cause or increase the risk of cancer, diabetes, heart disease, etc.

However, I propose that if we seek to improve longevity and the quality of life, we need to take genetics out of the equation and focus on what we can change—lifestyle. After all, we cannot change our parents, but we can certainly change our lifestyle. The lifestyle modification approach to slowing the aging process is based on the fact that the majority of illnesses and diseases that lead to our early demise are much more related to lifestyle factors than genetic factors. In fact, one can say that genetics is the gun, but it is our lifestyle that is the trigger. For example, if your relatives suffer with a lot of heart disease and they are all overweight from overeating or from eating the wrong types of foods, and they are smokers and are sedentary, then perhaps their cardiac problems deal more with lifestyle habits than genetics. This does not rule out that genetic factors may still exist, but improving lifestyle can compensate for poor genetics.

Research indicates that most serious illnesses and diseases caused by lifestyle are related to primarily three major factors: poor nutrition, lack of exercise, and excessive or chronic stress. With lack of exercise and poor nutrition, we can end up clogging our arteries with fat that leads to thickening and hardening of arteries with age. In addition, many of our smaller arteries, called capillaries, that deliver crucial oxygen to tissues, degenerate (a process I refer to as vascular atrophy). When you slow down blood flow to tissues because of changes that occur due to lack of exercise and poor nutrition, you deprive many tissues from oxygen and nutrients that we need to stay alive longer.

So one of the first things we can do is cut down on two well identified harmful substances in our diet—saturated fat, including deadly trans fats, and sugar. Of the two substances, sugar is suspected to contribute more to obesity and heart disease than saturated fat. The body, via insulin, actually converts excess sugar into fat that clogs our arteries. Elevation of dietary sugar from high glycemic foods (such as processed foods that break down into sugar rapidly) leads to a condition known as hyperinsulinemia. I believe hyperinsulinemia is much more harmful to us as we age than most people realize.

Hyperinsulinemia is a condition in which there are excess levels of circulating insulin in the blood. Insulin is a hormone secreted by the pancreas in response to high blood sugar levels. When we eat a lot of high glycemic foods, insulin levels in the blood increase. The problem with this is that insulin will inhibit the effects of fat-burning hormones like glucagon while converting excess blood sugar called glucose into fat called triglycerides. High levels of triglycerides are a known risk factor for heart disease. In essence then, insulin actually "insulates" us from burning fat while at the same time increases our fat storage! Therefore, hyperinsulinemia is considered to be one of the major contributors to obesity today. Other complications from hyperinsulinemia include:

- Hypoglycemia
- Diabetes
- PCOS (Polycystic Ovarian Syndrome)
- Hypertension or high blood pressure (insulin increases sodium retention by the renal tubules)
- Coronary Artery Disease (increased insulin damages endothelial cells lining the inside of the arteries)

As we get older, more fiber intake is extremely important. Eating raw vegetables and fruits are essential to a healthy diet. The problem with the way we eat nowadays is that we do not eat enough healthy vegetables and fruits. And even when we do put them in our diets we too often cook them until we destroy the fiber content and nutritional benefits that vegetables and fruits offer.

There are several books written today addressing the benefits of eating raw veggies and fruits. It is like going back to the way our great, great ancestors ate. If what you eat can be pulled off a tree, bush, or pulled out of the ground, and it's not poisonous, it's probably very good for you. Meat, egg, and milk products derived from free grazing animals that eat natural grass and leaves containing nutrients will help build our immune system, which becomes compromised with age. Vitamin supplements should be considered if the quality of food eaten is generally poor. Another benefit that people should consider is the exposure to sunshine without the effects of any sunscreen for about twenty minutes a day. This sun exposure is extremely important for converting Vitamin D for prevention of certain cancers and heart disease.

There is still debate on the true benefits of taking nutritional supplements regularly. A good general rule is to always take them when eating as digestion is the best route for proper absorption of vitamins and minerals. Very high dosages of vitamins should be avoided. Certain vitamins, such as vitamin A, can be harmful at high dosages. People should consult with a medical physician prior to taking any nutritional supplements if they have a medical condition or if they are taking medications.

Although we must obviously reduce fat and sugar in our diet, and eat more vegetables and fruit, we must also exercise regularly. In order to help get rid of excess circulatory fat and sugar that circulates through our body we must metabolize it, or in other words burn it off. It's no big secret that as we get older we become less active as more and more jobs are computer-based and sedentary. We sit much longer and research shows that people who sit for long periods of time each day will not live as long as people who do more daily standing and walking around. Remember, we are human beings who are physiologically designed for movement—to run through the woods, climb trees, tend to our crops, and hunt animals for food. We were never designed to sit in front of a computer or television all day.

So it is obvious that we need to become much more active. I know, we have all heard that a million times, but people continue to avoid exercise. After all, it takes a very active commitment to your lifestyle to get up and move. But the benefits are huge. For example, exercise lowers the risk of obesity and related cancers, improves bone density, which normally decreases with age, and boosts testosterone levels in men.

Aerobic exercise (walking, elliptical system, stair-stepper, etc.) should be performed at least thirty to forty-five minutes, seven days a week.

As we get older, of course, we have to change our aerobic exercise patterns from high-impact to low-impact. This means we should perform more low-impact, joint-friendly exercises such as swimming, walking, or working out on elliptical or gliding systems. This is much better for our joints as compared to running and pounding our feet on cement. Low-impact exercising reduces the effect on the joints and, in return, will help prevent development of arthritis.

Strengthening exercises are as important to health as aerobics. Strength training should be conducted three to four days per week. Strengthening muscle increases our calorie burning capacity, making it easier to control weight. Strengthening exercises increase bone density and stabilizes DNA activity. And stabilizing DNA activity reduces the risk of cancer!

Instead of using free weights that can cause a sudden tear of a muscle easier with age, we should use hydraulic exercise equipment or elastic exercise bands that have variable degrees of resistance. Variable resistance will allow the body to adapt to the actual force exerted at all points in the joint range of motion. When using a free weight, for example a twenty-pound dumbbell, the weight remains at a fixed twenty pounds throughout all points in the range of motion. As such, free weights offer no accommodation to weaker points in the range of motion as do elastic exercise bands. Therefore, you can actually overload the muscles at a certain point in the range of motion with free weights. As we get older, recovery from muscle tendon tears require more time. If there is significant vascular atrophy due to aging and lack of exercise, an older person can become disabled from a slow healing tendon tear for months, if not years.

Another important lifestyle factor that adversely affects the health of older people is stress. Stress hormones can do very bad things to your mental and physical state, and reduce your ability to cope. Circulating stress hormones have been shown by research to be higher in an older person than a younger person. As we pass fifty years of age, there are actual physiological changes in the brain that result in a higher baseline level of stress hormones such as cortisol and neurotransmitters such as adrenaline. So that means our threshold for stress becomes lower as we age. Older people often report that things that use to not cause them to feel stressed when they were younger, now cause them to feel much more stressed.

As I mentioned, cortisol is a stress hormone that is produced at higher levels when we age. It is important to understand that cortisol at high levels is very destructive to living long because cortisol has two major effects on our body. Cortisol converts protein into sugar and increases fat in our blood stream. Cortisol increases the bad cholesterol carrier called LDL that brings fat to the linings of our arteries. Why does cortisol do this? Remember, cortisol is a stress hormone and the purpose of a stress reaction is to prepare a person to run away from danger or to fight (the fight or flight response). I will call this the primitive stress reaction. Sugar and fat are the primary fuels for short-term and long-term muscle activity needed for fight or flight. This has never changed and that is why cortisol continues to increase fat and sugar in our blood vessels when we perceive stress.

In our modern world, most of our stress deals with non-life-threatening issues such as our economy, personal relationships, divorce, raising teenagers, etc. However, the brain doesn't recognize the difference between modern sources of stress and primitive sources of stress. So when we're under any kind of stress we experience elevations in blood levels of sugar and fat due to the effects of stress-induced cortisol production. If we had the stress control mechanisms to keep cortisol down that we had when we're younger, it would be easier for an older person to manage stress.

Another problem with having a higher level of baseline stress hormones as we age is that these hormones interfere with our abilities to focus and learn. Elevated stress hormones cause excitation of hundreds of thousands of nerve cells in our brainstem that are normally "quiet" when we are younger. The result is foggy thinking and short-term memory problems. It is like using a computer when the hard drive is 90 percent full. A goal for the older person then is to relax the excess brain activity and reduce the background noise. When this happens, we can concentrate and learn better. There is less memory loss. This can be accomplished by learning to better manage stress.

In order to better manage stress as we age, we must take two steps. The first step is acquiring a sheet of paper that has two columns that can be used to write down notes. Sit in a quiet place and be brutally honest with yourself as you write down a list of issues that are causing stress in your life in the left hand column. We will call these issues "stress factors." Once the stress factor list is completed, write down action steps to resolve each stress factor in the right hand column. For example, a stress factor may be excess body weight. The action step can be to start on a diet and exercise program immediately. People will often find that by systematically defining stress factors and creating action steps, the process of just doing this activity will actually lower stress. Managing and reducing stress occurs when we develop more control of our life.

The second major step to managing stress is to exercise and eat healthy. From a total health perspective, exercise is the single most important thing you can do, with more health benefits than any medicine. Exercise produces endorphins, a morphine-like substance in the brain that reduces the effects of stress hormones. It relaxes the arteries, lowers levels of stress hormones like adrenaline and cortisone, reduces blood sugar, and elevates HDL, the good cholesterol carrier.

HDL will bring cholesterol out of your blood vessels (thus cleaning them out) and bring it to your liver where it is converted into harmless bile. This is an exact opposite reaction to stress-induced production of the bad cholesterol carrier, LDL. Exercise also helps to prevent abnormal heart rhythms, heart attacks, and strokes.

WRIGHT

Interesting. So what can people do about the effects of aging on eyesight, hearing, and balance?

BUNCH

Loss of eyesight, hearing, and balance are some of the most common neurological problems that we see in the older person. At about the age of forty, on average, we start noticing changes in our vision. Glaucoma, cataracts, and macular degeneration are common aging eye problems that can seriously affect the field of vision and if not addressed, can even lead to blindness. Many of us begin to notice the more insidious changes in vision with age such as slower glare recovery time, poorer night vision, or impaired scotopic vision (reduced ability to see in dim light). This is usually most noted when trying to read a menu in a dimly lit restaurant. So taking care of our eyes becomes very important. The following tips for eye health are highly recommended:

- Increase ingestion of antioxidants.
- Take baby aspirin (eighty-one mg) daily before sleep if not aspirin sensitive.
- Avoid smoking.
- Control blood pressure and blood sugar levels.
- Reduce eye exposure to direct sunlight. Wear sunglasses and a hat with a brim.
- Wear safety glasses when working.
- Reduce alcohol intake.

- Avoid long-term use of corticosteroids.
- After age forty, undergo an eye exam every two years.

High frequency hearing loss is the most common hearing impairment we see in older people. People should always wear hearing protection in areas of sustained loud noises such as football games or when shooting firearms. Listening to very loud music destroys hearing over time, and many young people find this out the hard way as they hit their forties.

People should go for regular hearing checks every two years after age forty to check for high frequency hearing loss. Hearing aids are now becoming very small, cosmetic, and unobtrusive. Therefore, vanity-related reasons to not wear them are becoming much more difficult to defend. Hearing is one of our primary senses that is important to help protect us against accidents and can improve our abilities to learn and remember by hearing what is being said more clearly. Hearing and seeing better simply improves the quality of our lives as well.

We also see that people experience a degradation of balance as they get older and their reaction time when they're thrown off balance is slower. Older people are therefore more likely to fall when they stumble, trip, or slip. Slips and falls leading to hip fractures and subsequent blood clot problems constitute one of the most common causes of death in older people. The good news is that imbalance often improves with exercise! Balance exercises such as standing on one foot and trying to maintain your balance become increasingly important as we get older.

### WRIGHT

So it appears based on what you have stated so far is that we can fight declining strength and endurance that occurs with age. Is that correct?

BUNCH

Yes it is. We see a significant reduction in strength and endurance with age. As we age we will lose some strength, no matter what. However, if we perform strengthening exercises regularly, the amount of muscle tissue and strength loss is greatly reduced. Strengthening also stimulates branching out of blood vessels and capillaries. This helps blood to reach more tissues and bring to the tissues more oxygen. Consequently, this leads to better endurance during exertion.

As I said earlier in my interview, and I think it is worth repeating because it is so important, strengthening exercises have a stabilizing effect on DNA in our cells. Medical research indicates that strengthening exercises may reduce the risk of cancers more than aerobic exercise. More than 75 percent of all cancers occur after age fifty-four and about 90 percent of cancers are related to lifestyle factors, according to the American Cancer Association. Perhaps one of the most important lifestyle changes to help prevent cancer as we age is to start strengthening exercises more regularly!

WRIGHT

This is really good information and it has been a great conversation. I appreciate your answering all these questions here today and I could listen to you all day because I'm one of those aging Americans.

Today I have been talking with Dr. Richard Bunch, a licensed physical therapist with a PhD in human neuroanatomy and physiology. He is also an ergonomics specialist and professional speaker who has lectured to hundreds of thousands of people throughout the United States, Europe, Asia, and Africa.

Dr. Bunch, thank you so much for being with us today on *Health: Mind, Body, Soul.*

# About the Author

Dr. Richard Bunch, a native of Louisiana, is a licensed physical therapist, professional speaker, and ergonomic specialist. He served in the United States Army and attended undergraduate training at West Point United States Military Academy. He received his PhD in Human Neuroanatomy with honors from LSU Medical Center.

Dr. Bunch is the founder, CEO, and owner of ISR Institute, Inc. and WorkSaver Systems, LLC, that provides motivational injury prevention and wellness training, ergonomic consulting, and employee fit-for-duty testing for employers nationwide.

Dr. Bunch is the author of several publications and books on the topic of wellness, injury prevention, and ergonomics. He conducts keynotes and motivational injury prevention and ergonomic lectures throughout the United States, Europe, Africa, and Asia. He has won "Best Speaker" Awards at several national conferences.

Dr. Richard Bunch

985-791-4904

Bunchisr@AOL.com

www.ISR-Institu

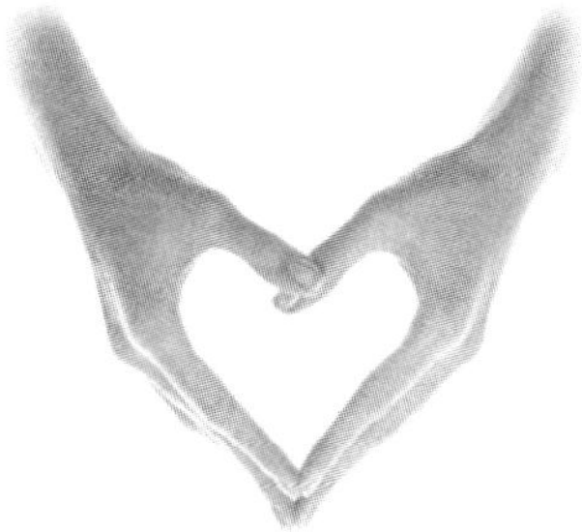

## Chapter Two

# Advice on Building Healthy Relationships

## with Dr. John Gray

THE INTERVIEW

DAVID WRIGHT (WRIGHT)

John, you've built a successful career as an expert giving relationship advice. I recently read a statement attributed to you: "A wise woman is careful not to pursue a man more than he is pursuing her." Will you explain why?

JOHN GRAY (GRAY)

When women make themselves too available to men, men get lazy. It's old-fashioned wisdom, but on a new level. We can understand it biochemically as well. Men bond with women when their testosterone levels go up. When there's a challenge, testosterone levels go up. But when things become easy, testosterone levels go down—so there needs to be a sense of the man initiating his own behaviors as to a woman doing it all.

The easiest way to make a man lose interest in you is to do everything for him. The most exciting thing to a man is when he feels that he is making a difference in a woman's life, as opposed to her doing everything for him.

WRIGHT

That makes sense. Perhaps definitions were different several years ago when I was single. Today, how does one determine if he or she is dating or in a "relationship"?

GRAY

Quite often women believe that when they are having sex with a man that they are having a monogamous relationship with him. They just assume that is his value system, and that's not always the case. I encourage women to assume that they're having a committed, monogamous relationship after a man has told them so.

The next question that comes up from women is, "Well, how do you bring up such a subject?" The best way to do it is to let him know at some point that you're not interested in having sex unless you're in an exclusive monogamous relationship. When he's ready to make that step she should tell him how she feels about it. That is certainly one approach.

WRIGHT

If someone is not sure that the person he or she is dating is "the one," how can that person get some help to sort through that uncertainty?

GRAY

Certainly feeling uncertain and doubting is a natural course of action in the dating process, and it's the first realization that's important. Sometimes people think, "If I don't know for sure, then maybe this is definitely not the right person for me."

One insight that is very important is that you could be with the right person for you, but still go through a period of feeling doubt and uncertainty. It's just a natural process, and while you are in that process it takes time before a part of you begins to sense that you're with the right person, or you begin to sense that you're with the wrong person. It just takes some time.

Couples who rush into making a commitment often make a mistake, and then feelings get hurt, so it's best to go slow when in doubt and not to assume that something's wrong.

### Wright

In the event of a cheating spouse or a lover, what should people do to learn to heal from infidelity in the relationship?

### Gray

It's an important concept to recognize that we all get our hearts broken, our partners make mistakes, and we experience disappointments. A part of growing in real love is the ability to forgive our partners for mistakes. People simply don't think sometimes and they make mistakes. By talking about it and sharing, people can understand what their mistakes are and make changes and grow from that. It's certainly a personal choice that some people make to simply exclude somebody who would ever cheat on them.

If someone has children I always encourage them to recognize that having an affair is a mistake, and people make mistakes—it's not a horrible, horrible mistake, it's just a mistake.

If someone's violent (that's more of a horrible, horrible mistake), even then it's forgivable if the person was to get help and recognize that he (or she) has a problem and overcome that problem.

The main question about being with someone is that after you have opened your heart and you've been hurt, if you take time to heal your heart, do you still want to be with him or her? That's the question. It's not for me or any other person to tell you whether you should be with that person; it's always an individual choice within the heart. The problem is that some people get caught up in this thinking that if someone makes a mistake then for sure I don't want to be with them. It's quite unrealistic to ever expect perfection in this world.

### Wright

In your writings you suggest using a relationship advisor or coach for those who need help. Will you explain the process?

GRAY

The process is simply talking with somebody who will ask you questions to help you to get in touch with your feelings. You can express your feelings without feeling that you're going to be judged or your feelings are going to hurt somebody or you're going to be held accountable and stand by those feelings. Often feelings need some room to flow and change as you grow in awareness. It's often not safe to show this with someone you're in a relationship with—the person might hold you to those feelings. So you go to a counselor to talk about those things.

Today it's becoming very popular to talk to coaches as well. One of the differences between a counselor and a coach is that a counselor is trained more academically in the process of analyzing what dysfunction you might have, and in providing a means to reflect on what's happening in your life related to things in your past. The counselor might even do more work on your childhood to rebuild self-esteem issues.

A coach is someone who is there to hold you accountable to do the things that you say you want to do by asking you questions. A coach can also become a sounding board who will ask you about what your feelings are, what happened, what you think should happen, what you think should not have happened, and what you think can happen. This type of exploration helps people find within themselves the wisdom to make better choices in their life. It also helps to motivate them to make better choices and follow up with action. So the coach tends to be more practically oriented.

A Mars/Venus coach adds to it an aspect of providing education as to the various insights of how men and women are different, how their emotional needs are different, and how they can motivate each other to be the best they can be in a relationship, rather than unknowingly pulling out the worst about the individuals in a relationship. I'm a big believer in education first, and then in coaching to motivate people. But often people don't even know what's going on, and some basic insights can help them make better choices and decisions. A coach can then assist them in staying motivated to achieve that end.

WRIGHT

I've heard the divorce rate is 50 percent. Is that true? And can a counselor or relationship coach actually help save a marriage?

GRAY

I've seen counselors ruin marriages, and I've seen counselors help save marriages. There are different forms of therapy. If you're in therapy and it doesn't feel right to you and you don't feel like you're making progress, you're probably in the wrong kind of therapy for you. There are some kinds of therapy where the opportunity is created for two people to sit and talk about how they feel with each other. This can result in arguments and fights in the counseling room just like the fights they have at home.

My Mars/Venus counselors are trained in ways to assist individuals in learning new ways of interacting, new ways of expressing their feelings, and new ways of avoiding arguments and fights. I think this is very important for a therapist to do. A Mars/Venus coach is going to focus more on assisting individuals in taking responsibility for how they're contributing to the problems in their relationship. This can simply be having someone to talk with to share what you're feeling. Sharing your feelings can sometimes bring about enormous insight into a situation, as well as helping you to feel better.

When you feel better you're able to respond in a more positive way. Our Mars/Venus coaches and counselors repeatedly receive stories and testimonials of couples who feel that their marriages were saved.

WRIGHT

I went on your Web site and I looked at some of the things that you're doing. I was really impressed. One thing that caught my eye was the Relationship Test. Does the Mars/Venus Relationship Test really work? What do you actually test?

### GRAY

There are different areas of relationships which could be stronger or weaker. What a Relationship Test does is allows you to become more aware of what you're experiencing every day. Often people do not take the time to sit down and reflect on what's working here and what's not working. Our lives are often so busy that we're just going from the *next* thing to the *next* thing to the *next* thing, and we don't sit back and reflect on what's working and what's not working.

By doing the test and answering the questions, you're having to take that time and reflect upon what really is going on in your relationship. The irony in relationships is sometimes couples will be fighting in counseling or they'll be fighting at home, and they don't even know what they are fighting about. They don't even know how the argument started! Everything was fine, and suddenly one little thing happens and one or the other is flying off the handle and they just don't know what to do about it.

Often these flying off the handle experiences are like the water boiling and turning into steam. Long before it boiled, it simmered, and long before it simmered, the water was heating up. So there's a process that leads up to uncontrolled experiences in relationships. When you become more aware of what's not working in a relationship long before it's boiling, you have a chance to easily make adjustments in your behavior.

When taking a Relationship Test you're able to see many places where you have confusion or you don't understand what is going on. Talking to a relationship coach you can ask questions, particularly in the problem areas. You can talk about what's going on so that you can make sense of what's going on in your relationship.

Often when we don't know what's happening or don't know how to correctly interpret what's happening because it doesn't make sense to us, we then assume the worst rather than assume the best. And what our Mars/Venus coaches do is help to point out the *good* reasons why people do what they do, and strategies to help bring out the best in them.

## Wright

Every time I hear a talk show host ask a guest about the most important attribute a person needs to have when considering a relationship, the answer from males or females are always the same: "A good sense of humor." Is that really true?

## Gray

Well, that's what everybody says, but when difficulties arise in relationships the women then complain that the men are not serious. Or the man could complain that the woman isn't serious. Generally it's the number one thing on the list for women to say "a man's sense of humor," and when I hear that I want then to educate that woman to recognize that she's looking for the wrong thing. The last thing you need is for a man to entertain you. What you want is a man to provide security for you, to be attentive to you, and to understand you. In that place of safety, then you will naturally be expressive of your femininity, which is actually quite entertaining to men. It's the woman who brings joy to life, not the man. So when women are looking for men to bring joy to their life, women are often just feeling insecure as though they can't provide enough, and they are looking to a man to provide that role.

I have a wife and three daughters. When I travel with them it's amazing how entertaining they are! The nature of femininity is that women talk, they share, they look, they comment, they respond, they laugh a lot.

But what *is* good for a woman to look for in a man is not entertainment. She may think she's looking for that, but she'll find herself being disappointed again and again. What she should be looking for is a man's sense of humor in that he doesn't take things too seriously. That's extremely very attractive to women. Not taking himself too seriously means that he's not defensive about things and he doesn't claim to be perfect or expect or demand that she believes him to be perfect. That is a very healthy attitude and attribute in a man. If he can, in a sense, "lighten up," that constitutes a good sense of humor. That is what creates a sense of security for a woman.

If women want men to entertain them all the time, not only will they be disappointed, but it puts way too much pressure on men—they'll come on really strong and then women will lose interest because men are just not entertainers.

### Wright

Is it possible to be too cautious setting your criteria too high when choosing a life partner?

### Gray

I think the idea that you are getting at is very healthy to examine. I hesitate to say, "Lower your expectations and find your ideal partner." That sounds like you're not getting the best. What is going on today with both women and men is that they have very unrealistic expectations of what they require and what they want in a partner.

Life is often a gradual process of humbling them and helping them recognize what's realistic and what they are really looking for. We often look to the cover of a book rather than to the substance of the book, hence the old saying, "Don't judge a book by its cover." In our society we have become somewhat superficial in how we look for people. It takes a little maturing before we begin to realize who a person is is much more than how they look or how they react in certain situations or what they have or what they can do.

And yet those are all a part of the picture. I focus on helping couples change their expectations just in a sense of what a healthy relationship looks like. It doesn't mean that he's being romantic all the time, and it doesn't mean that she's happy all the time—two people really need to learn how to be happy on their own and then want to share that happiness with someone. That becomes the foundation of a relationship. When we are looking to someone to fill us up and make us happy, we will be disappointed later on. When we are somewhat happy and fulfilled in our own life, then we can find extra happiness through sharing our happiness with someone else. When that happens we are much less needy and our expectations tend to be much more realistic automatically.

WRIGHT

Almost everything you've said has hit me personally, especially the aspect of education. You see people who say, "This is my life-long partner" and they talk about all kinds of things, but it seems like you're talking about education.

GRAY

I feel that what's missing most in the world today when it comes to relationships is insight and education into understanding how to create healthy relationships. And why we need this education now more so than a hundred years ago, is that people didn't take courses even fifty years ago in improving their relationships. That's because there were hundreds of years of tradition where women had certain roles and men had certain roles. Men interacted in certain ways and women interacted in certain ways. As long as everybody acted according to those established patterns, everyone got along quite well.

Then the world changed. Now the world is different and yet no one has defined new roles and how men and women are supposed to interact and what works best for them. To a certain extent there is no "best"—it's a world of tremendous freedom and choice and we have to define those roles ourselves. But in defining those roles there's a certain amount of freedom to create those roles, and there's also a certain lack of freedom.

I might wish to walk through a wall, but I just can't—certain realities don't change. So in this world where we are "making up" relationships in a new way, there are certain realities that have not changed. There are certain ways that men interact and there are certain ways that women interact. There are certain needs that women have and certain needs that men have. The needs men and women have are different. By understanding those differences we can then realistically work with those differences to support each other better at this time of enormous change and enormous stress in our lives due to that change.

And what is interesting is that men and women react differently to stress, so most of the differences that cause frustration between men and women are simply differences that we don't understand, and those differences that we don't instinctively relate to are particularly how men and women react to stress.

For example, men will often become quiet or distant under stress, whereas women will want to open up and share and talk under stress. And then, taking another step that stresses even more, women will then *not* want to talk because they'll feel that they've tried to talk and no one listened so they begin to close up, and then they have no way to effectively cope with stress.

On the other hand, you've got men who tend to naturally pull away and mull things over to feel better under stress. If they are really under a huge amount of stress, these men don't even take the time to pull away. They go into a more talkative mode—they just want to complain and point out how they are victims in life. This becomes very distressing to women, and they go further and further away. That's what I would call "role reversal," which is another problem occurring today.

There are a lot of combinations in men and women and we just don't understand how to make sense of it, but by having a basic understanding of how men and women are different and how they cope with stress differently, we can then be better equipped to support our partners when they are under a lot of stress.

For example, if my wife doesn't want to talk about something, I can be helpful to her and be cooperative, which will lower her stress level. She will then begin to open up and talk, which will lower her stress level even more—as long as I make it safe for her to talk.

If a man is stressed and is complaining a lot and talking a lot, then what a woman can do is instead of trying to be a good listener, she can simply ask him to talk with his friends and give her some room to do what she wants to do. She should not encourage him to talk about all the things that are going wrong in his life. As she leaves him alone he will then be able to cope with stress better. He will then "come out of his cave" so to speak and be much more friendly to her. Women have to recognize that when men are in a bad mood or when they're stressed out, it's not up to her to do anything for him. Men have to come out of this primarily on their own, otherwise they tend to become weak.

So these are primary differences that a woman wouldn't think of. Another example is if a woman's feeling stressed out and he comes to her and asks her questions to help open her up and give her support, it will actually empower her. And doing so empowers the man. But when a woman is too much like a mother to a man, it will weaken him and she will resent it later as well, that's a no-win situation.

### Wright

I have known you for several years and I have always been impressed by your ability to stay on the leading edge of the subjects you are passionate about. Have you found any new information about relationship-building in the past few of years that might help people make fewer mistakes in the search for love and companionship?

### Gray

I think that in a sense I was touching on that a few minutes ago when I mentioned the subject of stress. Stress has become so high that not only do men and women have strong stress reactions, they actually go further into a role reversal where women are so stressed that they feel they have to do everything themselves and they become very much like a man. Men become so stressed that they begin to complain about their lives and feel like they're not responsible for their lives anymore. This is the wrong direction, and yet it's a natural stress reaction.

Today we are experiencing unprecedented amounts of stress with longer commuting hours and higher costs of living, balancing work and home life, increased information, and cell phones, talking, and being connected to work all the time. All this is putting a huge new burden on our lives and on our relationships.

What I have done is help to point this out, which can help couples enormously. Couples can recognize that there are ways to lower stress. If we are going to have more dramatic stress, there are more dramatic ways that couples can lower the stress levels for each other. Those ways happen to be women learning to ask for help—that's a real big issue—and men being more responsive to give help. That's not to say they have to do it every time she asks as if he's supposed to "jump to it." There are times when you are supposed to take your rest, so there needs to be understanding of that.

Women often resent having to ask for help, and that is something that has to change. She has to recognize that when you grow up in this world you have to learn how to ask for things, particularly in the business world. Likewise in relationships, if a woman wants her partner to change his natural mode of behavior she needs to *ask*. She shouldn't expect him to be like a woman who would just tend to think about everything that needs to be done until overwhelmed doing it—men typically don't fall into that role. So she needs to ask him, and when people ask others to do something, when they do it they need to let them know it's appreciated.

This is a new skill for a woman. While women sometimes resist this, once they practice it they realize, "Wow, this isn't that hard, and it works!" So that's one way to lower stress in life—if women are not feeling supported to *ask* for it in a way that will work rather than the way that they do ask, which often doesn't work. Practice "realistic expectations." Instead of complaining that "I can't walk through this wall" and "Why doesn't the wall open up for me?" you've got to find the door and learn how to open it!

The second important area to lower stress is in the realm of communication. Women want more sharing and more communication and men aren't providing that. There's a way that men can provide it—if women cooperate. As I said before, women should ask for what they want. Maybe a woman could say something like, "I'd like for you to listen to what is going on in my life." Let him know that he doesn't have to say anything. In fact, I encourage that in the beginning—he should say nothing, and let her talk for five or ten minutes. She then thanks him for listening, and then walks away. While this seems very unnatural, it is a super stress reducer once people start to experience it. It's quite amazing.

I didn't invent this—this is what has been going on for years in the therapy office. Women come in and they talk about what's going on in their lives and they feel better. The therapist doesn't say much at all. And the better the therapist, the less the therapist says and the more questions the therapist asks.

So the secret here is learning how to talk about what is bothering you without expecting a solution or without expecting your partner to "fix" you or fix the situation in some way. So she can set up that conversation and she will feel better; he'll feel better too because he helped her. And men like helping their wives.

The third area is romance. Again, in this area couples stopped having romance, and romance is actually one of the most strong and powerful stress reducers. It's just that when we're under stress the last thing we think about is romance, both for her and for him. Yet the difference is women will often think about how much they miss it. They're not necessarily feeling romantic, but they often complain that "he's not romantic," implying that she wants him to be romantic so she can feel good again. I understand that and I respect that. And I have a solution for that, but it's not waiting for him—you have to ask! Now, what woman would ever think to ask for romance? Well *you* can. It's a very simple thing.

To solve this problem women have to learn how to ask, and men have to learn how to respond. Women then have to learn how to appreciate that, and the solutions do occur. Women can't expect a man to be a mind-reader. He doesn't know what's going on inside her head and in her heart. Asking for romance is something so foreign that women need a few examples of it and then they can get the hang of it.

For example, she shouldn't say, "You're not romantic, we don't experience romance anymore, we never go out anymore, we're not having fun anymore." Those are just negative complaints. Instead she needs to focus more on what's positive. For example, "Hey, this particular band is playing in town this weekend. Would you get tickets for the concert?" The woman asks the man—that's it. It's a very simple thing. The woman could say, "Oh, we haven't gone out this week, would you get tickets for this or that?" or simply, "Would you pick a movie and we'll go see the movies?" or "Would you make reservations and let's go out to eat?" The man could say, "Where would you like to go?" The woman could say, "Whatever you want to pick."

Women can start defining romance as letting him decide where to go, her asking for it, him deciding, and her having a good time just being with him! And gradually that moves into more discretion about what you're going to do and so forth. This process will begin to restore the woman's confidence in the man. All the woman needs to do is to just ask and let him know that whatever he does will be fine.

Just as it was in the beginning when he was so romantic, men often become unromantic because they try, but after a while women start picking out what he did wrong. And men will think, "Well, she's so picky I'll just let her decide." And that's the end of romance because part of what reduces stress for women is that she does not have to decide. And when a woman comes back to the realization that having the man make some decisions and she doesn't have to decide will actually lower her stress enormously. It also lowers a man's stress enormously when he knows that whatever he decides she's going to like, as opposed to feeling that he's going to put his best out there and she's going to step all over it by pointing out what he did wrong. She doesn't mean to do that, but that's the net effect.

So these are extra additions, extra awarenesses, and insights that can help couples to cope with the extra stress they're experiencing in their lives today.

WRIGHT

If you had to "bottom line" the reasons for the success of your Mars and Venus books, products, ideas, and counseling help, what would the main reason be?

GRAY

I think that because the world has changed, people are eager and hungry to have a new way of understanding the world in a positive light. When we don't understand what is going on around us, we just assume something's wrong. By learning the new insights regarding how men and women are different, and how we look at the world differently in a *positive* way, they are released from having to blame their partners or blame themselves. They are motivated to find creative solutions that make their relationships better. So in one aspect, what I do is give people permission to make mistakes, and give them insight to solve the problems.

WRIGHT

An interesting conversation! I always learn so much when I talk with you. It's just incredible. I really do appreciate this time that you've spent with me today, and I really think the readers are going to get a lot out of it.

GRAY

Well thank you so much. It's a pleasure.

# About the Author

Dr. John Gray is the author of fifteen books, including Men Are from Mars, Women Are from *Venus* (Harper Collins 1992), a number one best-selling relationship book. Over thirty million Mars and Venus books have been sold in over forty languages throughout the world.

Dr. John Gray, a certified family therapist, is the premier Better Life relationship coach on AOL. In 2001, he received the Smart Marriages Impact Award. John Gray received his degree in 1982 from Columbia Pacific University. He has authored fourteen other best-selling books. His book, *The Mars & Venus Diet & Exercise Solution* (St. Martin's Press 2003), reveals why diet, exercise, and communication skills combine to effect the production of healthy brain chemicals and how the need for those chemicals differ between men and women.

An internationally recognized expert in the fields of communication and relationships, Dr. Gray's unique focus is assisting men and women in understanding, respecting, and appreciating their differences. For decades, he has conducted public and private seminars for thousands of participants. In his highly acclaimed books, audiotapes, and videotapes, as well as in his seminars, Dr. Gray entertains and inspires audiences with his practical insights and easy to use communication techniques that can be immediately applied to enrich relationships and quality of life.

Dr. Gray is a popular speaker on the national and international lecture circuit and often appears on television and radio programs to discuss his work. He has made guest appearances on such shows as *Oprah, Good Morning America, The Today Show, The CBS Morning Show, Live with Regis, The View, Politically Incorrect, Larry King Live, The Roseanne Show, CNN and Company,* and many others. He has been profiled in *USA Today, Newsweek, TIME Magazine, TV Guide, People, Forbes,* and numerous other major publications across the United States.

Dr. Gray's nationally syndicated column reaches millions of readers in many newspapers, including *The Atlanta Journal/ Constitution, New York Daily News, New York Newsday, The Denver Post,* and the *San Antonio Express-News.* Internationally, the columns appear in publications in England, Canada, Mexico, Korea, Latin America, and the South Pacific.

Dr. Gray lives with his wife and three children in Northern California.

Dr. John Gray

www.askmarsvenus.com

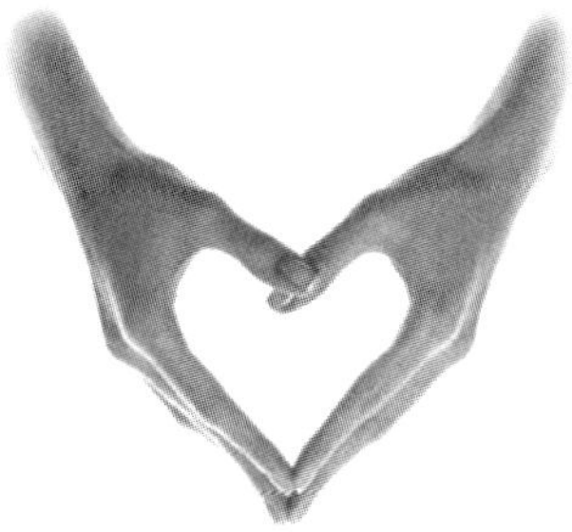

## Chapter Three

# Health: A Journey To Self

## with Beth Welton-Miller

THE INTERVIEW

DAVID WRIGHT (WRIGHT)

Today we're talking with Beth Welton-Miller. Beth is the founder of Vibrant Living LLC, an organization providing transformative education and healing practices to enliven body, mind, heart, and soul. She brings with her an extensive twenty-five-year background in adult learning, somatic psychology, mindfulness, energy medicine, shamanism, intuition, bodywork, and ritual. Beth's presence, and insight help individuals and groups build alliance with their healing intelligence so they can manifest a life that is most vibrantly healthy.

Beth, welcome to *Health: Mind, Body, Soul.*

BETH WELTON-MILLER (WELTON-MILLER)

Thank you.

WRIGHT

Beth, you've been working in the holistic health and healing arts field for twenty-five years; how would you define health?

WELTON-MILLER

Health is a process of discovering and reclaiming our authentic self. This self is where our core truth resides. When we develop a relationship with our authentic self, we have contact with our inner wisdom. To make this journey to our inner wisdom successful, we must give attention to the many parts of our lives—the physical, mental, emotional, and spiritual. They form a dynamic system that affects one another. This system has an intelligence that knows how to heal, regenerate, and be in wholeness. When we deeply listen to and honor each of these aspects, we have vitality. When we get sidetracked on our journey, struggle and suffering are created.

In my experience with transformation—both personally and professionally—the journey to self consists of five principles: inclusion, awareness, curiosity, self–responsibility, and self-compassion. Below is a description of each of the the five principles.

1. We need to include all the many parts of our lives. When we embrace the full range of our emotions, our beliefs, and our body sensations; we learn from every moment.

2. We bring awareness to all aspects of who we are—our body, our mind, our emotions, and our soul. As we are mindful and shift from unconscious to conscious, we discover important information for our lives.

3. We approach life with curiosity and wonder. Like a child who has a sense of open-hearted innocence, we live in creative discovery.

4. We take self-responsibility for our reality. We claim our body, mind, emotions, and core beliefs as our own. We move from blame, rescue, and victim behavior to taking ownership for our life choices and situations. This is how we gain true power and happiness.

5. We have self-compassion for these parts—body, mind, and soul. We bring empathy and understanding to ourselves, knowing we are not broken and there is nothing to fix. Instead, we are continually moving toward greater awareness and understanding of our wholeness.

These principles help you develop a relationship with your core self. By doing this, you have access to your highest wisdom, which guides decisions in your daily life and helps you gain happiness, peace, and vibrant health.

In this chapter we are taking a journey together. Think of me as your guide—someone who will provide information, provoke thought, and invite discovery. This chapter is interactive in order to provide you with the opportunity to experience the power of the five principles in your life right now. I will be by your side and walk you through each process by asking you experiential questions that help you gain awareness and deepen into your authentic self.

My request is that you be intentional about engaging yourself in the questions and exercises presented in the chapter. This format fosters self-guided behavior, which is essential for developing a relationship with your inner wisdom. My hope is that this inspires you to incorporate these transformational practices into your life. I invite you to relax and get comfortable. Have a cup of tea or cocoa, a journal close by, and settle in for an adventure!

#### Wright

It's interesting to think of health as a journey to self. Will you expand on that?

#### Welton-Miller

Imagine yourself as an adventurous explorer, very curious and open, like an inquisitive child. Imagine you are this child going on a journey and exploring the inner landscape of your mind, your thoughts, your cells, your DNA, and your energy field. You look at everything with a sense of newness. Nothing is off limits. You have a genuine interest. You are great at non-judgmental observation and want to understand what is going on and how everything works. When we explore life like a curious child, we can discover so much about our self and our inner wisdom. This wisdom is an internal guidance system and like a GPS, when listened to, can guide us on our journey.

A significant reason we disconnect from our internal GPS system is that at an early age we were criticized or discounted. This causes confusion in the child and we start second-guessing our inner wisdom. The child develops limiting beliefs that gets etched in the neural pathways of the brain and are lived out during life.

As adults, we need to reclaim this powerful part of ourselves so we can make decisions that serve and nourish our soul. We then can stand firm in our own knowingness about what we truly need. We cannot know what's right for us and our soul unless we are in deep contact with it. When we are adventurous like the child, we can call on our curiosity and openness, which allows us to look at what is going on and make discoveries in ways that are compassionate and more light-hearted.

WRIGHT

The internal guidance system seems very important when building a relationship with self. What are some practical ways a person can develop this?

WELTON-MILLER

To be happy, connected to our needs, and to know what we want, it is essential we are present and compassionate with ourselves on a regular basis. We build a strong relationship with our self, much like we would in relationship to someone we deeply care about.

In this relationship with another person, our focus and intent would include the following: regular contact, active listening, asking questions, curiosity, understanding, and empathy.

We would keep agreements by following through on what we said we would do. This builds trust in the relationship. Much like we do with someone we deeply care about, we do this in relationship with ourselves. Also, if our inner wisdom makes a request, such as exercising or not eating sugar, we follow through. This builds trust and connection with ourselves.

Start developing this relationship right now. Close your eyes, breathe, and ask yourself what you are experiencing in the present moment. Take time and be patient with yourself. What are your body sensations? What are your emotions? What do you need? Listen for the answers.

We also need to be intentional. Being intentional is focusing energy, clearing time, and creating space to activate intention. I like to start my day with meditation and prayer in a specific place in my home. I give gratitude and call on my authentic power and connection with all. Some may call this connection with higher truth, universe, or God. It helps me to recognize who I truly am, even amid any inner "stuckness" and the happenings of everyday life. Start gradually by setting aside five minutes a day to state your desires to know and connect with yourself. You then may want to expand this and check in at different times throughout your day. The purpose of this is to help you develop a sacred container that holds you in your new intention. This is a place to call on and anchor yourself in your soul's wisdom.

Developing a deeper relationship with yourself provides greater contact with your intuition. I call this my "niggles" and "nudges" and they guide me in decisions. "Niggles" tell me when something is not quite right. They are like a warning sign. I stop, breathe, and pay attention. Then, I ask myself, "What am I noticing?" I pay attention to my thoughts, body sensations, and emotions. I then ask, "Does anything need to happen?"

On the other hand, "nudges" encourage me to move forward, even when I am afraid. When I follow my intuition, there is a flow. Like most of us, I have avoided what I knew because it was scary to make a change when I didn't know the outcome. We can keep ourselves in situations that are extremely stressful and energy-consuming when we don't follow our intuition. Following our intuition is a continuous process and provides us with a dynamic feedback loop. Sometimes we follow our intuition and it works for a while, or until the next step gives us more "nudges." We follow these "nudges" also.

We just don't receive information from our internal guidance and that's it. We pay attention, checking in daily, moment by moment to see what may have changed. Following our inner wisdom provides clarity.

### WRIGHT

Tell me more about paying attention to body sensations.

### WELTON-MILLER

The body is a wealth of information and does not lie. It is a phenomenal gauge of our happiness and distress levels. We all know the sensation of a full bladder and we pay attention to that. It's equally important to pay attention to other body sensations in the exploration of self.

Are we feeling tight, relaxed, hot, tingly? We pay attention to these sensations to connect with ourselves. When we explore body sensations, we help ourselves relax and our brainwaves to move into alpha, which is a slower rhythm. In this brainwave, we have more access to clarity. When we are tight, worried, and try to figure things out, it is extremely hard to solve problems and have clear and creative thinking.

In certain meditation and mindfulness practices, noticing the breath come in and go out is a way to pay attention to the body. Paying attention to this very important part of your health—breathing—can give you valuable information.

Ask yourself, what is my inhale like? Is it full? Is it tight? What is my exhale like?

Taking this a step further—expressing the sensations noticed in the body—this expression of a deeper truth connects you with your integrity. If I notice tightness in my chest and say, "My chest is tight." I'm connecting with myself. With this awareness, I can explore the emotions and needs associated with that tightness. "My chest is tight and I notice I am feeling sad and needing some love and connection."

My clients are amazed at how powerful connecting with and naming sensations can be. When emotions are named and felt, pain in the body has a possibility of going away and relaxation ensues. Clarity is found amid confusion and overwhelm.

Let's explore this. What sensations are you experiencing in your body right now? Take time. Breathe. Is it associated with an emotion and what is it?

Usually body sensations are connected to emotional states. Let yourself feel this emotion. There is nothing to figure out. You are being with yourself in a compassionate and curious way.

Continue to pay attention to your body sensations. What needs may you have right now? Say it to yourself or write it down.

When doing the above exercise, you are exploring your deeper wisdom through your body sensations.

### Wright

It sounds so doable. What, then, keeps people from developing clarity and intuition?

### Welton-Miller

Clarity and intuition are always possible. Many things contribute to people not developing a relationship with their intuitive self—lack of time, core beliefs, shame, or fear of what we will find when we look in the mirror, or what may have to change. When we act from our intuitive power, it can contribute to others having feelings and sometimes we don't think we can handle their reactions as we express our full self. We also use addictive and compulsive behaviors to numb pain and discomfort, which keeps us from connecting with our intuition.

There was a time in my marriage when I became quite shut down. I could react to something as simple as the way my husband squinted his eyes. The squinting reminded me of my father when he would get angry. This activated the fight or flight response in me. I then did not bring issues to my husband when they needed to be discussed. In order to make a change, I had to take responsibility for my fears and consciously engage with myself. As I separated from the old past history, I was able to interact with him with clarity and compassion.

Emotions are a part of life. They are a pathway to experience our intuitive self and wholeness. The pain of shutting down our authentic self is, in a sense, a death of what is most precious—our essential nature. As we discover and share this essential nature, we experience true freedom.

### WRIGHT

You talk about the power of changing our minds. Will you explain more about what you mean?

### WELTON-MILLER

The power of thought can have a major influence on our current experience as well as our future experience. Much research has been done verifying how our thoughts influence our reality. Our thoughts can change our bodies, our DNA, even the crime rate in a city or the shape of water molecules. Our thinking changes our mood, our energy levels, and the feelings in our body. In order to change, we need to be aware of what we are thinking.

In this moment, think the following thought, "There is never enough time and I'll never get it done right." What do you feel in your body when you say that? What sensations do you experience? Are you tight or relaxed? What emotion do you feel? Joy? Fear? Hopeless? Now change that thought to, "I have plenty of time to do my excellent work and time for relaxation and play." What do you feel in your body now? What emotions do you feel? Try this with other limiting thoughts you have. Make a game of it with your curious child. I invite you to take a moment to ask yourself, "What's my limiting thought and what thought do I want to have instead?" Be sure to see and feel the changes you want to become.

Our thoughts create an energetic field around us that vibrates in a certain way. This energy field creates our current reality and life situations.

Take a look at your life right now. Ask yourself, "What are the thoughts I am thinking that are creating what's happening in my life?"

Be extremely compassionate toward yourself in this process because it can be easy to judge what is happening in your life. Include the adventurous, curious person so you can discover and play with these thoughts. Discovering our unconscious core beliefs provides us with the illumination we need to make conscious changes.

### Wright

From the clients and groups you have worked with, what are the most common limiting beliefs you see that people have and what are new beliefs someone could incorporate to make the most significant positive change in his or her life?

### Welton-Miller

Limiting beliefs, although common, are different for each person. In my experience, the reoccurring themes are: my safety, lovability, belonging, and power.

Here are some predominate, limiting belief statements:

- It's not safe to fully express myself.
- I'm not lovable.
- I'll never get it right.
- I need to do something to get approval and love.

- I am alone.
- My needs are not important.
- I am powerless.
- My power will hurt someone.
- There is no support for me.
- It won't be done right unless I do it myself.
- To be successful I have to sacrifice what I love.
- To be successful I have to work hard.

Beliefs and thoughts make a significant difference in how we view our self and the world. To change limiting beliefs, we must change our thoughts. Formulating new thoughts can best be done by wording statements as though they are in the present moment. Use words that juice you and that stimulate your senses and create sensations in your body. For each person, the wording may be a little different. I encourage you to play with a new belief that creates more of what you want.

Some possible new beliefs are:

- I feel loved when I fully express the depth of myself.
- My gift to the world is my full expression.
- What I want is important and brings me joy.
- I relax and let others support me.
- I reach out for support on a daily basis.
- I have the power to co-create a life that is nourishing.
- My authentic power is beautiful.
- I am successful when I follow my natural rhythms.
- I am wildly successful when I follow my intuition.

Changing limiting beliefs is not just saying the words—it is feeling it in every cell of our bodies. When we are able to vibrate like the new beliefs, they become alive in our life.

WRIGHT

I thought it was good to focus on the positive. Why would I want to dredge up the dark, which is associated with pain?

WELTON-MILLER

The shadow is the messy, raw, forbidden parts of us that we tend to hide from others and ourselves. Our shadow consists of patterns from our ancestors and early life. These patterns from our ancestors are passed down through the generations in DNA and the energetic field. When we solely focus on the positive and attempt to hide the shadow, we don't get to discover what's blocking our way to wholeness. By denying its presence, we give energy to the shadow and it can take control of our lives.

We see the shadow at home or work when we are reactive. It's the moments we are judging others, thinking we are right, or looking to blame and find fault. Because the shadow becomes an invisible influence in our daily routines, it is hard to identify. We get used to it and believe this is the only way it can be.

It's usually uncomfortable to look at the dark, messy, and unpleasant situations we've created in our lives. Letting go of the past and its effects on our life can be difficult. What we don't realize is that this dark, lesson-rich place in our lives is the ground in which new seeds of wisdom can germinate and sprout. Our adversities, weaknesses, and traumas are usually the biggest opportunities for learning. They are callings to health and wholeness. Until we look with the heart and wonder of a child, we remain stuck there. If we can look with self-compassion and curiosity, knowing there is nothing wrong with us or other people, then we open up a door to more possibility.

WRIGHT

Do we really have that much influence to change our lives?

WELTON-MILLER

Research and science demonstrates that we do have the power to influence our self and others. We co-create life from our thoughts and beliefs. So the question is, if we have this much influence, how do we want to use it? What do we want to create with each and every moment? How do we want to feel? How do we want to respond to life's situations? Do we want to stay stuck in our life, feeling like a victim or blaming others? Do we continually tell the same old stories and expect things to change? We give away our authentic power and happiness when we think someone else is doing it to us. On the other hand, we can choose to be in the driver's seat of our life and create the changes we want. To take responsibility for our lives and change our belief system is empowering.

If you want a different outer world you need to change your inner world.

Ask yourself what you want to see in your world? Write it down as a first step. Get comfy and allow yourself to dream about your life and what most enlivens you. If you want harmony in your relationships, then how do you have peace and harmony within yourself? If you want a world without war, then how do you end the war within yourself?

If you want to have relationships you can trust, and are reliable, then how are you reliable to yourself, doing what you say you will do? If you want a vibrant body, then how do you eat healthy foods, think nourishing thoughts, and follow your body's innate wisdom to live in wholeness?

I encourage you to think about what you want to see changed in relation to your family, friends, and the world and then start making those changes in yourself. Be specific about the behaviors you may be changing. Write this down. Take action until you embody it so it becomes a solid part of yourself.

Watch for the changes in your life.

WRIGHT

Beth, will you give me a personal example of your journey to self?

WELTON-MILLER

I struggle with my relationship to food. Food is a chemical, which affects physiology and mood. Just cutting out processed sugar and reducing the glycemic index reduces the ups and downs of my mood and energy. For me, this is important for my happiness and health.

For years, I have struggled with overeating and being compulsive with food, especially when feeling stressed. The thirty pounds I gained started feeling less and less like me. Overeating seemed to be a way to sabotage myself and dull my "light" and full essence. I was tired, could not think as clearly, and was not as "easeful" in my body. My expertise in health and nutrition did not stop me from overeating. As I aged and my hormones would fluctuate, I had more cravings.

I played with my relationship with food in various ways. I experimented with techniques such as loving the food I ate, abstinence from certain foods, detoxification, being with feelings, and asking myself what I truly hunger for. The strategies worked for a while and then I would return to overeating. I tended to fluctuate between strength and control with eating and then feelings of deprivation and rebelling. This was definitely not the peaceful relationship I so wanted with eating and food. I knew I was the one to break my code to peace.

In my class called "The Power of Presence," I teach people to be with self, look inward, and be with the uncomfortable. People learn to be in their bodies, listen to what is going on, and be exquisitely self-compassionate. I needed to stop avoiding this aspect of my life and go to another level of presence in my inner journey. I was out of integrity with my work and myself. I knew facing my dragons would make a difference in my life, but avoided consistently going there, and facing the discomfort. I was not stepping into my full power. It became clear that something needed to shift and I felt more space in my life to take action.

Throughout the process of facing my compulsive eating I made sure I was connected to my intuition. I made a structured food plan with no processed foods. I paid more attention to my eating and hunger. I was present with and got more pleasure out of what I did eat. I learned what foods affected my cravings. I stopped myself, breathed, and was the curious explorer when I so much wanted to go for the half-gallon of chocolate chip ice cream or bag of potato chips. It was uncomfortable and brought up pain. I stayed present and did not run from the emotions that emerged. There were feelings of guilt, boredom, loneliness, and anxiety. There was the fear of success as well as failure.

What I found, when I started going to this new level of presence with myself, was inner relaxation. The anxiety in my gut lessened or went away. My thinking became more flexible and I could see more options. It felt miraculous in a sense. In the grip of my compulsion, I hung in there and felt the power of being with myself.

I also got support from a close friend whom I checked in with regularly. This helped me let go of the shame of secretive overeating. I would tell her what I ate or check in before I ate something that didn't support my intention. Talking to my friend gave me a deeper sense of connection. I also sought out a Naturopath for the physical support needed to detoxify my body. I did this so my body could be the "light" it wanted to be.

In this process, food lost some of its draw. I found more ways to meet my needs for nurturing and pleasure. I still remain in the process of choosing what is best for me. I overeat past full and eat sugar occasionally and I then see what it does to my body and energy. I am in better touch with what I most need to honor my destiny and to have a clear mind and a radiantly healthy body.

By being inclusive, aware, curious, self-responsible and self–compassionate, I was able to lose the weight and gain a different relationship with food and myself. Amid all the choices and complexities in life, I'm willing to stand more with myself and be conscious.

The next time you do something that is compulsive in nature, I invite you to pause, breathe, and connect with your body, emotions, and beliefs. Ask yourself, "What is here for me to learn, honor, and be with?"

Transformation occurs when we pay attention to what's happening in the present moment.

### WRIGHT

It sounds like there is a lot that I can do. What if I want to take responsibility for energizing myself and feeling good? Can I do that?

### WELTON-MILLER

There are many ways you can increase your energy and create "natural bliss." It is helpful to experiment with techniques that change your brainwaves, modify your mood, and increase your well-being. I encourage you to find out what works the best for you.

Breathing exercises oxygenate the blood and move our energy. It is a way to relax deeply and move any stuck feelings in the body or psyche. You can take a few in-the-moment breaths or breathe for five intentional minutes or more.

Movement is helpful, whether it be dancing to music, exercising, or passionate lovemaking. Moving is helpful to get energy unstuck and to increase "feel-good" hormones.

In the morning, I put on music to dance and jump on my rebounder. Certain tunes pick me up so I can fully say yes to the day. I get creative with new thoughts. I also do movement activities as a way to take breaks in my day.

Music is a vibration that helps us evoke those places in us that are rich with creativity and information. Experiment with music. Collect music that evokes your energy, touches your tender heart, or inspires your passion. Play with surrendering to it and it will give to you.

I also use music to "tone." Toning is repeating a sound with my voice over and over again. I like using the Indian Tambura F sound that I have on a CD. It helps me resonate with my heart. As I wrote this chapter, I toned to have clear thinking and come from my heart. It helps me be in a flow in my right brain.

I love being in the peace and beauty of nature. I live in the country with a mountain, huge trees, and water surrounding me. Being a part of nature feeds my spirit. When I connect with the birds, the trees, or the wind, I experience relaxation and the sense that all is well. I encourage people to slow down, get into nature, and be nourished.

### Wright

In the process of discovering more of your authentic self, what if someone is afraid to change because it may disrupt his or her relationships or family? Help me understand what happens when a person changes in a family dynamic.

### Welton-Miller

This may be a particular struggle for women because of their more predominant role as the nurturer of the family. In relationships, we don't have control over others. When we change ourselves we don't know how others, especially others we love, will respond. This unknown can be scary. What we do have control of is how we respond to others and the actions we take on our unique journey.

When I react less and show up more from my authentic self, there is the possibility to effect change in others. Research validates that when I calm down the reactive part of my brain, I shift to my prefrontal cortex, which is where my clear thinking and wisdom reside. This shift helps others come from their prefrontal cortex also. So, when I grow and change my mind for happiness, peace, and abundance, I help others do the same.

My deeper journey involved making significant changes. My spouse was likely to react to these changes and could be defensive. I kept remembering that I have a choice to react to him defensively or stay connected to myself. When I developed a deeper relationship with my authentic power, I was less likely to lose myself when he reacted. There are times he was motivated to change as he saw how it helped me. Did that happen overnight? No. In relationships, we have the opportunity to learn patience as we are committed to our evolution. We learn about ourselves in the process of being in relationship with others and using each other as our sacred mirrors.

Developing regular gratitude for the ones we love and expressing it is helpful. We can choose to be thankful for all our relationships, including the challenging ones. This is a way for us to see where we still need to heal and grow. These relationships show us our beliefs about life and ourselves. I am thankful that my spouse and I are committed to our evolution together and have created a sacred partnership where I can experiment, be authentic, and consciously engage with the present moment .

### Wright

If people were to take four steps today to head them in the direction of their health and happiness, what would those steps be?

### Welton-Miller

If we want to create different results in our life, we need to do things differently. What can you do differently today, tomorrow, and the next day? How can you develop a relationship with yourself so you don't abandon yourself and you learn from all the opportunities that present themselves in your life?

These are four steps you can do in just minutes and that produce instantaneous results and shifts:

1. Take a pause, breathe, and pay attention to the present moment. Allow it to be there with nothing to do but be curious.
2. Take ownership for your reactions, especially when they are defensive or they bring strong emotions or energy. Be curious.
3. Be extremely compassionate and tender toward yourself.
4. Reacquaint yourself with your curious explorer child, who is open to wonder, discovery, and possibility.

I wish you well on your precious journey. May you know and experience your inner wisdom.

If you have questions I encourage you to visit my Web site: www.vibrant-living.com or give me a call.

### Wright

Well, what a great conversation, Beth. I really appreciate all the time you've taken with me to talk about this important subject. I have taken notes as you have been talking and I've got a lot to think about. I'm sure our readers will get a lot out of this chapter.

### Welton-Miller

Thank you. I've thoroughly enjoyed the conversation also, David.

# About the Author

Beth Welton-Miller, MS, LMT, assists people in cultivating and experiencing connection with their life force essence and the clarity, power, and well-being it creates. She is a holistic therapist, intuitive, shamanic practitioner, and teacher providing transformative education and healing practices to enliven body, mind, heart, and soul. She brings with her an extensive twenty-five year background in personal development, somatic psychology, mindfulness, universal spirituality, intuition, bodywork, ceremony, and ritual. She has a master's degree in Education and certifications in Training and Organizational Development, Body Centered and Conscious Relationship Transformation, and she is a Master Practitioner of Energy Medicine and Healing the Luminous Energy Field. Beth's compassionate presence and insight help individuals and groups build alliance with their divine innate intelligence so they can manifest a life that nourishes and expresses their soul.


Beth Welton-Miller, MS, LMT

*Vibrant Living, LLC*

503-680-5810

beth@vibrant-living.com

www.vibrant-living.com

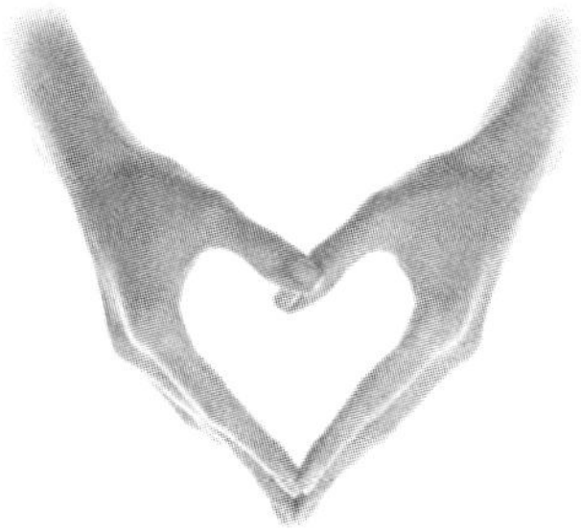

Chapter Four

# NLP: Your Ticket to Body-Mind Wellness

## with Philip Mandel

THE INTERVIEW

### David Wright (Wright)

Today I'm talking with Philip H. Mandel, who is a Master Practitioner of Neuro-Linguistic Programming (NLP) as well as a Certified Destination Method® Coach. He works with individuals of all ages using the body-mind connection to facilitate deep, personal change. As an author, speaker, and Principal of Phil Mandel and Associates, he has spent more than fifteen years helping people find solutions to their health challenges, whether mental or physical. His goal is to help create positive, lasting change. His compassionate attitude and commonsense wisdom put people at ease, and his can-do outlook inspires people to better health.

Phil, welcome to *Health: Mind Body Soul.*

### Philip Mandel (Mandel)

Thank you, David. I'm thrilled to be here!

### Wright

And welcome back to Insight Publishing. You already have chapters with us in *Nuts and Bolts: Business Edition* (2007) and *Getting Things Done: Keys to a Well Balanced Life* (2008). Those are primarily business- and success-oriented books, yet here you are, contributing to a book on health. Care to explain?

MANDEL

Sure, I'd be happy to. My father was a physician, so I had health and healthy habits taught to me since birth. My passions have always been related to health, inspired by my father and the dedication he showed toward his patients and his research. Chapters in the business books came about because businesses need to be healthy, too! In fact, businesses consist of people, don't they?

WRIGHT

You mentioned your father was a physician. What kind of medicine did he specialize in?

MANDEL

He specialized in internal medicine.

WRIGHT

That sounds like it's primarily focused on physical health. What made you want to be in a book that focuses on mind, body, and soul?

MANDEL

My dad always wanted me to be a doctor and follow in his footsteps. I resisted because I really didn't want to go through another six years of school plus internship and residency, then work the kinds of hours I saw him work. I managed to sidestep that and went into biomedical engineering instead. I earned bachelor's and master's degrees at MIT and Northwestern University, respectively, and did engineering work for quite a few years.

Then, in 1986 I came across this incredible field called Neuro-Linguistic Programming (NLP). What I discovered is that we can do amazing things with our minds to help heal our bodies because the body and mind are tightly connected. Not only is NLP used for issues that are emotional or mental—depression, anxiety, fears, phobias, and so on—but also it is used for physical ailments.

WRIGHT

It almost sounds like a slap in the face to your father; his medical training was purely physical.

MANDEL

I certainly don't mean to be disrespectful. I cherish his memory and the time I got to spend with him. Unfortunately, he died in 1983 thanks to coronary artery disease.

Physicians are, indeed, trained almost exclusively in physical health. They measure this and prescribe that or they perform surgery. I mean no disparagement to him or to the medical profession whatsoever. In fact, I take medication myself when appropriate. It's not about that. It's about this: We have other tools to help people heal using the body-mind relationship without having to rely on physical substances like medications. I think of it as being *in addition to* or *complementary with* Western medicine.

WRIGHT

I wonder if you could say a bit more about the body-mind relationship.

MANDEL

If you look at your hand for a moment—the part before the knuckles—and try to move it without moving your fingers, you'll find that you can't. The fingers move anyway. If you try to move your fingers without moving your hand, you can't do that, either.

WRIGHT

You got me. I just tried it.

## Mandel

To me, the body and mind are related like the fingers and the hand. Whatever happens in the body affects the mind; whatever happens in the mind affects the body. It's not so much that there is a relationship between the two—it's more that they're parts of the same fully integrated system.

We are body, mind, soul, and spirit. Part of us happens to exist in three-dimensional space such that we can look at the body, touch it, or measure its temperature. Part of us we call our mind. The mind isn't just in the brain—the mind includes the brain and encompasses more than the brain. Beyond that there is soul, spirit, and our connections with other human beings and all that lives.

The common vernacular is "body-mind connection." To me, body and mind are just components of a whole system that is called "you" or "me." Just as you have a left hand and a right hand, you have a body and a mind—but it's all still you. You are not only a collection of parts—you are a fully integrated human being. Body and mind are parts of the same system and intimately affect each other.

One of the groundbreaking books on this subject is *Molecules of Emotion: The Science Behind Mind-Body Medicine* (Simon & Schuster, 1999) by Candace Pert, PhD. Pert is a research professor in the Department of Physiology and Biophysics at Georgetown University Medical Center in Washington, D.C. She gives strong scientific support for the body-mind school of medicine.

Another book is *The Biology of Belief: Unleashing the Power of Consciousness, Matter, & Miracles* (Hay House, 2011) by Bruce Lipton, PhD, cell biologist, and former professor at the University of Wisconsin School of Medicine. He writes about new discoveries regarding the interaction between body and mind and the processes by which cells receive information.

### Wright

So what are some of the physical symptoms or ailments you have been able to help people resolve using just their minds?

### Mandel

One of the ailments for which we commonly use NLP is allergies.

Think about this for a minute. Let's say you are allergic to cats, but you're perfectly okay with dogs. The question is this: is cat dander actually dangerous? Well, I've got one of my two cats sitting on my lap as I write this. I frequently put my nose in his fur, give him soft kisses, and inhale his dander. It doesn't bother me a bit. There are millions of people in the world who are perfectly fine with cat dander.

In other words, the dander itself is not dangerous. However, some people's immune systems have gotten confused. They overreact by responding as if the dander were dangerous, when in reality it is not, but the reaction to the dander can be dangerous.

In other words, an allergic reaction is just a mistake of the immune system. Think of kids trying to put a square peg in a round hole. They either learned and forgot or they haven't yet learned how to do it right. The same with cat dander, it is just as safe as dog dander, but with people who have an allergic reaction, their immune system seems to have forgotten that fact (or never learned it correctly in the first place).

What we do with NLP, then, is use the mind to retrain the immune system. We teach it that cats are just like dogs—cat dander is just like dog dander. Cats purr and dogs bark, but both their danders are safe. When the person is taken through an allergy resolution process, the immune system relaxes and thinks, "Cat—big deal, dog—big deal, they're both the same to me. Why react to cats when they're not actually dangerous?"

I created a Web site dedicated to resolving allergies. You can see my Web site addresses, which are listed at the end of this chapter. People can actually eliminate their allergic responses by going to my Web site, following the allergy link, investing a small amount (less than most people spend for a month's supply of allergy medicine), downloading the *Allergy Resolution Process* e-book, and following the instructions therein.

It takes about two hours to do the *Allergy Resolution Process* thoroughly. Approximately 80 percent will no longer react to their previously dreaded substances—cats, dogs, milk, pollen, wool, you name it. Whether an environmental, animal, or food allergy, the process usually works quite well.

Naturally, results will vary. The disclaimer at the Web site is important for people to read carefully, especially when it comes to safety.

Here is another example of using the mind to resolve physical symptoms: A man with low back pain went to his primary care physician who didn't find anything physically wrong. He prescribed a pain killer and an anti-inflammatory. The man also went to a chiropractor who wasn't able to help, either. Suspecting a possible emotional cause, however, he referred the man to me.

The man said that his back pain bothered him for about a month every year—from Thanksgiving to Christmas. I found it interesting that it was so seasonal. I've heard of seasonal allergies but never seasonal back pain.

He talked about holiday stress. When he was a kid, his family got a little weird that time of year. We delved into those memories, and I took him through an NLP process known as a "visual swish," which is effective in helping people resolve anxieties. His back relaxed and the pain went away almost immediately. When I saw him again about five years later, the seasonal back pain still had not returned.

One more example, if I may—migraines. Migraine headaches afflict about thirty million Americans, according to the National Headache Foundation. The medical community has made great strides with regard to pharmaceutical treatment over the years, which is a very good thing. Sometimes, however, we can help resolve the symptoms without meds by just using the mind.

I recall two incidents when I was able to assist people with migraines. One involved a former girlfriend who had such bad migraines that she had to stay home from work as often as twice a month. After I took her through an advanced process called Releasing Emotional Enmeshment created by Dr. Robert McDonald as part of The Destination Method (please see Acknowledgements and Resources at the end of this chapter) to unravel some long-standing issues with her father (who was long gone, by the way), her symptoms were significantly reduced—75 percent better, according to her—and less frequent. In fact, she did not have to miss work anymore due to migraines.

The other migraine incident was at an NLP workshop I gave called "NLP Play Day." In front of the group, I worked with folks one-on-one with whatever they wanted to resolve. The first person, as it turned out, was a woman who had awakened with a painful migraine. In fact, she sounded so bad on the phone before the workshop that I tried to convince her to stay home for her own safety. She assured me she would be able to drive to the workshop, but if the NLP we would do at the workshop didn't work, she would get a ride home.

Fortunately, we were able to resolve the headache completely by doing Six-Step Reframing, a powerful and common NLP process. She was able not only to sit through the rest of the workshop but also drive herself home. Though a bit sleepy during the workshop because of her ordeal, she was thrilled that the pain was gone. I have to tell you, David, I *love* it when that happens!

WRIGHT

Remarkable!

Now, you've talked about thoughts and you've talked about beliefs; are those both components of the mind? How are they related?

MANDEL

A thought is something like this: “I think I’ll have a turkey sandwich for lunch” or “My socks don’t quite match my slacks.” They tend to be fleeting rather than pervasive. They’re just concepts about something. They don’t run our lives in any significant way and don’t go much beyond the subject of the thought itself.

A belief, on the other hand, is more set in stone. We have beliefs about God and spirituality, about equality, wealth, relationships, identity, and so on. Beliefs are pervasive and long-lasting. They color and organize our thoughts. In a very real sense, our beliefs run our lives, yet we’re often not aware of them until we take the time to examine them.

**Beliefs–Values**

↓

**Thoughts**

Notice that beliefs and values are at the same level. They’re how we know what is important to us. If we value education, for example, then education is important to us and we will take steps to ensure that our kids get a good education. If we believe that health is a high priority, we will be sure to eat well and take care of ourselves to maintain good health.

To reiterate, thoughts are fleeting and temporary; beliefs and values are pervasive and long-term. The relationship looks like this: Our thoughts are organized by our beliefs and values.

Let me give you an example. Let's say that a person has certain political leanings, and two candidates come up for election for the same office. If candidate A has the same political views as the voter and candidate B does not, that difference in values is going to run the voter's thoughts. The voter will think, "When Election Day comes, I'm going to vote for candidate A. Not only that, I'm going to contribute some of my hard-earned dollars to the campaign."

It bears repeating: Our beliefs and values organize our thoughts. They're all components of the mind, but beliefs are more *significant* than thoughts. At the same time, thoughts are more *fundamental* than beliefs.

To look at it another way, consider that this sentence consists of words and the words consist of letters. Which are more significant, the words or the letters? The words are more significant; unorganized letters are just alphabet soup such as we might feed to our kids.

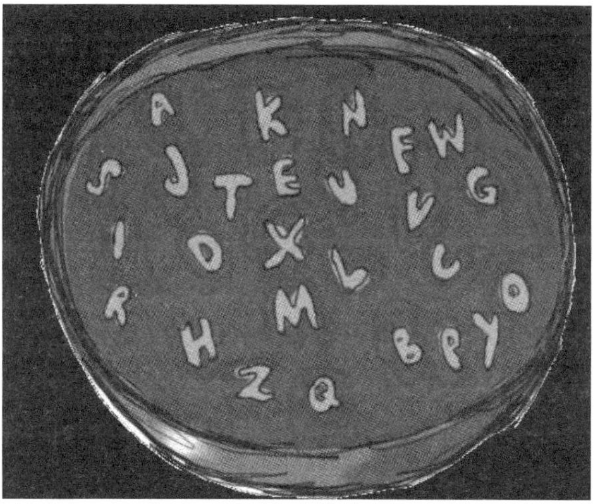

Letters, on the other hand, have little significance unless they're organized into words. Words, then, are more *significant*—they transcend and include letters. Letters, however, are more *fundamental*—they are the building blocks of words. You can have letters without words, but you can't have words without letters.

The same goes for thoughts (or letters) and beliefs-values (or words). Beliefs and values are more *significant* than thoughts (transcend and include). Thoughts are more *fundamental* than beliefs (building blocks). You can have thoughts without beliefs, but you can't have beliefs without thoughts.

Ken Wilber discusses these hierarchical concepts in great detail in his wonderful book, *A Brief History of Everything* (Shambhala, 2001).

### WRIGHT

The title of this book is *Health: Mind, Body Soul.* We've touched on the mind and body; how does the soul fit in?

### MANDEL

I think of the soul as being beyond belief, so to speak. It's even beyond identity, at the same level as spirit.

We all have physical bodies, we all have thoughts, we all have beliefs, and we all have a sense of identity. These are all entirely about the individual—about you and me separate from each other and separate from everyone else.

When we run out of "me," what else is there? I think of soul or spirit as a way of connecting with other people and with the larger systems of which we are a part. Body, mind, and spirit-soul are intimately connected as aspects or levels of the individual.

### WRIGHT

Let's get back to allergies. I've gotten to be an old man now with no allergies for most of my life. All of a sudden I've developed allergies in the spring. I take a little pill every day, but I don't know if it helps or not. Are you actually able to cure allergies using the mind?

MANDEL

First, I have to say that the literal answer to your question is "no" because of the word *cure*. Let me explain.

If I were to represent that I am able to cure something, I would need FDA approval. The medical community would have to share that conclusion and there would have to be studies to prove it. Since it's not an FDA-approved process and most allergists would say allergies can't be cured, I'd have to say "no." That's why I use the term *resolve* rather than *cure*.

Consequently, I think of it as changing your relationship with, or changing your body's response to, an allergen. We're really just re-educating your immune system to do something different.

Notice that this so-called allergen is just as safe as another similar substance. Some people are allergic to cow's milk, some to soy milk. However, there are billions of people in the world who aren't allergic to either. It's not normal to react negatively to either of those substances since billions of people don't have those reactions. Happily, we have used NLP body-mind techniques like my *Allergy Resolution Process* to resolve these types of allergies and many more.

The answer to your question, then, is that we don't actually cure allergies, but we aim to change your response to the pollen to a *null* response. For example, do you respond to flour if you walk into a bakery and there is flour dust?

WRIGHT

No, not really.

MANDEL

Good! So why would your immune system react to flower dust (pollen) when it doesn't react to flour dust? Those are similar substances in a sense that they're both tiny, airborne particles. We can re-educate your immune system to ignore the flower dust just as it ignores the flour dust.

WRIGHT

So FDA approval notwithstanding, the bottom line here is would my eyes quit tearing up?

MANDEL

As mentioned previously, the NLP Allergy Resolution Process is about 80 percent successful. The way I offer it on my Web site is this: There is a nominal cost to download the e-book. You work the process on your own in the comfort of your own home. In the off-chance that you're not completely satisfied, I will either talk with you one-on-one by phone to find out what we can do to make it work or refund your investment. The choice is yours.

I take all the risk. If it doesn't work, I'll either work with you individually or give you your money back!

WRIGHT

That's a generous offer, Phil. I'll definitely consider it.

On a different note, I've heard that two-thirds of Americans are overweight or obese. Of course, that has significant health implications. What can we do with our minds to help get our bodies into better shape?

MANDEL

That's my favorite question of all, David, since overweight and obesity are destroying the health of our society.

We all have unique relationships with food. Interestingly, food in the physical sense is just a set of substances that nourishes us and keeps us alive. Trouble is, sometimes people eat for the wrong reasons. Isn't that amazing?

Let's say you have a belief in God. If I were to ask you, "Why do you think God put food on the planet when He created everything?" you might say, "To make me happy; to keep me from being depressed!" But if you really think about it, food is here to nourish our bodies—to make us healthy and strong so we can live productive, vibrant lives.

WRIGHT

Only the pie was there for the happy part.

MANDEL

Or dark chocolate, in my case.

When people eat because they're depressed or because it's Tuesday or because they're happy or because they're sad, it leads to being overweight or obese—and associated maladies like heart disease, high blood pressure, diabetes, and so on.

So, what can we do with our minds to help get our bodies into better shape? We can change our relationship to food. We can notice that even if we do get some relief from emotional distress by eating, it's just temporary relief—but it has long-lasting effects that are often far worse than finding another way to handle the distress.

I suggest that people find different ways to deal with their stresses, anxieties, and depression. Becoming overweight often starts a nasty downward spiral. They begin to feel bad physically, they're depressed because they keep expanding into bigger pant or dress sizes, then they need to eat more to stuff those feelings and handle the depression that is now worse because they ate more.

Fortunately, I'm lucky enough to be associated with a system called Take Shape For Life that addresses these issues in a very effective way (see my Web sites at the end of this chapter). I work nationwide with folks to help them adopt healthier lifestyles, change their relationships with food, lose their excess weight, and learn how to keep it off for life so they can enjoy longer, healthier lives.

### WRIGHT

How about some of the other major diseases such as cancer, multiple sclerosis, or lupus?

### MANDEL

Oh gosh, those are biggies. I would love nothing more than to tell you we can reliably resolve those diseases. Sadly, that is not the case yet.

Cancer is almost the opposite of an allergy. Remember, an allergy is, loosely speaking, the result of a hyper-vigilant immune system. In other words, the immune system is reacting to something as if it's dangerous even though it really isn't. With cancer, on the other hand, the body's defenses ignore something that actually *is* dangerous.

Believe it or not, every one of us has potentially cancerous cells in our bodies nearly all the time. Some of our cells mutate and could start growing without restraint, but the surrounding cells say, "This isn't right. You don't belong here. Goodbye!" and they dismantle and eliminate the misbehaving cells.

When something goes wrong, however, these runaway cells take hold and start to grow. The body's defenses ignore them, and *voila*, there's a tumor.

What we can do is help people use their minds to try and get in touch with what is going on with the cancer. We have various ways of trying to shake up the immune system so it will start paying attention to that crazy growth that doesn't belong. Sometimes we're able to help a person get better.

Again, I'm not going to use the word *cure*, but there are many anecdotes describing people who had remarkable recoveries using body-mind techniques. Nothing I've just said, however, should preclude readers from taking appropriate action and following the advice of their physicians.

There's an entire field nowadays called Psychoneuroimmunology (PNI) that addresses body-mind healing using scientific methodology.

Let's break down that big word, shall we? *Psycho* relates to the mind, *neuro* refers to the nervous system, and *immunology* has to do with the immune system. PNI, then, studies the relationship among the mind, nervous system, and immune system.

PNI specialists use a variety of techniques aimed at promoting health such as deep breathing, guided imagery, relaxation therapy, meditation, and yoga. Using these techniques, mind-body medicine helps direct a person's energies toward health and healing.

Multiple sclerosis (MS) and lupus are other diseases in which the immune system has gone awry. They're more like allergies in the sense that the immune system attacks good tissue instead of letting it be. What we want to do is use the body-mind relationship to remind the immune system that the tissue is good stuff, not bad, and to please leave it alone. Anecdotally, there are many cases when folks have been able to improve their condition using NLP, PNI, and other body-mind techniques.

The first such case I can recall was a fellow NLP Practitioner I met at a conference. I had no idea there was anything wrong with her since she seemed like she had more energy than most people, including me! When her husband told me she had recovered from MS using NLP, I was stunned. Her diagnosis was chronic progressive MS, the same type my sister, Jill, had until she died from complications at just fifty-three. If only I had had some of these tools while she was still alive, I might have been able to help her.

WRIGHT

Phil, I'm so sorry about your loss.

Now, we've talked a lot about the mind, what about the relationship between the mind and the brain?

MANDEL

If I were to ask you to point to your brain, I don't think it would be difficult. You'd probably point to your head, and you'd be right.

The brain weighs about two pounds; it's this wide and that long and thusly tall. If you'll forgive my being graphic, when a coroner does an autopsy he or she can open the head and take out the brain, and there it is.

You can't do that with your mind. If I were to ask you to point to your mind, where would you point? As you know, sometimes you might be anxious and get butterflies in your stomach. Is your mind in your stomach? Some people may get heartburn or pain in the chest, or their heart starts to flutter when they're nervous. Is the mind in the heart? Some people have inklings or premonitions—they just happen to be thinking about someone and the phone rings; it's the person they were just thinking about! Is the mind in the phone? (Just kidding.)

Clearly, the mind extends beyond the brain. It includes the brain and also includes the entire body—everywhere to which the nervous system extends. I may get a bit "woo-woo" here, but my belief is that it extends even beyond the body, which is how the premonition just mentioned is possible. Perhaps it's one of the subtle ways we're able to connect deeply with others person-to-person—the fact that our minds include and extend beyond our physical bodies.

### WRIGHT

There is one word I come away with that has woven itself through everything in this conversation—*relationship*. You talked about relationships with food, with pollen, with all kinds of things. So when you are engaged in mind, body, and soul, are you really changing relationships? Is that the crux of the matter?

### MANDEL

I would have to say "yes," David, because we're either changing our relationship with ourselves or changing our relationship with someone or something external to us.

If I change my relationship to cat dander so my immune system understands that cat dander is just as safe as dog dander or dust or flowers or flour, I've accomplished something. If I change my relationship with myself to get my immune system to pay attention to a tumor it was ignoring, I've accomplished something. If I change my relationship to food, then I can enjoy food for purposes other than comfort and the illusion of love.

### Wright

While sitting here listening, knowing that I am overweight, thinking about some of the things that I eat, well, it's hard to get excited about something that you do twenty-one times a week (three meals per day) or, as many doctors say, we ought to eat four times a day. I do find myself eating a lot when I'm tired, especially during this time of year (winter) when I do a lot of music-related activities during the evenings. If I'm lucky, I get home before ten o'clock perhaps two nights a week. At my age, seventy-two, everybody says I'm a ball of fire. Well, no I'm not. I'm tired all the time, so I find myself eating because I'm tired or because I have no energy, which sometimes has nothing to do with being hungry. I'm rarely ever hungry. The only time I get hungry is when I don't eat breakfast. Along about noon I get hungry, but I know I should eat breakfast every morning. When I did on a regular basis, I was a lot healthier. It's like that spiral you were talking about. I was carrying out the thought you had. After a while it just gets ridiculous; it gets completely out of control.

### Mandel

I understand, David. I can give you some suggestions in that regard, as long as you understand that I'm not a physician, nutritionist, dietician, nurse, personal trainer, or any other licensed practitioner in the medical field. I am, however, certified as a health coach affiliated with Take Shape For Life, which I consider to be the premier health and weight management program in the country. I retired from engineering to join the company. I can make some suggestions that have worked for thousands of clients and health coaches I've worked with over the past five years, if you'd like.

First of all, how much water do you drink in a day?

### WRIGHT

That is one of my problems!

### MANDEL

The suggestion I've heard from several physicians is to take your weight in pounds and divide by two. Drink at least that many ounces of water per day.

For example, let's say you weigh two hundred pounds. Half of that is one hundred, so you should be drinking a minimum of one hundred ounces of water per day. That sounds like a lot, but it translates to six common 16.9-ounce water bottles—just one every couple of hours while you're awake.

I'd bet you would feel better and have more energy from day one if you were to drink at least that much water every day. (Naturally, anyone contemplating this should check with a health care provider first.)

Next, let's talk about what you said a moment ago. Part of the problem is that you don't eat breakfast! Even if it's just a banana, or egg whites and a slice of toast, anything healthy first thing in the morning (within thirty minutes of getting out of bed) will have you feeling better and more energetic throughout the day.

I'm not sure where you heard about eating four times a day. In our program (Take Shape For Life), we eat six to seven times a day. Generally speaking, the more frequently you eat little nibbles here and there, the better off you'll be.

Let's talk about insulin for a moment. The secret to weight control is this: keep your insulin at a stable level. If you don't eat for several hours, your blood sugar starts to get low. Then, when you finally do eat, your insulin pump goes, "Oh goody—there's a bunch of sugar in the blood stream. I'd better store it quickly before it goes away!" The insulin pump kicks in and you store like crazy. In fact, you're already in starvation mode so that whatever you eat is going to turn into storage first. Then if you're lucky, there is a little bit left over to get you through the next two to three hours so you can burn some of it off *before* it gets stored as fat.

To summarize, drink three to four quarts of water per day (more if you're—um—heavier than 200 pounds); eat a modest, healthy breakfast *every day*; then eat every two to three hours throughout the day no matter how busy you are, even if it is just a glass of low-fat milk or piece of fresh fruit. That's not the end of my coaching for you, but at least it's a start!

WRIGHT

Well, even though we finished the formal interview a while ago, I just thought I'd get some free advice.

MANDEL

Happy to do so!

WRIGHT

Phil, thank you again for participating in *Health: Mind, Body, Soul*. It's been a pleasure talking with you.

MANDEL

The pleasure is mine, David. I look forward to seeing the finished product and reading my co-authors' chapters!

# About the Author

Master Practitioner of Neuro-Linguistic Programming (NLP), Certified Destination Method® Coach, Certified Flight Instructor, long-distance cyclist, accomplished pianist, and recovering engineer with degrees from MIT and Northwestern University, Philip H. Mandel coaches individuals and leads workshops on topics ranging from motivation and getting things done to losing weight and reducing stress.

"Phil is sincerely interested in helping others with their goals. He has a unique sense of humor and style that makes him stand out and shine. Working with him is always interesting and uplifting, and his caring manner makes his 'space' a safe place to be. I give him my highest recommendations and will continue to make referrals to him."—Michael Underhill, D.C., Beaverton, Oregon.

"Phil's NLP sessions have helped me make better cold calls, improve my level of confidence, and increase my sales."—Kelly Critser, Beaverton, Oregon.

## Acknowledgments and Resources

Over the years, many wonderful people have helped educate me with regard to the material presented in this chapter. With apologies to those I inadvertently leave out, I want to acknowledge selected individuals and offer the reader resources for further study.

Dr. Robert Dee McDonald and Rev. Dr. Luzette McDonald, founders and principals of Telos Healing Center (www. teloscenter.com), Yorba Linda, California. Robert is creator of The Destination Method®, which includes the Releasing Emotional Enmeshment process mentioned in this chapter along with several other deeply transformational processes.

Tim Hallbom (NLP Institute of California, www.nlpca.com), Suzi Smith (Suzi Smith and Associates, www.suzismith.net), and Robert Dilts (NLP University, www.nlpu.com), co-developers of the NLP Counter-Example Process from which I developed my *Allergy Resolution Process* e-book.


Philip H.Mandel

*Phil Mandel and Associates*

Beaverton, Oregon

503-887-0889

phil@philmandel.com

www.philmandel.com – speaking, training

www.resolveallergies.com – *Allergy Resolution Process*

www.shapewithphil.com – Take Shape For Life

health and weight management

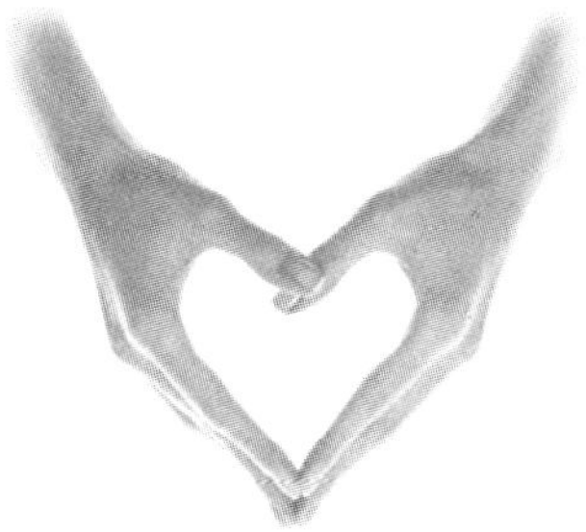

Chapter Five

# Holistic Integrative Healthcare: A Healing Practice for the New Millennium

with Barbara Ford-Latty

## THE INTERVIEW

DAVID WRIGHT (WRIGHT)

Barbara Ford-Latty is the president and founder of The Haelen Group, an integrative health collaborative. Barbara specializes in energy therapies, including energetic touch, aromatherapy, and sound therapy. An RN with a master's degree in Holistic Wellness, she is fully grounded in traditional allopathic healthcare as well as holism. Believing passionately in preserving the balance in our natural environment and living in balance within that environment, Barbara is an educator, lecturer, author, and integrative health facilitator. She also works one-on-one with her clients to improve their quality of life with heart-centered care and in partnership with traditional healthcare.

Today I'd like to welcome Barbara Ford-Latty to *Health: Mind, Body, Soul.*

BARBARA FORD-LATTY (FORD-LATTY)

Thank you.

WRIGHT

I know you have had experiences with many facets of healthcare. How do you define "integrative health"?

FORD-LATTY

I think the integrative approach to healthcare applies the knowledge of conventional Western medicine with natural, noninvasive, complementary health practices.

For example, some complementary energy practices include acupuncture, Qigong, healing touch, meditation, yoga, and body work. These are just a few of the various practices that support and enhance the body's natural healing process.

The strength of the integrative approach lies in its holistic view of wellness. Unlike other cultures, Western healthcare has drifted further and further away from the holistic treatment of health issues. I purposely do not use the term "disease" here because as a society we tend to equate that word with only physical ailments, losing sight of the fact that we are energetic beings, connected in all ways with the universe around us in mind, body, and spirit. We are more than a collection of machine parts, each part working in isolation from the others.

In the complexity of today's world, your healthcare should not add to the confusion, but present options in an informed stress-free manner and these options should be grounded in an understanding of both traditional and complementary therapies in order to move out of a *sick-care* system into a true *health-care* system. The integrative approach guides the individual to take control of her or his own health, thus making appropriate lifestyle changes that help improve quality of life.

The bottom line is that integrative healthcare partners the best of both traditional medicine and complementary therapy—the best of both worlds—to make a healing process, not just a quick fix.

## Wright

With your background in traditional healthcare, what influenced you to explore alternative health practices?

## Ford-Latty

This metamorphosis has evolved over many years. In the years that I have been involved in the health arena, I have seen a gradual depersonalization of our healthcare. There is less and less room for the person in the process of healing. Most of us in the health field have been programmed to view ourselves as did Descartes and Newton—the body is a machine with separate parts and Western medical science took this on as a guiding philosophy.

It was obvious to me that our obsession with science somewhat obscured the fact that, yes indeed, we are physical beings, but we are energetic and spiritual ones as well; we're not just a collection of body parts. I, like so many of us in healthcare, have come to agree with the Einsteinian paradigm: we are matter as expressed by a continually changing, complex system of interconnected energy and this system is connected to the universe around us. We now understand that wellness depends upon the integration of complex needs with the inherent resources of the human being.

But there are other, more mundane reasons for me. As a nurse, I've always been in the caring dimension of healthcare, but I am aware of a shift from caring, comforting, and healing to technology, documentation, and tasks. The emphasis in healthcare today is focused on the many requirements that are placed upon us by a corporate system of healthcare. We are pressured to meet so many expectations that we have become purely task-oriented.

Technological advances are magnificent but without addressing the whole person we only create more problems. We've all seen the increase in giving a *"pill for an ill,"* so to speak. In the search to find cures, we administer more medication. As a result, many elderly and not so elderly come into hospitals taking a plethora of different medications for a wide range of disorders. The effect of these medications is cumulative—they build up over time, especially in the elderly and in children.

The more medications we put into our body, the more interactions they produce, and believe me when I say that they do have repercussions whether we feel them immediately or not. I have seen elderly patients taken out of their familiar territories who become agitated when they cannot understand what is happening to them in the hospitals. To calm their agitation they're given more medicine and they develop reactions, sometimes quite severe ones.

The Agency for Healthcare Research and Quality reports that the number of drug-related hospitalizations in the United States increased from 1.2 million to 1.9 million from 2004 to 2008 and patients age sixty-five and older accounted for 53 percent of these hospitalizations. I feel that we have become a society of excess and this is reflected in our methods of treatment.

The final reason is that healthcare has become big business and this business is the prime mover for the industry. It may be masquerading as patient centered care, but to stay viable, business has changed the scene in healthcare. I feel that alternative therapies such as healing touch, sound therapy, acupuncture, and mindfulness meditation bring us back to the person. They allow me once again to touch the patient in mind, body, and spirit; to calm, to reassure, to offer aid, and to heal. For me, I feel that I have evolved into a higher sense of my profession and my goal is now to heal safely and to nurture rather than cure.

### WRIGHT

How do you explain the new interest in alternative health therapies and integrative health?

### FORD-LATTY

I think a paradigm shift is slowly beginning to emerge in Western society and it is changing the meaning of health today. As we are shunted from one specialist to another, from one diagnostic test to another, we feel separated from healing, not connected to it. People are looking toward the complementary healthcare practitioners for this connection. The relationship between the practitioner and client is vital to the process of healing. This partnership is a synergy of awareness, compassion, intention, sincerity, and presence, which form the foundation of all other interactions and from which trust evolves.

Secondly, I believe there is growing dissatisfaction with the results and the safety of allopathic healthcare. Doesn't it make sense that people prefer to try a natural product or a noninvasive therapy before they surrender to more invasive therapy or stronger medication? As a society we need to work harder to prevent catastrophic illness and this work needs to be recognized as appropriate treatment by insurance companies and the government agencies responsible for our well-being.

The National Center for Complementary and Alternative Medicine (NCCAM) study in 2008 found that more than 38 percent of the population age seventeen years and older report using CAM. The complementary therapies included natural supplements, meditation, energetic touch, and yoga.

As a society, we're finally moving from a cultural perspective that focused purely on the physical lack of disease and are moving toward the idea of health as a balanced, dynamic, open, living system that exists in synergy with all other life forms. We are moving forward into a new era and we are pulling the traditional healthcare community with us.

### Wright

With all the theories of health that we read about, hear, and see in the media these days, what is the significance of integrative health?

FORD-LATTY

I think there are three significant precepts that form the foundation of integrative health and I think these are why it is so significant, relevant, and necessary in today's world. Integrative health is a holistic process implemented by qualified practitioners who understand that health is multidimensional. These precepts are:

1. A balance of elements is essential for healing.
2. Care, which includes love for the person and protection, is the thread that weaves the tapestry of whole healing.
3. It is based in Holism. This is enabled by a supportive partnership between a holistic practitioner who understands traditional medicine and complementary therapies and an individual who is empowered to take responsibility for his or her own health.

So I'd just like to take a moment and explain why these three tenets are significant. First of all, let's talk about balance. This is the concept that Hippocrates and Plato espoused centuries ago and is called homeostasis. The term itself was coined in 1926 from two Greek words; homeos meaning of the same kind, and stasis meaning standing still. In other words, all like components remain stable, while those that are unlike, change, move, and become unstable. The body continually strives for stability—balance—even in the face of change.

This principle is the basis for all integrative treatment. An individual's lifestyle, genetic makeup, and state of being are all considered. In order for this principle of homeostasis or balance to maintain health, it must be present at all levels: mind, body, and spirit. Each level connects and supports the other and with the universe around us. Our body is made to heal, to rebalance itself.

Imbalance happens when we do not pay attention to our body or give much thought to our choices.

The second piece is caring. In this context, caring is love in the highest sense of compassion, genuine care, and concern for a person's highest good, and it's a powerful component of healing. The ability to love ourselves and our life in the present moment leads to a healthy way of living.

For example, research shows that the immune system is stimulated by love and support. These positive feelings can reduce the risk of angina, and it can promote longer term survival from serious illness such as cancer. Love is deeply related to what keeps us well and what makes us sick and is one of the most powerful interventions that I can offer to those I serve. Caring also includes protection from harm, which mandates that as healers, we hold ourselves to the highest credo—we shall do no harm and work only for your greater good.

Caring also defines the integrative relationship between the practitioner and the client. It is through caring that trust is established, and it is a reciprocal relationship. As much as the individual receives from the practitioner, the practitioner also learns and draws energy from the individual. The following model of Holistic Synergy visualizes the concept where the energies combine, informing the healing relationship between the two. (See Diagram 2 below.)

Now we come to the third piece, where we bring all of the

THE SYNERGY OF HOLISM

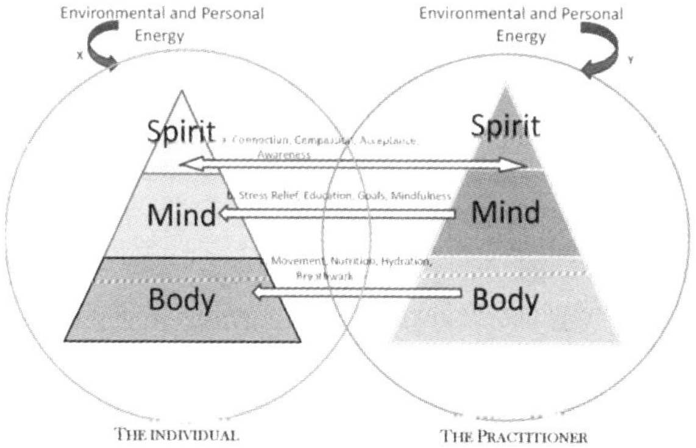

elements into balance—holism. It's up to the practitioner to guide the individual toward achievement of his or her own personal goals. In the holistic approach, the individual is a full partner working toward whole balance.

### Wright

What do you mean exactly by the term "holism"?

### Ford-Latty

Holism is a word that has been bandied around for quite a while. A holistic approach looks at the entire dynamic state of being. It's all about the balance that I mentioned previously. Fundamentally, holism incorporates certain essential elements for wellness:

- Fresh, pure water
- Deep and restful sleep
- Safe and nutrient-rich food
- Adequate physical activity
- Micro environmental protection, which means lack of chemical pollutants in food and water and air
- Complete, dynamic, and positive energy fields
- A connection with spirit

There is no *one size fits all* in holism, it is individual for each person, but without each of these elements you are out of balance. The awareness of these elements, and an informed understanding of their role in health, is the fundamental concept of holism. Each individual's needs at a particular time and in a particular space are a reflection of his or her balance, or imbalance, at that instant. Holism takes into consideration all the factors that influence health for that person.

Let me give you an example. In osteoporosis, products such as supplements or medications are but one part of the treatment. We also have to understand the need for whole food nutrition and the movement of energy through our being and how it affects the absorption of these nutrients by body. This energy flow is integral to wellness, and there are different methods of enhancing it. To move gently without pain is one goal of therapy.

Physical exercise enhances the flow of energy and takes many forms. It can be Qigong, sports, dancing—there are many avenues to enhance this flow of energy through the body, but the important point is to understand all of the needs in reestablishing the balanced self. The holistic practitioner looks not only at the area of the body where a problem occurs, but the entire energetic system, the other physical systems, and the quality of the seven elements. It's like a puzzle—what is missing, what can be improved, where are the blocks, what's working well? In this way, you get a three-dimensional approach to the person.

I think that this holistic paradigm is sorely needed, as health concerns become more and more complex and the allopathic or traditional perspective of looking at each disease as purely a malfunction of a body part managed by a pill for an ill is no longer sufficient. Holism takes all the factors that influence the health for that person into consideration and this management of wellness is orchestrated by the knowledge that imbalances to any of these essential elements are common to most, if not all chronic disease. It makes sense to look at the whole person and that is the holistic approach.

WRIGHT

What are some of the reservations you have concerning the food we eat?

FORD-LATTY

As we are all well aware, along with pure water, safe nutritious food is crucial to our health and well-being. Books have been written about this topic, so most of us are familiar with the new dietary recommendations and low-salt, low saturated fat, low carbohydrate—the new millennium mantra for healthy eating. There are additional recommendations that I think are extraordinarily important for us to confront in today's society.

First, the way we choose the food we eat in combination is important for digestion. Food combining is complex, but the basic theory holds that certain rules are important for optimum digestion and utilization. In today's world, seven out of ten people have some type of digestion upset, whether it's irritable bowel syndrome, acid reflux, gastric ulcers. This type of disorder is predominant in our society. Doesn't it make you wonder what is going on with our food?

There are some types of food that are best eaten together, some are best eaten alone. Here are some basic rules of food combinations:

1. Fruits should be eaten alone because they are easily digested, eaten in the morning or several hours after other foods. Melon should always be eaten alone and not combined with other foods.
2. Starch and protein should be eaten together. The reason for this is that proteins require an acid digestive medium and starches require an alkaline one, so when combined, they interfere with each other and lead to chronic GI upset. What is our Western diet, if it isn't meat and potatoes?
3. For adults, milk shouldn't be used as a beverage but counted as a food, not as a liquid with food.

As important as food combining is for our gastrointestinal health, the safety of our food and the processing of our food create new risks to our general health. We need to scrutinize food additives and how our food is grown, raised, processed, and transported. For example, certain substances have been added to our food storage materials such as PDE, BPA, PFA, and Pthalates. These are chemical substances that cause cancer, endocrine disruption, and neurodevelopmental issues, but they are allowed to pollute our foods. Don't you want to know why?

There are also certain substances called excitotoxins that cause the neurotransmitters in our brains to work rapidly overtime. Examples of these are aspartame and monosodium glutamate (MSG). Low doses of MSG slowly overwork the neurons in our brain to death, which can result in neurodegenerative diseases. Even low doses of MSG in the diet of children, whose developing systems are more vulnerable to influence, can cause abnormal development in glands and neurons with delayed direct toxic effects on the nerve cells of the hypothalamus. Up until 1967, MSG was routinely added to baby food until legislation brought this practice to an end—an end for baby food, but not for other foods.

Current research is being done on the neuron changes from excitotoxins and their link to Alzheimer's disease. We need to pay close attention to food labels and demand accuracy. We need to understand that just because some additives are deemed safe by regulators does not hold true long-term. We need to know exactly what we're eating and why food processing companies are so resistant to giving out this information. Doesn't that make you wonder about safety?

Genetically Modified Organisms (GMOs) also compromise food safety. A GMO is a living organism that has been altered by inserting genes from another species. This has been done for a variety of reasons, but the most publicized one has centered on feeding the starving world populations by producing fast-growing, heavy-yielding super crops. To test this assumption, the Union of Concerned Scientists completed a study and found that despite twenty years of research and thirteen years of promotion, genetic engineering has failed to significantly increase U.S. crops, yet today more than 80 percent of U.S. soybean and corn crops are GMOs.

What is the risk of these crops to consumers? For one, we are seeing more food allergies, especially in children. Additionally, there is depletion of crop diversity, which has resulted in super weeds and the companies that have genetically modified the organism produce super weed killers. These weed killers cause birth defects. Other risks are yet unknown but if the past is any indicator, that which we believe is harmless usually turns out to be either carcinogenic or otherwise harmful.

Do we have the right to know if the food we eat has been genetically modified? Ninety percent of the United States consumers say they want these foods to be labeled, but so far the FDA has not made this a requirement.

Finally, public health experts have been warning the industry about antibiotic use in factory farms for years. These antibiotics are administered in low doses to make the animals we eat grow faster in crowded, unhealthy conditions, and these conditions are breeding grounds for drug resistant bacteria that move from animals to humans. E. coli, Staph resistant bacteria and other bacterial diseases are becoming more and more difficult to overcome.

Because of these issues, it is imperative that we stand up and find out exactly how our food is processed, what has been added to it, and how the animals or plants are raised. Perhaps then we can pick up a container in a supermarket and understand what we are actually eating.

### Wright

You've mentioned energy work as an alternative therapy. How does our energy affect our state of balance and health?

### Ford-Latty

Energy therapy is a relatively new component of the Western understanding of wellness, although it has been an integral element in other cultures' concept of health and wellness for generations. For example: *prana* is the concept of the breath of life in Ayurveda or Indian medicine; *qi* is the energy that provides the life force in Chinese medicine. *Huaca* is the term used by shamans in Peru, *ton* and *wahkan* is the force in the Dakota and Lakota tribes here in the United States. For me, the ancient knowledge of past civilizations need not be discarded as inferior to our own. We need to open our minds and hearts.

Throughout the world there is ongoing research into energy medicine, and the general consensus is forming that energy is indeed an essential conduit for wellness. For example, it is now recognized that the energy of our emotions does actually affect our health and the more subtle energy of life force is growing in acceptance as well. As research continues, it is apparent that there is something essential we have overlooked in Western medicine for quite a while.

Just as we require an uninterrupted flow of pure clean water, the vital force of energy must have an unimpeded flow as well. Unfortunately there are many issues that can impede its flow on all levels. In physical illness there can be blockage of arteries and veins. In mental illness there can be blockages of behavior, emotions, moods, and cognitive ability. In spirit, there can be a lack of connection to a universal force or a creator. This energy, as well as our physical energy, has to be expressed. If it remains blocked, the energy builds into high levels of internal stress that implodes, resulting in high levels of external stress.

For example, the gentle, two-thousand-year-old Chinese internal martial arts of Qigong and Tai Qi are based on this idea of energy flow, or qi (chi). This practice has been linked to health benefits across the spectrum of life for everyone from children to seniors. Studies show that these internal martial arts improve the quality of life for those suffering from menopausal symptoms, sleep problems, breast cancer, arthritis, circulatory issues, and Parkinson's. The combination of gentle movements and deep breathing can be adapted even for people in wheelchairs and others with disabilities. Actually, its benefits can be felt by anyone, not only those who have physical problems. Pain, stress, and anxiety can be lessened with the regular, consistent practice of Qigong or Tai Qi. Flexibility, balance, and cardiovascular health all can be improved with consistent practice over time.

I spoke earlier of the concept of a life force. Another path of connection is through the chakras. With today's media exposure, chakra is now a word that is so overused that it has almost lost its sacred meaning. In actuality, chakras originate in ancient sacred traditions. The seven major chakras come from these sacred traditions and exist in the subtle energetic body that overlays the physical body—one's energetic field. We now know that these seven chakras also bear a relation to important physical parts of our body. It is interesting that each chakra point lays over an essential gland or organ and corresponds to major ganglia, or neuron networks, in our nervous system.

Each chakra imbues a certain type of energy to the person and in balancing the chakras the body comes into balance and alignment. With touch therapy, sound therapy, or Qigong, the energy gates of the body open, and this insures a continual flow of energy.

Let me make a disclaimer: no one is saying that this is a quick fix, which we in the West love so much. Energy work requires intent and commitment to a lifestyle that allows regular practice, whatever method you choose to improve your flow of energy in your life, whether it is internal martial arts, yoga, healing touch, sound therapy, or meditation.

### WRIGHT

You use both sound therapy and touch therapy in your work. How do these modalities help to relieve stress?

FORD-LATTY

Earlier I spoke about the blocking of energy channels causing internal stress expressed as external stress. Energy work, such as touch and sound are methods of unblocking that energy beyond the intervention of a medication or a specific technology. One method is through connection to another person, a caring advocate, who holds the intent to heal. Through the conduit of the healing practitioner's energy, the individual's energy fields become stronger and less obstructed. This is a loving intervention that has been a part of man's evolution since the beginning of time and now we are beginning to see the science behind it as well. Energetically, we are enjoying a harmonious revolution where trust in this creative process of healing is beginning to take its place.

There are four consistent and highly reliable results of a healing touch. One is relaxation and stress relief. This can happen very rapidly, in as little as two to four minutes. Another is pain reduction. I am speaking of clinically significant pain relief where analgesics are no longer necessary.

Touch accelerates the healing process, so it has positive benefits to the immune system, nurturing a fertile ground so that healing can take place and improves the results of traditional treatments. It alleviates psychosomatic illness, because the healing touch affects the autonomic nervous system, which is at the heart of psychosomatic illness. There are measurable benefits to touch therapy, and research is ongoing through incredible organizations such as HeartMath and Healing Touch International, along with the healthcare institutions that support these therapies.

In sound therapy we're also dealing with energy, but this time as vibrations. We all know how music from our past invokes memories, feelings, and actual physical symptoms. We cry, we laugh, we feel good, and we feel bad, all because of the music. The premise behind sound therapy is that specific vibrations of pure sound in increments of fifths can affect the energy field and the physical systems within our bodies and can be experienced by our senses. Our universe resonates in the cadence of fifths—it is the song of nature. Breathing in and out to a count of five reestablishes your connection to the universe around you and the same effect is seen with pure sound, only magnified.

This intervention results in a reestablishment of balance through specific tonal vibrations. The new studies are discovering that music activity throughout your life improves your thought processes and helps the brain adapt to the changes of aging, while sound therapy via the tuning forks' pure sound can actually reach specific areas of weakness inside the body by rebalancing, calming, and clearing the mind.

WRIGHT

So if our energy fields are important for balance, where does intent fit in?

FORD-LATTY

Intent is the foundation of all healing. Think about intent from the standpoint of purpose, focus, and centering. When I enter into a client relationship, I do not do it lightly. Every word, gesture, and nuance becomes important. I am completely focused on the client.

Intent = mindfulness. It is an immersion into the awareness of person and energy. It is the complete focus of one's entire consciousness to the healing process. It is never entered without a sacred commitment, or a centering of one's own energies. So what do I mean by centering? This is the ability to bring a total concentration of energies to the quiet place within—a place of deep unification and awareness of life. In this process, practitioners display certain qualities. They include compassion, authenticity, and mindfulness.

Intent also includes a deep understanding of the tools. Meditation, deep relaxation, energy work, and prayer are all tools of deep healing, but the goals of each are different.

- Meditation empties the mind of all distractions so that we can be totally in the "here and now." Its goal is to arrive at "oneness with the universe."
- In deep relaxation, the goal is the reduction of tension in the body, to relieve stress, and create a receptive, focused mind.
- Energy work opens the energy flow within the body to facilitate healing.
- Prayer is the method by which we connect to a deeper communication with a higher power. Intent pulls this all together. We approach this healing session with our entire focus on the individual and our own inner energies.

I will interject here a few words about the individual's intent. This has to do with the attitude you have toward this type of complementary therapy and your attitude toward your life—your intent. It includes self-awareness, or mindfulness. Mindfulness is the third piece of the holistic puzzle.

Mindfulness Based Stress Reduction (MBSR), introduced by Jon Kabat-Zinn in 1979, is a clinically standardized meditation that has proven effective in alleviating stress, anxiety, and depression. This intense self-awareness of all aspects of self—body, soul, heart and mind—is facilitated by yoga, transcendental meditation, and breathing exercises. In a study by Kabat-Zinn, the response of meditators was compared with non-meditators after receiving an influenza vaccine. Significant positive increases in left-sided brain activation and antibody levels were documented in the meditators. These findings support the theory that mindfulness meditation may positively alter brain and immune function.

The responsibility for developing a genuine intent to receive a navigable path toward healing is shared between the individual and the practitioner.

WRIGHT

When you talk about caring for the whole person, will you explain where the concept of soul or spirit fits in?

FORD-LATTY

Many times, when people talk about soul and spirit, they equate spirituality with religion. They are related but are not synonymous. What we talk about in healing is spirituality, which encompasses a deepened experience, difficult to define—an all-encompassing awareness of the interconnectedness and mystery of life. It's the essence of who we are, unlimited by space and time. It is an expression of souls. Religion is dedicated to the observance and practice of beliefs based on the teachings of a higher being; or god figure. A religion is a specific path to express the soul but also to explain the cause, purpose, and nature of an omnipotent god figure, adopted by a group and practiced via ritual and worship. It is a structure and a process to connect people with this deep mystery of life.

So spirituality is the essence and mystery; it may or may not be expressed through simple traditions and practices but it usually is. Religion is but one vehicle for the expression of spirituality but it is not a prerequisite for this expression. There are many ways of understanding and expressing spirituality that transcend religious practices, but one thing is certain, without a connection to something greater to ourselves, the healing process becomes futile, like planting a seed in the desert without water, without nutrients. The connection becomes a life force in itself, and without it life becomes meaningless. The connection with spirit is one of the foundations of healing.

WRIGHT

As a nurse and educator, what do you see in the future for complementary therapies?

FORD-LATTY

I am optimistic with the direction we are taking in mainstream healthcare, as alternative therapies become accepted as partners in wellness. Medicine has always been in agreement of the concept of homeostasis of the physical body, but in the holistic approach to wellness it becomes multidimensional. Western society is coming to the realization, described by Richard Gerber, of the human as a being of unlimited healing and growth potential. I think that in the future we will continue to learn from other cultures as we grow in our understanding of human beings in relation to the universe.

On a mundane level, we will begin to view healthcare in a prevention management mode rather than the crisis mode we practice today. Even now, insightful employers are seeing the benefits of a balanced, healthy workforce through integrative health coaching and this will only continue to grow, drastically reducing medical costs. I believe we will begin early teaching of healthy lifestyles to our children and will return arts programs and physical education as requirements of our school curriculum.

As a society, we will view alternative health practices not as alternative, but will consider them a beneficial complement to traditional healthcare. Energy and other modalities will be the norm, and insurance will reimburse us for these, reducing the drain on resources that crisis management takes.

I see a movement of the people to take responsibility for their own health. As an informed population, we can cause sweeping changes in our healthcare system. By embracing that concept of balance in mind, body, and spirit, people will quietly forge changes in the healthcare system—the future rests with us.

WRIGHT

So put all this together for us. Do you have any suggestions of ways to change our lives and achieve wellness?

## FORD-LATTY

I think the concept of Joseph Campbell on following your bliss is simple but profound. For example, if you are determined to remain healthy and so fill your life with exercise, vegetarian diet, no caffeine, low fat, no trans-fat, and you are miserable every step of the way while you're trying to be healthy, then you are not healthy. Each person has to choose a path to health that fits his or her goals and that permeates the self with joy and a sense of well-being—one size does not fit all.

It's better to feel that our lives are over too quickly than to face the end filled with regret at how we lived—living unfulfilled. To make sure this doesn't happen, we must take responsibility for our own health and well-being. Your lifestyle choices are just that—your choices.

We do have a major obstacle in our way—we are bombarded with too much information, too fast, on too many subjects all at once, without any careful thought or purposeful rationale on the part of most media. According to recent media reports, we should drink coffee; no, don't drink coffee. Don't drink alcohol but drink red wine. Exercise thirty minutes every day; no, you should exercise thirty minutes three times a week; then again, you should exercise five minutes every three hours. Take a multivitamin daily; no, don't take a multivitamin daily. Now a new study tells women that calcium causes strokes, so let us all stop the calcium now—or should we? Is this from the same people who told us not to have yearly mammograms after age forty? What's a body to do?

Be guided by your own pathways to peace and health that have emerged in your life. I do feel there are five keys to wellness that are simple and easy to incorporate into any lifestyle. As you reap the benefits of these lifestyle changes you'll be motivated to try more!

1. Move and open up the energy flow in your body. Take part in Qigong, walk, jog, or bike—just make some active movement part of your day.

2. Pay attention to what you eat, and don't eat anything you don't know the ingredients of. Grow your own, eat organic, or eat local, and if you're not a big fruit eater, make a promise to replace one snack (such as potato chips) or one sweet with one fruit a day.

3. Breathe, breathe, breathe—deep and long, several times a day. Take long deep breaths to nature's rhythm (inhale to the count of five, hold to the count of five and exhale to the count of five) while you are driving, watching television, or when you are at the computer.

4. Move away from the computer desk and go outside and be still, even if it is for a minute, even if you are in the middle of the city. Go outside and take your shoes off. Never totally separate yourself from nature. Feel the energy of the Earth. Can you hear your heartbeat? Can you feel the blood coursing through your veins? Can you feel the power of the Earth filling your body? Listen to yourself—the most amazing being in the universe. Listen to your body, your dreams, your senses, and come back in touch with who you are.

5. Cultivate gratitude: Do you look at your life as a precious gift, or a routine, mundane state that you can do nothing about? Do you see the ever-changing beauty in the world around you? Do you appreciate what we (collectively, as a civilization and individually as *you*) have been given? Develop an attitude of gratitude and say "thank you." Feel it, mean it, and say it out loud.

No one has to run a marathon, go on a six-hundred-calorie diet, or meditate for an hour to feel the results of these positive lifestyle changes. Start small, stay steady, and as you change these random acts into habits, you will feel better. Your energies will flow, your heart will sing, and you will feel whole.

"Remember me," the Buddha said, "as the one who woke up."

Are you ready to wake up?

# About the Author

Barbara Ford-Latty brings more than twenty years of experience in health care and education for hospitals, individuals, colleges, and corporations. An RN with a master's degree in Holistic Wellness, she is fully grounded in traditional healthcare as well as holism and serves as a Network Leader in the American Holistic Nurses Association. Believing passionately in preserving the balance of our natural environment and living in balance within that environment, she works with clients through integrative health coaching, energetic touch, and sound therapy to relieve stress and to improve their quality of life with heart-centered care.


Barbara Ford-Latty, MA, RN

*The Haelen Group*

Roanoke, Virginia

(540) 966-6173

bfordlatty@haelenhealth.com

www.haelenhealth.com

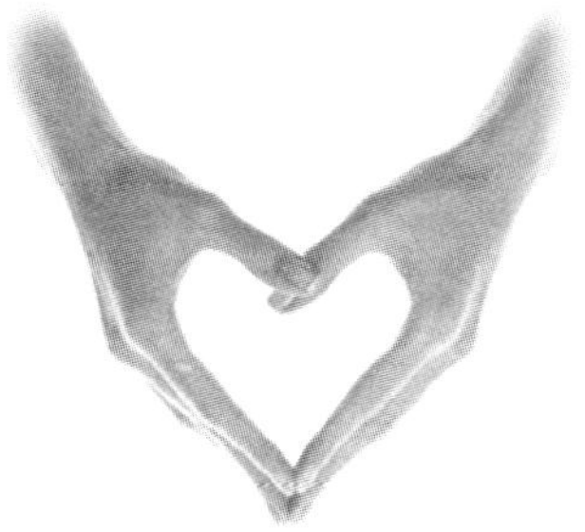

Chapter Six

# Mind, Body, Spirit: Approaches to Stress Management

with Jon Seskevich RN

## THE INTERVIEW

DAVID WRIGHT (WRIGHT)

Today we're talking with Jon Seskevich. Jon Seskevich RN, BSN, BA, CHTP, is a nurse clinician and certified stress management specialist at one of the country's foremost medical centers located in Durham, North Carolina. Since 1990, this trailblazer in integrative healing has provided a stress and pain management education service for more than thirty thousand patients and families in the hospital. An award-winning nurse, he is a graduate of the University of North Carolina School of Nursing and has a BA in Religion from Goddard College. He has authored chapters, presented hundreds of talks, recorded five CDs, and has participated in and published research on stress management techniques.

Jon is the author of *Mind, Body, Spirit: Approaches to Stress Management*. He will share with us jewels of stress management that help with life's biggest stressors. Anyone can benefit from this, I'm sure.

Jon, welcome to *Health: Mind, Body, Soul.*

JON SESKEVICH (SESKEVICH)

Thank you very much.

WRIGHT

So would you tell our readers about your viewpoints on the subject of stress?

SESKEVICH

Most people, when considering the subject of stress, think of problems, worries, tensions, or pressure. As a nurse healer, I think it's more practical and valuable to see stress as simply relating to change. Whenever there is change in life, even good change, it can cause stress. Some examples of good changes are important holidays, a wedding, moving, starting a new job, having a child or a grandchild. All of these are good and positive but certainly can cause stress because of the changes in people's lives. Of course, there are some people who would appreciate some "good stress" for a change because their stressors haven't been very good at all.

In our society, there are some people who actually thrive on stress. Firefighters, military personnel, police officers, business people, hospital intensivists, and emergency department staff are easy examples. These people, whom we appreciate for helping make our lives better, can have high stress every day and love it. It's what they do. There are going to be other individuals who hate change, they'd rather have things stay the same.

The common ground, whether one loves stress or hates it, is that stress is physical. It is not imaginary. The human stress response sends powerful chemicals into the body that can affect the whole person. Adrenaline, noradrenaline, and cortisol affect the body, can make the muscles tense, and drive blood pressure and blood sugar up.

I'm not saying the stress response is bad. I was driving in the country at night, and a deer came running out of woods. I totally wanted that stress response so I could have sharp vision and quick reflexes to miss the deer. After that emergency passed, it was good to have tools to recover to cut down on the wear and tear that stress causes.

I recently attended a conference at Harvard Medical School titled, "Building Resilience: The Mind Body Revolution in Health and Healing." The latest research in the stress response shows that stress tends to affect a person in genetically vulnerable areas. For example, one person might have a predisposition for headaches, and when stress comes on, their head is killing them. For others their blood pressure rises. Others might get back pain or their stomach may give them challenges. Health problems can become chronic, which unfortunately gives a person more stress!

The stress response affects the emotions and the mind as well. It can cause worry, anger, forgetfulness, and trouble concentrating. There is an increased risk of making mistakes or having an accident because mental drift can happen. Stress can affect the emotions. One illustration I use considers a person as a cup of water. When our cup is full of stress, like a full cup of liquid, anything added will overflow. There can be an easiness to experience anger, anxiety, sadness, or other difficult feelings. So when we explore this "full cup" scenario, our real problem might not be the one thing that causes our cup to overflow. It is that our cup is already full and anything else can upset us. Stress management approaches empty out the cup, so we have some energy and reserve as new changes or challenges arise.

Stress can affect a person spiritually. As stress causes wear and tear spiritually, people can lose their faith, hope, meaning, or purpose in life. Stress affects the mind, the body, the spirit. I'll go so far as to say it affects the family, it affects our work, our hobbies, and our creative activities.

I think in the hospital and in life, what most people get for "stress management" encouragement are the words: relax, don't worry, breathe. But they have never effectively been told how to do that.

What many people don't understand is that it can be really hard to relax when dealing with an unwanted illness or when there has been an entire series of changes in life. It can be very hard not to worry when one is waiting and not knowing. I teach people how to relax and decrease worry. In my career, I have found "waiting and not knowing" to be the biggest stress of all. I've had so many people say to me over the years, "Even if it's cancer, at least I would know; the waiting is the hardest part."

One Friday afternoon a few years ago, I went into a forty-year-old woman's room. She said, "Jon, even if its hospice—going home to die—at least I would know. The waiting and not knowing is driving me nuts." So I have learned that it's not the what ifs of the future that is the stress, it is being in limbo! Sharon Salzberg recommends that people recognize that "something will happen" to decrease this stress.

I never really say "stop worrying" to anyone, because as a nurse, I get paid to worry. When I was working with cancer patients on the evening shift, one could ask every one of my patients, "Do you want Jon to worry about you?" If that patient didn't say yes, you know the family member sitting in the chair would have said, "Yes, worry about my dad" or "Yes worry about my wife." The relaxation technique that I will teach here helps to decrease worry by letting go of unneeded thoughts when we want to. This is a cool skill to have.

I see the field of stress management as containing powerful tools for the prevention of health problems, as well as for healing, recovery, and management of chronic illness. For a healthy person, stress management is seen as "primary prevention"—a way to help prevent an illness. An example of this would be utilizing stress management approaches to help stop smoking such as the QuitSmart program. Some people think they smoke to relax, but it is actually nicotine withdrawal that smoking soothes. Stopping smoking is actually a "good stress" because you're going to lower your risk of health problems as well as actually decrease your body's overall stress.

Some people who are reading this chapter or a family member are already facing health problems, some with chronic, long-term conditions. Stress management can be viewed as a healing tool of secondary prevention. I have a working definition for the word "healing." Healing means improving quality of life and/or physical function. Goals of healing can be to cut down on the severity of an illness, decrease the number, or shorten the duration of severe flare-ups.

### Wright

Would you tell us about yourself and your career in nursing?

### Seskevich

I love being a nurse. In my early twenties we were having difficult economic times with a recession and lack of jobs. I worked delivering flowers, picking apples, etc., and sometimes was unemployed. In my free time, I volunteered with telephone crisis counseling lines and began to study meditation. This taught me excellent skills that served me quite well in my later life.

I didn't have a car, and hitchhiking was a popular means of travel. While hitchhiking during a two-week period, I kept getting rides from people who were nurses or worked in a hospital. This happened so much that one day as I got into a car, I asked, "Are you a nurse?" The man was somewhat startled. He said, "Well, no, but I work in radiology in the hospital, how did you know?" So I interpreted this series of coincidences as actually "a calling" for me to become a nurse. I really liked helping people, and the idea of working in an environment with both men and women felt balanced. So I went to school and in a short time became a nursing assistant.

Earlier I had read a profound book called, *Be Here Now,* by Ram Dass[1] that changed my life and stimulated a serious interest in exploring the deeper meaning of life. It presented ideas on how to quiet the mind and open the heart in order to live more fully by being in the present moment. The author's main message was to love everyone, serve everyone, and remember God. It taught about

Eastern and Western spirituality and opened the entire study of death and dying for me. My perspective from this book contributed to my attraction to hospital work.

In 1975, I started working in a small hospital and the next year continued my education to become a licensed practical nurse. During the next nine years, I gained a lot of great experience in bedside hospital care and being able to help people with their day-to-day health problems. For three years during this time period, about once a month I assisted a pathologist with autopsies. This helped me work with my fears and apprehensions about death and helped me gain a deeper understanding of the body and the impermanent nature of life.

Ram Dass became a mentor and guide in my life during that time. He encouraged me to keep going with my education. I completed a degree in religion and started thinking I might become a minister, a counselor, or social worker. As I was searching my soul to hear the direction I needed next, I went to Insight Meditation Society in Barre, Massachusetts. I did a meditation retreat with Sharon Salzberg. During this retreat, I kept hearing the word "nursing" again and again in my mind. This felt like a further calling for me to continue in my nursing career. So a little while later I moved to North Carolina, kept working as an LPN, and began school to become a registered nurse.

After graduating in 1987, I began working in the medical center in an innovative mind/body medicine inpatient unit called the Combined Medical Specialties Unit (CMSU). People who were dealing with chronic pain and psychosomatic illnesses came from all across the Southeast. People who have difficult health problems often hear the encouragement, "Learn to live with it," but nobody teaches them how! The nursing staff on our unit actually taught people how to live with serious symptoms and long-term chronic illnesses.

We called it psychosomatic medicine from the Greek roots, meaning mind/body medicine. In the earlier days and even now, psychosomatic has carried an implication of imaginary illness or that the person's pain and suffering weren't real. Our forward-thinking medical staff realized this was a misunderstanding. Psychosomatic illness is really about fundamental interconnections between the mind and body, through the brain/nervous system, immune, and endocrine systems.

In one of the CMSU classes, I shared a vignette. A man came to the hospital emergency room three days earlier having chest pains and was diagnosed with a heart attack. He had EKG changes and blood chemistry changes. I would ask the patients in the class, "Did he have a psychosomatic illness?" Almost always everybody would say, "No." Then I would say, "Well, let me tell you a little bit more about this gentleman. For the last three months, his job has been getting tougher; his boss has been giving him a very hard time. They have been talking about layoffs. He's been fighting more with his wife. He has been increasing his smoking, drinking more, and then last Friday night he found out his seventeen-year-old daughter was pregnant. Chest pain began. He went to the ER and was diagnosed with a heart attack. Did he have a psychosomatic illness?" I would again ask, and everyone agreed he did. The stress in his life caused tremendous wear and tear and then it manifested in his body as a heart attack.

So the nurses on that unit taught about stress management, depression, and assertive communication skills. Psychologists taught relaxation techniques. Patients had counselors and psychiatrists and there were medical support groups. We had a full multimodality treatment approach with the best of conventional medicine. People with long-term problems were sometimes getting better.

Then in 1990, I moved over to the main hospital and, with nursing leadership, created a position teaching patients stress management on busy inpatient units. I began working on a cardiac unit, an oncology unit, a pulmonary unit, and a gastrointestinal medical-surgical unit. We found that not only did I help the patients feel better and do better, but I also helped the staff do their job.

For example, a nurse might be working with a patient on night shift, and the patient was crying and upset, and then a referral was made. The next night the patient would report that it helped and it would be noted that he or she slept well. The nurse's shift would go better, or at least he or she would be able to focus more on other patients. A patient might be dealing with a lot of pain and be very worried. I would visit, listen, and teach skills. The patient might then find his or her pain medicine working better, lasting longer. Stress management education is a win-win situation for patient and caregivers. A patient might have difficulty walking after surgery, dealing with a lot of anxiety and shortness of breath. After our session, he or she would have tools to breathe better and have less fear and anxiety. This can help the patient walk better, which assisted the nurse to do his or her job and getting the person home sooner.

Also at this institution I have been blessed to participate in research studies that tested the value of the modalities that I teach. I worked on the famous MANTRA study, the Monitoring and Actualization of Noetic Training, conceived and led by Dr. Mitch Krucoff and Suzanne Crater NP[2]. Among many interesting results, we showed that my relaxation approaches decreased worry for patients waiting for procedures. I was involved in another study where we taught mind, body, spirit interventions for people with congestive heart failure[3]. Also, in the Calm Down Study Dr. Jim Lane and I investigated meditation for both stress relief and blood pressure control[4].

WRIGHT

What is your vital quartet of stress management?

SESKEVICH

The first quadrant is called mind/body approaches and psychological support. The second quadrant is called spiritual approaches. The third is good nutrition, and the fourth is exercise and physical approaches.

I believe that all stress management approaches can be organized into one of these groups. This vital quartet of healing modalities was first categorized by Michael Learner, PhD[5]. He is a MacArthur Genius Award winner, and is one of the leading proponents of sensible, sane, complementary therapies for cancer. There has been a great deal of research individually into these modalities that show that they help a person to become healthier. You can ask any doctor if he or she believes that a healthier patient will do better with his or her treatment and the answer would be *yes!* We wonder if people who choose a combination of these four approaches might experience an even greater synergistic healing response.

WRIGHT

Will you share more about mind/body approaches and psychological support?

SESKEVICH

There are many different mind/body approaches that people can use for healing and stress management, and there is good science to support them. These approaches promote resiliency, brain health, and functioning, allowing the body to return easier to a healing balance of homeostasis. They can help with multiple physical problems and symptoms. Regular practice is recommended, with at least ten to twenty minutes once or twice a day.

Meditation is the practice of focusing oneself in the present moment. There can be a specific focus of attention—repetition of specific words or phrases, prayers, breath awareness concentration, sound, and progressive muscle relaxation. Or the focus can be on simply being present with your direct experience without clinging or aversion. Mindfulness meditation[6] is very popular with a lot of ongoing research. Many practices comprise mindfulness, including choiceless awareness, walking meditation, breath focusing techniques, eating meditation, body scan, and loving kindness meditation popularized by Sharon Salzberg[7].

Guided imagery or visualization is picturing in the imagination, for example, a peaceful soothing place and being there consciously. In guided imagery, you are present with what you see, what you hear, what you smell, what you touch, what you feel, or any combination of these.

Prayer is universal and most religions teach this practice, which can bring physical and mental benefits as well as spiritual ones.

In childbirth classes, people learn Lamaze and Bradley breathing techniques and focal point concentration.

Progressive muscle relaxation involves going through the entire body, first tightening then softening and relaxing the muscles.

The main technique I share in the hospital with people has three distinct steps. Step one I call "soft belly breathing" inspired by Stephen Levine[8]. It involves placing one hand on the abdomen, noticing that touch and then aiming the breath softly for the belly and for the hand. What you start to notice is your abdomen rises with the breathing in and gently falls with the breathing out. You don't have to breathe deeply or work hard, just simply aim the breath toward the belly.

Stress tends to make us breathe short and quick or to hold the breath. A challenge is that both of these types of breathing signal danger to our body, so stress tends to go up as control goes down. With soft belly breathing, as the belly gently rises, the lungs fill with good air, signaling the body that it's safe and okay to relax. The abdomen gently rises with the breathing in and gently falls with the breathing out.

Step two involves feeling the support of the bed or a chair, letting your body be soft and heavy, letting the bed or chair hold you. It is nice to have the head upright and not hang over if sitting in a chair, or well supported if you are in bed. The tension can begin to drain right away from the body.

Step three is to silently repeat a short positive thought over and over again. Each time you notice your mind wander, kindly and gently let go of the thought and return to your "relaxation words." Sometimes, this is called a mantra. I did some research on the word "mantra," and I learned that it is something that protects the mind.

WRIGHT

I've heard of this concept. What is the best phrase to use?

SESKEVICH

Because I'm a nurse, I get to look at people holistically—we are our body, we are our mind, but we're also our spirit, our soul. I've developed a spiritual assessment[9] that I have used in the hospital many thousands of times, and I will share it with you. The assessment question is, "Is religion or spirituality important to you? For some people it is, and for some it isn't, how about you?" I find I get four answers. One answer is yes; one answer is something like, "I don't go to church but I believe in God;" a third answer is, "I'm not sure about God but I think there is something spiritual or a higher power," and the fourth answer is "no."

I know that each person reading this chapter will give one of those four answers. So if the answer is number one or two (and for some who choose number three), you could use a short spiritual thought for your relaxation words. Examples for a Christian could be, "God is with me," "The Lord is my Shepherd," or "Hail Mary, Mother of God." If you are Jewish it might be a phrase like "Shema Yisrael," or the word shalom.

In the hospital, we had a patient from Turkey who had fought for us in Afghanistan, and he was having major surgery. He chose the relaxation words "La Ilaha Ill Allah," which in the Muslim tradition means, "There is no God but God." We had a Buddhist patient from Korea who chose the words "Om Mani Padme Hum," which means, "Compassion dwells within the heart." We had a Native American woman who chose the words "Wakan Tanka"—"Oh, Great Spirit." You get the idea—choose a short spiritual thought that has meaning to you.

Now, for some who are not sure if spirituality is important to them and for those who report that religion isn't important, I would suggest using a positive phrase like "easy does it," or "I can do this." So you choose a certain phrase for your relaxation words and then silently to yourself repeat them again and again. The key to the technique is, with patience and kindness, to return to the relaxation phrase each time you recognize your mind wanders. You can try out different phrases, but I would suggest that by your third or fourth days of practice, settle on one phrase for at least a month.

Let me share now about what could be seen as the toughest of all the stress management strategies of the vital quartet and that is psychological support—letting people help you, letting people give to you, letting people love you. This is the toughest because for many of us it's actually easier to give to others, but harder to let people give to us. It's easier to give to others and harder to let people give to us. If you need to receive support or help due to life's changes, please reflect. When you give to other people, how does it make you feel? I've asked this question to many people and they say it makes them feel good to give to others. So another way of looking at it would be, when you let other people give to you, it makes others have the same good feeling. But the receiver sometimes has the harder job, because he or she has to learn to accept and receive.

There was an example once in the hospital, on the oncology unit. The doctors were coming around on morning rounds and went into a woman's room. She had cancer that had spread to the spine and had became paralyzed; she also had severe nerve pain. When the doctors came in, they asked her how she was doing. She said, "I want to see Dr. Kevorkian." They laughed, thinking she was joking, but the lady looked at them right in the eyes, and very seriously repeated, "I want Dr. Kevorkian!" Because Dr. Kevorkian was known as the suicide doctor, the physicians decided to get a psychiatric consult to rule out suicide and help with depression. The discharge planner was aware of the stress management consultation service available and so instead of Dr. Kevorkian the lady got to see Jon Seskevich.

As I walked into the room, the first thing the woman said after I introduced myself was, "I don't have any stress, it was just a bad night."

"Oh, that's great you are not stressed."

I look at stress a little differently than most and I shared with her about how stress comes from change. She could really relate to that. Also she said that during the night she had a lot of pain but "didn't want to bother the nurses." I sensed trouble receiving support was part of her stress. As part of our discussion, she shared that at one point she had gone to Central America and helped build churches for people.

"How did that make you feel?" I asked.

"Well, after we built the churches, they had big fiestas for us. The people were so happy! It made me feel good to give."

"Okay, so if you go home now and let your family help you, how will that make your family feel?"

"Good," she replied. I agreed.

She was able to go home a few days later with the support of hospice and her family, feeling better about it all.

Psychological support can be achieved in many ways. For some it's going to be talking and sharing with a family member or friend.

Others might not want to talk completely with their family or friends so they might go to a professional therapist or spiritual support person. Others might want to be in a support group with others dealing with a similar illness or life challenge. I've had people say they don't like to talk very much. They've found that journaling and writing about their experiences as very supportive. Some make a list of needs and let volunteers or community members help.

WRIGHT

Will you explain to our readers about the second of the vital quartet—spiritual approaches?

SESKEVICH

Yes, I think that most people, looking at spirituality first, think of religion, and religion is obviously a way to deepen their connection to their soul. What I would recommend is exploring the aspects of religious faith that brings you closer to God. For one person it's going to be going to church temple or synagogue; for another person it's going to be reading the Bible or holy book in his or her tradition. For another it's going to be prayer, having that quiet time, meditating, reflecting on God. For others it's going to be doing good works or helping the poor or maybe sacrifice and giving up something and offering it to God. Whatever it is—whatever part of your spiritual practice brings you close to God—I would say take time to do it.

Other people find spirituality in different ways. One example can be beauty, nature, art, music, poetry, dance, or creative expression. By doing this, people nurture and feed their spirit and soul. For others difficult life experiences can be a way to tap their spirituality. We don't have to look any further than twelve-step groups for examples of this. The twelve-step groups originated with Alcoholics Anonymous (AA), but today there are twelve-step groups for drug addiction, overeating, gambling, sexual addictions, and for families and friends of alcoholics. For very challenging life experience that society doesn't have easy answers for, the twelve steps have been found to be valuable. What happens when it works with twelve-step programs, is the person hits bottom because of their problems and then reach out for help and work the twelve steps and come through with transformed lives.

For example, in one of the publications of AA[10], the author says "Thank God I'm an alcoholic." It wasn't because of the misery that happened in his life but he said it was because he discovered the fellowship of AA and he was able to transform his life in a very positive way with the twelve steps.

So religion, beauty, and painful life experiences can be ways that people experience a deeper spiritual self.

### WRIGHT

Would you say a few words about the third and fourth vital quartets—good nutrition, and exercise and physical approaches?

### SESKEVICH

I know good nutrition will be covered in great detail in other chapters of the book, so I will refer the reader there. Exercise itself has been found to have so many positive health benefits for the whole person. Exercise three times a week for twenty to thirty minutes, even with something as simple as walking or swimming, has been shown to have positive health outcomes. If someone is dealing with acute illness or a flare-up of symptoms, "pacing activity and rest" can be a very skillful physical approach.

In this paradigm a way of looking at activity is having your feet on the floor, for example, sitting, standing, and moving about can be seen as being active. Resting is simply when your feet are off the floor. Lying down in bed, feet up in the reclining chair, feet up on the couch at home—feet off the floor is resting. What we see a lot with illness and pain problems is that when the person is feeling good, they tend to go, go, do, do, push, push, but then they pay for it with more symptoms. What that does is knock them in back to bed, hating it and frustrated. Then they start to feel better, so the pattern continues—go, go, do, do, push, push, and then they pay for it.

What is better would be to have a plan for pacing activity and rest. For example, if you live with pain every day and you are having a bad pain spell, you might start off with fifteen, twenty, or thirty minutes of being active followed by two or three hours of rest. Don't just stay in bed because staying in bed after a while starts to drain you and make you weaker and weaker. So get a good rest period but then get up again and move around for fifteen to thirty minutes. Then as your condition improves, slowly increase the amount of activity, slowly decreasing the amount of rest. If you have been up thirty minutes, resting two and a half hours and you feel better, maybe bump it up to staying up for forty-five minutes or an hour and decrease the rest to two hours or an hour and half. Slowly increase activity and decrease rest as you recover. If the illness flares up, increase the rest and decrease the activity.

Massage can be a great physical approach for stress management and supporting health. Also, acupuncture has demonstrated evidence of pain relief and symptom management.

### Wright

In your daily work with people, how do you listen without taking on the pain?

### Seskevich

This is one of the most valuable skills that a helper or care-giving person can learn. If you followed me in the hospital one day, you'd see I'm walking into one room and maybe there is a twelve-year-old boy with leukemia; I'm walking into another room and maybe that person has had two major heart attacks and he or she is never going to be able to work again; I'm walking into another room and a woman has been paralyzed by a car accident; I'm walking into another room where someone is waiting for a lung transplant and doesn't know if he or she is going to live another day. If I took on the pain of each of those situations, I would not be able to go to work the next day. If my heart was shut down and didn't care, I wouldn't be able to relate or really help other people. So I've learned this idea and developed the skill of listening without taking on the pain.

Steven Levine, one of the founders of research in the field of death and dying, was coming to a workshop and I met him at the airport. I said, "Steven, where is Ondrea, your wife? I thought she was coming."

"She just found out she had lupus," he replied, "and she wasn't able to make it."

My face scrunched up, my heart was hurting, and sadly I said to him, "Oh."

He looked at me, got close to my face, and said, "Wrong answer. It is another new moment—ah, lupus."

My mind started racing, I was hurting there in the airport, but was I helping Ondrea in New Mexico? The answer was no, I wasn't helping Ondrea. Was I helping Steven, her husband? The answer was no; he was having to comfort me. Here I was hurting, feeling pain, and I wasn't really helping anyone at all.

My mind was racing. I considered the difference between pity and compassion. Pity is looking at a person with an attitude of, "Oh, you poor thing," but secretly inside thinking thank God it's not me. There is distance there. Compassion, I was learning, is having the courage to touch pain with love. It doesn't mean we're going to fix or actually change the situation, but when we have courage to really be present and care, we're touching that pain with love and healing can happen.

So now, in the hospital, if someone is sharing a story of sadness or tragedy, what I do is nod my head, and I quietly say, "Okay." That "Okay" is a signal for me to care and use supportive listening skills.

There are certainly many listening skills and strategies. One group is our nonverbal communication. Eye contact, leaning forward, and nodding invite the person to share more of what is going on. Having periods of silence, not feeling the need to jump in and talk, and just being silent, gives the person space to think. There can be a validation of another's feelings. Restating or paraphrasing, gives the speaker a great signal that you heard what was said.

### Wright

Well, to conclude the interview, is there another stress management story you want to share with us?

### Seskevich

Yes, I'd love to. Many hundreds of years ago there was a kingdom and a king. When he was young he was very benevolent, but as he got older, absolute power corrupted him absolutely. He became mean and tyrannical. There was one group in the population he really didn't like, and one day he called forth leaders of the group. He said, "People, I want you to give me something that will make me happy whenever I am sad. If you don't, I'm going to wreak havoc on all of you." So they all went out. They were scared, struggling. Some prayed, and others read and studied. They stayed up all night trying to figure out something that would make the king happy whenever he was sad.

At the chosen hour, they came back in and one of the leaders, a woman, stepped forward. The king said, "I want you to give me something that will make me happy whenever I'm not." She walked forward and handed him a coin. At first he laughed and laughed, "I'm the king, I make all the money, what is this going to do?"

"Turn it over," she said.

"Okay," he said, "whenever I'm unhappy, I'm going to turn this coin over and it will make me happy." He turned it over and it said, "This too shall pass." He thought out loud, "We had this famine that was such misery, but that passed. I was happy again. When my father died, it broke my heart; but it's true, over time it passed. I was happy again. Okay. I don't believe this, but you've done it, you're free to go!"

They all left, went outside and started high fiving each other. They laughed at the trick they played on him. They said to one another, "Wait until he reads it when he's happy—this, *too,* shall pass."

### WRIGHT

What a great conversation, Jon. I really appreciate all the time you've taken to answer these questions. I have learned a lot, and I'm sure that our readers will, too.

Today we have been talking with Jon Seskevich. Jon is the author of *Mind, Body, Spirit: Approaches to Stress Management.*

Jon, thank you so much for being with us today on *Health: Mind, Body, Soul.*

### SESKEVICH

Oh, it's been a delight. Thank you very much.

References:

1. Dass, Ram (1971). *Be Here Now*. San Cristobal, New Mexico: Lama Foundation.
2. Seskevich, J. E., Crater, S. W., Lane, J. D., Krucoff, M. W. "Noetic Therapies as Adjuncts in Stressful Medical Procedures: Beneficial Effects on Mood Prior to Percutaneous Intervention for Unstable Coronary Syndromes," *Nursing Research, 53,* 116–121 (2004).
3. Seskevich, Jon. Gabert, Helen. Charles, Ann. Cuffe, Mike. "Integrated Healing: Helping patients with heart failure manage stress." *Holistic Nursing Practice* Vol. 18#2, page 49 (2006).
4. Lane J. D., Seskevich J. E., Pieper C. F. "Brief meditation training can improve perceived stress and negative mood." *Altern Ther Health Med.* 2007 Jan–Feb;13(1):38-44.
5. Lerner, Michael (1996) *Choices in Healing: Integrating the Best of Conventional and Complementary Approaches to Cancer*, MIT Press, 1996.
6. Kabat-Zinn, Jon (1991) *Full Catastrophe Living: Using the Wisdom of Your Body and Mind to Face Stress, Pain, and Illness,* Delta Trade Paperbacks.
7. Salzberg, Sharon (2005) *The Force of Kindness: Change Your Life with Love and Compassion.* Boulder, CO: Sounds True Inc.
8. Stephen Levine (1987) *Healing into Life and Death.* Anchor Books, Random House.
9. Seskevich, J. E., "Assessing Spirituality with Grace." *Integrative Nursing* Vol. 2, No. 1 (March–April, 2003).
10. Anonymous (1985) "Best of the AA Grapevine," *The International Journal of Alcoholics Anonymous* Volume 1 pg 153.

# About the Author

Jon Seskevich RN, BSN, BA, CHTP is a nurse clinician with the stress management consult team at one of the country's foremost medical centers in North Carolina. This Great 100, Alumni of the Year, and Friends' of Nursing award-winning nurse is a graduate of the University of North Carolina School of Nursing and has a BA in Religion from Goddard College in Vermont. He is a Certified Healing Touch Practitioner and Certified Holistic Stress Management Instructor. One of Jon's mentors, Ram Dass, Richard Albert, PhD, has written, "Jon is a truly brilliant example of compassion in action."


Jon Seskevich, RN, BSN, BA, CHTP

*Stress Management Education*

1017 Iredell St.

Durham, NC 27705

919-286-1207

jon@managestressnow.com

www.ManageStressNow.com

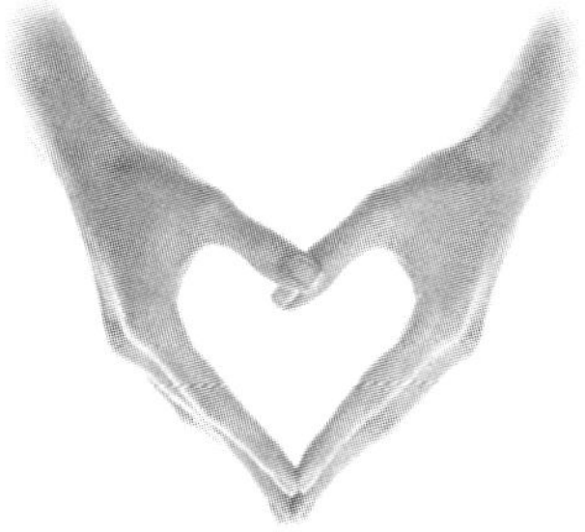

Chapter Seven

# Syncing Up for the Perfect Partnership

## with Rita Rizzo and Lou Vincent

THE INTERVIEW

---

DAVID WRIGHT (WRIGHT)

Today we're talking with Rita Rizzo and Lou Vincent. Rita and Lou are partners in the firm of Rizzo and Associates LLC, a management consulting and training firm established in 1984. They have also been married for the past two decades and work together as co-facilitators. They address even the stickiest topics with wit and humor. Experienced in addressing gender, racial, generational, ethnic, socioeconomic, and religious diversity topics, Lou and Rita both bring a depth and breadth of knowledge to the larger arena of organizational consulting. Their clients are often known to say that Rita and Lou are simply a breath of fresh air.

Lou, Rita welcome to *Health: Mind, Body, Soul.*

RITA RIZZO (RIZZO)

We appreciate your having us.

LOU VINCENT (VINCENT)

Thank you very much, glad to be here today.

WRIGHT

Why and how do perfect partnerships begin?

VINCENT

Health is rooted in balance and harmony. The soul inspires, the mind imagines, and the body behaves and takes action. When all three of these elements align with each other in harmony, balance is created and is experienced as health. A perfect partnership is a healthy one.

RIZZO

Partnerships between people, regardless of whether we are speaking of marriages, friendships, or business alliances, are needed when people envision a goal they believe they cannot achieve alone. When a person feels the need to find a partner, the selection criteria are frequently based on one or more of these four subconscious motivators: attraction, admiration, attributes, and attitude. The perfect partnership is born when all four factors are realized on the levels of the mind, the body, and the soul. When two people mesh on all points, at all levels, the dynamic duo is unleashed!

VINCENT

Attraction is basic to all relationships. On the body level, it might be experienced as physical attraction or chemistry. On the mind level, it might manifest as an attraction to another's intelligence or ideas. On the soul level, attraction is expressed as magnetism. In other words, the other person feels right to you. Perfect partners know when the feeling is right because they begin to love each other either romantically or intellectually or both.

RIZZO

Admiration is the recognition that your perfect partner possesses assets that match or are exemplary to your own. On the body level, that person might be a good physical fit with you insomuch as he or she values heath and pursues it in similar ways to you. The person may even demonstrate self-discipline in his or her diet and exercise that you wish you could master. On the mind level, you might admire the person's manner of perceiving the world, or expressing their thoughts. On a soul level, you might admire the reverence your partner shows for life, and the gentleness with which he or she nurtures it. Great partners teach you things that fill in the gaps in your own soul development.

VINCENT

That leads directly to the next motivator, which is to find a partner whose attributes compliment and reinforce your own. On the body level, it might mean finding a partner who has stamina in the same or different areas than you. On the mind level, it might entail noticing the relevance of another's knowledge, skills, abilities, and awareness to the task at hand. On a soul level, one partner's attributes may trigger attribute development in the other.

Rita has this "refuse to lose" attitude that makes me a stronger person. I would likely abandon my efforts on a worthwhile project far too soon except that the way she never gives up has rubbed off on me!

RIZZO

Thank you Lou, that's quite a compliment! It is true though, isn't it? Your partner's attitude about life can influence the way in which you think about yourself and your own talents and possibilities.

Something that I appreciate about Lou is that he wakes up every morning in a great mood. He puts his body in motion the moment his eyes open and is obviously glad to begin another day. His mood influences my mood on the mind level, his activity spurs me on to throw back the covers and begin to move, too, and his "happy to be alive" attitude reminds my soul to rejoice in the opportunity each new day brings.

Attitude really is everything in life. Essentially, we each live our lives in the space between our ears. It is a true blessing if you can find a partner who stimulates a positive attitude in you and makes you believe that together all things are possible for the two of you.

### WRIGHT

So Rita and Lou, would you say the two of you have the perfect partnership?

### RIZZO

Well you have to be careful with the word "perfect" but we do think we are perfect for each other. We sync up in a variety of ways—as business partners, facilitation partners, life partners, and parenting and grand-parenting partners. The coolest of all of our partnership roles is that we're best friends. Of course, it also helps that we love each other deeply. Thus far it's taken a couple of decades to perfect all of our various partnership roles and sand away at the fault lines that appear every now and then, but we are getting better at it every day. We started out with attraction, admiration, and a fairly good attitude about our relationship, but it took us a while to develop some of the attributes we needed to fully bond.

### VINCENT

At first it was a struggle. Each of us was concerned about our own individuality and didn't want the other person trying to change us. In past relationships, both of us had a history of others attempting to mold each of us into what they called their "perfect partner" and it didn't work out very well. We both thought it was important to adapt to each other without losing our own identities, and we found that to be a challenge at first. Although we are both half of the same whole, we are also independent individuals.

RIZZO

The concept for this chapter—the notion of "syncing up"—came to me one day as I was connecting my cell phone to my laptop for a data transfer. I remarked to Lou that much like our electronic devices, he and I had learned to "sync" pretty efficiently over time. We each go out into the world and make our individual impact and then we come home and connect. The mind-body-soul connection we make enriches and strengthens each of us. We exchange information to promote mutual learning, we pamper each other to make the other feel cared for, and we give each other the empathy and encouragement needed to empower us for the next venture out into the world. We get our mind-body-soul fix from one another, and then we disconnect and go back out there and handle the next big challenge each on our own.

WRIGHT

So how has your twenty-year journey towards the perfect partnership progressed?

RIZZO

When we met each of us was searching for our own purpose in life. Neither of us was looking for a mate but we found that we had this instant attraction to each other. We just weren't clear why we were supposed to be together.

Since then, we have done a lot to clarify our purpose and direction. We began by conducting our spiritual studies together. We discussed our individual values and beliefs and we found common ground there. To me, likeness in spiritual beliefs is a strong common ground issue on which to base a relationship.

Since our values are our basic marching orders, we felt we were able to use our shared value system as a basis for our partnership. We also noticed that both of us are "happiness seekers" and we were both the happiest when we were in service to others. We began working together before becoming a couple, so our next step was to try and discover an equitable division of labor.

VINCENT

We actually took a three-day retreat out away from our work and family to relax, focus, and create a plan. We visualized ourselves being successful. From that vision we set our combined goals, and divided our task list according to who had the most competence and the best skills, knowledge, ability, and willingness to do each task. We also drew some terrific pictures of ourselves sitting on the beach somewhere with umbrella drinks enjoying the fruits of our labor. Eventually, we developed our daily motto, "Have some fun and get something done!"

WRIGHT

So what do you mean you are both happiness seekers?

RIZZO

I think the thing that attracted us most to each other is that we both just love to have fun and also enjoy being highly productive. I met Lou when he was a participant in one of my classes. The first thing I noticed about him is what a fun and lively sense of humor he had. I think that was the genesis of my attraction to him. Luckily, he seemed to enjoy my sense of humor as well. We also admired one another's intelligence. We were able to find mutual happiness by making a mind, body, soul connection that has led to a wonderful harmony between us. I think we dance well together, whether it's on an actual dance floor or during our ongoing daily banter that keeps us both in stitches or while mingling our talents and ideas to manage our family or to create our best work product. We tend to joke and laugh through major portions of every day and make every attempt to not take ourselves too seriously. We have had many opportunities to sit on the beach with umbrella drinks as we initially projected that we might, but more importantly, we are usually successful with making each day a mental "walk on the beach" by simply enjoying our small successes as they come.

### Vincent

Imagine for a moment that the whole of your life consists of one trip to the grocery store and then a meal to consume what you buy. At the close of the meal, your time on Earth ends—it's over. So here you are in the market, filling your basket with everything you want for your big meal. Maybe you have selected steaks, russet potatoes, sour cream, butter, salad, your favorite dressing, a bottle of bubbly, and chocolate fudge cake to compliment a cup of gourmet coffee.

Just as you are about to check out, you see an acquaintance walking toward you. Quickly he or she talks you out of your selections, citing cholesterol levels, sugar content, empty calories, and tooth decay as reasons to rethink your purchases. This conversation prompts a second trip through the store that results in the return of all your favorite items to the shelves to be replaced with the selections your friend believes are better for you.

Now how do you feel about your life as you cook your Tofurkey, sprout salad with low-fat dressing, plain brown rice, near beer, and sugar free Jell-O? Are you satisfied with the results of a life lived for others? Did you make your best choices while focused on winning the approval of others? Have you entertained the world with your own song or are you just dancing to the tunes that others put forth?

Remember that you are paying for the meal just as you do for your choices in life.

Rita and I tend to make our own choices and create the music we wish to dance to, which leads us to be happy with our lives most of the time.

### Wright

Well said.

How did you decide on your particular method of creating harmony in your partnership?

### Vincent

We believe it takes a team to make a dream. We fully acknowledge that each person in our partnership has particular needs on the mind, body, and soul levels.

Rita is a natural born leader and I respect her need to lead. I need to read and study to develop my mind while Rita Googles and converts information into ideas at light speed. I tend to our nutritional needs by cooking a balanced meal for us every day, while Rita maintains the pool so it is available for daily exercise. I am well progressed in my formal spiritual studies, while Rita tends to learn as much from observing nature as from conducting regimented spiritual readings. The guys at our neighborhood drive-through describe me as "calm and laid back" and Rita as "a bundle of energy who is always in a hurry." I guess that says it all. Learning to integrate these differences requires that we learn to cooperate with one another. To accomplish this, we decided to follow the *Cooperation Model* that we often teach to managers in the workshops we conduct.

### Wright

Would you talk more about the *Cooperation Model?* It sounds intriguing.

### Rizzo

The Cooperation Model is three-pronged. It consists of negotiating for: 1) shared desired results, 2) shared power, and 3) shared trust.

Think about the last time you voluntarily cooperated with another person. Were these three elements in place? Did you want about the same outcome? Did you share power by allowing the other person to influence your thinking? Were you able to influence his or her thinking? Did you conclude the cooperative effort by each committing to taking certain actions and then following through on those commitments? If so, you demonstrated shared trust. We use this system to make plans, solve problems, and anchor our decision-making.

### Wright

This all sounds almost too good to be true. Are there any bumps in the road as you go about your journey together?

### Rizzo

Of course! That's why forgiveness, an important soul function, is an essential part of any partnership or relationship. Durable partnerships develop the ability to accept the fallibility of both partners.

Beyond forgiving your partner for their shortcomings, I also think it's important for each person to be able to forgive themselves. There is no place for ongoing blame and regret in a productive relationship. I believe it's essential not only to forgive, but to also allow your mind to forget as well. By this I mean that once a mistake has been corrected or an issue resolved, it should be laid to rest and not resurrected at the next sign of disagreement.

In the beginning, our relationship was difficult because I just refused to let conflicts end, but thankfully now neither of us has the time or the energy to keep a grievance going beyond a very limited life span. I now understand that every circumstance Lou and I face in our lives are a result of the mutual karma we have earned with our choices, or due to what we have asked for in our prayers and projections, so it is best to just roll what is happening today.

### Vincent

One's ability to love is based on one's capacity to forgive and yes, the road to success is always bumpy, curvy, ruddy, and full of potholes.

As we reflect on our tough times, they almost always involve other people. Fitting other's needs into our partnerships has created some worthy challenges. Attempting to budget our time, put aside our own needs and reconcile our differing sense of responsibility to others has been the source of a number of heated discussions in our home and business. Often, when partners are involved in a conflict, they get caught up in pushing each other's hot buttons, because they know where they are. This behavior almost always makes the conflict worse, and never resolves it. In order to maintain a solution focus, Rita and I have developed what we refer to as a "Hot Button Free Zone," within ourselves. If we don't have hot buttons, no one can push them.

### WRIGHT

This information sounds like it would be great for not only couples, but corporations. I'm sure you do a lot of work in both areas. Do you always work together or do you work separately as well?

### RIZZO

We work separately as well. We're currently blessed to have a very large contract in the South where we are working together every other week. On alternate weeks, we travel and work separately. It's really fun to be able to share the stage because we learn a lot from each other when we get to work together. It makes us each better and gives us more material to offer our audiences on the weeks that we work apart.

### VINCENT

When I'm out, I'm always picking up new stories and new ideas from my participants and I just can't wait to get home and tell Rita the new learning I've encountered while I was on the road. I think it's the same for her, because it seems she has always saved a few special tales to share with me.

WRIGHT

Well, before I interrupted your train of thought with that question, I was just curious, earlier you stated that you were happiest when you were in service to others, does that contradict what you had stated?

RIZZO

Well no, as Lou stated, our biggest problems and worthiest challenges almost always come when we are in service to others. Overcoming these challenges spurs our individual and mutual growth. We really are happy being in service to others. As a matter of fact, we refer to it as being "God's work." We regard helping others to learn and grow so they can live better lives as the best extension of themselves. Unfortunately, helping others isn't always convenient, it's not without resistance, neither can it always be done efficiently and effectively.

We've struggled to decide what others really need from us and a lot of times Lou and I, coming from different cultures, tend to see that differently. I tend to be more of a rescuer and an enabler, and he tends to be more of an assigner. He is famous for asking others to do certain assignments that will make them more self-sufficient and independent, while I am more willing to take on their responsibilities as my own. This is one area where we disagree about how to use our attributes to benefit others, but we have both moved to a middle position during our time together. It is just another example of how we have allowed ourselves to learn from one another.

WRIGHT

As you mentioned, you are from different cultures, does that ever cause issues?

### Rizzo

Let me be very clear about that, yes and no. There are times when it creates some very distinct perceptual differences for us, but then anytime two individuals are acculturated in different ways there are collision points. There are also more perspectives on how to solve problems, how to make decisions, and how to formulate plans.

Our cultural differences are really more than skin deep, which is what people notice when they see our pictures. We are from different genders, and different regions of the United States. We have different traditions, we are from different socioeconomic groups, and we have extremely different life experiences. All of these diversity factors can lead to dissenting points of view in assessing whatever situation is at hand. We even find differences in assigning motives to other people who are involved with us. My read on what's happening in any given situation might be vastly different than Lou's due to our unique acculturation.

### Vincent

One's viewing point is equal to one's point of view. Early on in our relationship we learned that when an issue arises where we don't see eye-to-eye, it's always best to rise above our own individual points of view and form a mutual viewing point where we can examine the issue at hand for a variety of different perspectives instead of depending entirely on what we were taught was correct as children.

### Wright

That makes a lot of sense.

So do you think you have a unique effect on others due to your diversity?

RIZZO

Probably. I think that people learn something about racial unity and intercultural communication as much from watching us together as from anything we attempt to teach as part of a curriculum. We're always modeling how to get along cross-culturally, even if we are not totally aware of it.

Everyone is diverse from one another in one way or another and each person has a different effect on the world based on who she or he is. I think the thing we do that has the biggest influence is to truly relate to and connect with others on a very human level.

Just last week, a gentleman approached us after class and stated, "You two wore me down. I came in this morning fully prepared to reject you and everything you had to say. I just couldn't hold it. You won me over with your warmth and acceptance toward everyone in the room."

We considered that a high compliment. It is exactly the result we are working toward—to foster more unity in the world despite our differences.

WRIGHT

My wife and I have been arguing for many, many years about which one of us is the smartest. Does that ever come up?

RIZZO

Oh absolutely, yes, but we have another motto for that. We're big on mottos around here. We've got them hanging on all the walls and on Post-it notes everywhere. The one that pertains to that particular conflict says "Neither of us is as smart as both of us!"

WRIGHT

Well, I guess that brings us full circle then. What advice would you offer others who would like to perfect the various partnerships in their lives?

## Vincent

As Shakespeare said, "To thy own self be true." That involves both knowing who you are and knowing how the other person perceives you. None of us can get all of our needs met entirely alone. It works best if each partner comes into the relationship with a clear sense of what they may have to offer to the world and engages in collaboration with another to realize that vision.

We have developed something we call the *Five Magic Questions* to help us think collaboratively.

## Rizzo

I'm glad you mentioned the *Five Magic Questions,* Lou, here they are:

The first question is, "Given the situation that we're in, what would we like to see as a result?" Again, think about beginning with the end in mind.

The second question is, "What are the three options available to us for getting the outcome that we want?" We have noticed when answering that question, the first two options usually come easily but we really need to dig deeper to come up with three options. Diving deep for the third option helps us analyze all aspects of the situation.

The third question is, "What risks are involved with implementing each of our options?" Lou likes to say that the trick in problem-solving is to solve one problem without creating three more, so we do a risk analysis to assure that we are able to avoid any unwanted future repercussions.

Question four is, "Which set of risks is most under our control and how will we control them?"

After we have finished the risk analysis, we move on to question five, "What is our plan?" Answering the final question involves listing out the activities we're going to do, setting a time line, and dividing up the tasks based on who has the time and the talent to execute each activity.

Any type of partnership, whether it is personal or professional, works best if the partners possess overlapping value systems, can recognize one another's attributes and talents, and are able to negotiate an equitable distribution of work based on those talents. It really helps if the partners genuinely admire and respect each other and enjoy being together.

To be highly productive partners, each one must have common goals, shared trust, shared power, and the ability to forgive and move on when missteps occur.

From time to time you need to recall what attracted the two of you to each other in the first place, and strive to maintain a positive attitude to create an unstoppable will to succeed.

Beyond that, knowing how to assist your partner in fulfilling his or her mind, body, and soul needs will cement the partnership. In a productive partnership each mind needs education and stimulation, each body needs nutrition, activity, and nurturing, and each soul needs care, concern, and love. The trick to a lasting and satisfying partnership—the perfect partnership—is to discover the needs of your partner's mind, body, and soul and then be able to fill in the gaps when your partner can't provide what he or she needs.

VINCENT

The law of reciprocity is always at play, you reap what you sow, love is harmony, harmony is love, and all else is chaos.

WRIGHT

I may take your mantra to have common goals, shared trust and shared power and the ability to forgive and move on. I may put that on my wall.

VINCENT

That sounds good to me.

**WRIGHT**

This has really been a good a great conversation. I have not only enjoyed it but I have learned a lot. I'll bet your clients really do learn from you. I can imagine spending a lot more time with both of you; it has been a real pleasure for me.

**VINCENT**

Back at you, David.

**RIZZO**

Thank you so much, we have so enjoyed talking with you and wish we had more time to spend with you as well. We'll just have to look forward to working with you again on another project.

**WRIGHT**

Today we have been talking with Rita Rizzo and Lou Vincent; they're both partners in life and partners in the firm of Rizzo and Associates LLC, a management consulting and training firm. They're experienced in addressing gender, racial, generational, ethics, socioeconomic and religious diversity topics. Rita and Lou both bring a depth and breadth of knowledge to the larger arena of organizational consulting. Rita, Lou, thank you so much for being with us today on *Health: Mind, Body and Soul.*

**RIZZO**

Thank you, David.

**VINCENT**

Thank you, David. As they say in Tennessee, bye ya'll.

# About the Authors

Rita Rizzo is the Principal of Rizzo & Associates LLC, an Ohio based consulting and training firm established in 1984. She holds a master's degree in Training and Human Resource Management from University of Leicester in Leicester, England, and received her undergraduate education in the field of psychology. Rita is a Certified Management Consultant (CMC), an earned distinction awarded to her by the Institute of Management each year since 2002. She is also certified as a conflict mediator. Rita has provided training and consulting services for more than twelve thousand audiences from corporations, associations, and government. Each and every presentation Rita delivers is done with warmth, wit, and sincerity, and she never fails to engage her audience in fun and fulfilling ways.

Lou Vincent is the Vice Principal of Rizzo & Associates LLC. He has also served the firm as a trainer and consultant for more than two decades. He holds a certification in Organizational Behavior from Heriot Watt University in Scotland and is currently a Master's Candidate in their MBA program. Lou's "pleasing personality" and down-to-earth wisdom make for a pleasant, yet insight-provoking, training experience. He has conducted more than nine thousand seminars with audiences from governmental institutions, health care facilities, and associations. Lou specializes in the topics of diversity, human resource development, systems approaches, and workplace violence.

*Rizzo & Associates LLC*

ritar@rizzoandassociates.com

www.rizzoandassociates.com

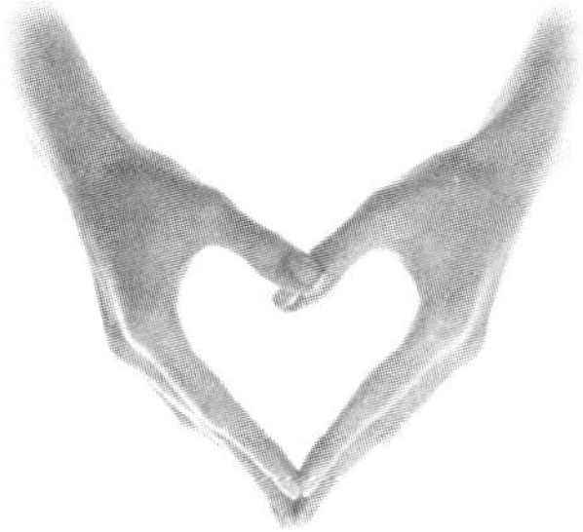

## Chapter Eight

# Taking Responsibility for Your Health

## with Dr. Earl Mindell

THE INTERVIEW

### DAVID WRIGHT (WRIGHT)

Today we are talking with Dr. Earl Mindell. Like Drs. Spock, Edell, and Ornish, Dr. Earl Mindell has become a household name to millions of North Americans. When the *Earl Mindell's Vitamin Bible* exceeded seven million worldwide and published in thirty languages, he had become a phenomenon. Currently it has sold over ten million copies worldwide.

Some of Dr. Mindell's previous books include *Earl Mindell's Soy Miracle, Earl Mindell's Herb Bible,* and *Supplement Bible, Safe Eating, Food as Medicine*, and *Shaping Up with Vitamins.* He conducts nutritional seminars around the world and makes daily appearances on radio and television programs.

Dr. Mindell holds a Ph.D. in nutrition and is a professor of nutrition at Pacific Western University in Los Angeles. He is a California registered pharmacist and a master herbalist. He is a charter member of the American Academy of General Practice of Pharmacy as well as the American Pharmacists Association.

Dr. Mindell, welcome to *Health: Mind, Body, & Soul.*

### DR. EARL MINDELL (MINDELL)

Well, it's a pleasure to be on the show. Actually I should add some of my other books too: *The Prescription Alternatives, The Diet Bible,* and

*The Allergy Bible.* I have forty-seven books as of today and I'm working on a few more. I'm always working on more books.

WRIGHT

I went to Amazon.com just to check your book titles a few days ago.

MINDELL

It's a little embarrassing. On Amazon they have about ninety-five things. They are not all books; some are tapes etc., but they've got almost everything. Well, you know some are, of course, out of print now because I've been writing for more than twenty-five years.

WRIGHT

Dr. Mindell, millions of people are taking vitamin supplements today. However, in a recent article in *Biography Magazine*, you were quoted as saying, "Vitamins are no substitute for eating well." So, how do vitamins help the body?

MINDELL

Well, let me say this. It's pathetic that the United States—one of the richest nations in the world—is a third world country when it comes to nutrition. Vitamins don't replace a terrible diet, but boy, you sure do need supplementation because of this horrific diet we're eating. I call it the 'standard American dieter's fad'—it's more like pathetic. I also call it the "Twinkie, Ding Dong, doughnuts, pizza, Prozac, Pepsi" diet.

Basically, vitamins work *with* food to produce energy. They are necessary for optimal health, which means your body is working as efficiently as possible, and for life as we know it. So it's important to get all the necessary nutrients. If you're lacking one vitamin it can cause a problem with the other ones as well.

WRIGHT

In the same article, when asked about the secret to your success, you were quoted as saying, "I simply tell people the truth about how to take better care of themselves." From whom do people get erroneous information about their health?

MINDELL

Well, they don't get *any* information about their health. They only get information about their sickness. I mean, all you have to do is watch commercial television any particular night and you are inundated with all these drug ads for sickness. You don't hear anything about health. You know we call it "health insurance," but it's not health insurance—it's sickness insurance. We only hear about what to do in case of sickness and what to do. No one tells about health or preventing sickness and keeping this incredible body healthy.

Life expectancy is I guess about seventy-seven years on the average for male and female, doing what we do. If we were to be really educated about how to take care of ourselves, 100 would be the normal life expectancy.

WRIGHT

When the first edition of your book, *The Vitamin Bible*, came out in 1979, the medical community scorned you. They said they thought you were a fanatic. In the past ten years, though, major research studies have changed—even the medical establishment's attitude. That must give you a tremendous satisfaction.

MINDELL

Well, it does. In fact, in *The Journal of the American Medical Association*, October 2002 edition, came out with a research article stating exactly that—everyone should be taking a vitamin and mineral supplement.

As I mentioned I'm an antique collector. I have quite a collection of antique pharmacy and medical things. I have a book published in 1938 by the American Medical Association showing they were very big on vitamins back then! Of course, after the Second World War with the advent of the utilization of synthetic drugs like penicillin, etc., the drug companies said, "Let's dump all of these old remedies and just concentrate on these synthetic drugs." And boy, they've done a pretty good job in the last sixty years. So it's not a new concept, but because diet and lifestyle has changed so dramatically in this country, even the so-called "establishment" is becoming aware that there's no way you're going to get enough nutrients in your diet.

WRIGHT

In 2002 the *Journal of American Medical Association* reversed their twenty-year-old stance against vitamins.

MINDELL

Correct.

WRIGHT

What affect did that have on the public's attitude towards adding vitamins to their diet?

MINDELL

Well, I think it definitely helps when you have the so-called establishment saying that it's imperative people take a supplement. For instance, the March of Dimes (which is a pretty "establishment" charity) has ads going all over the place telling women of child-bearing ages that they should be supplementing their diet with folic acid, one of the B vitamins. Lack of folic acid can cause incomplete development of the brain, spinal cord, and/or their protective coverings—a defect called spina bifida. A lack of folic acid, which just about everyone in the country has, causes the body to produce an over abundance of a toxic amino acid.

Amino acids are the building blocks of protein called homocystine and that is probably a greater contributor to heart disease than elevated cholesterol. So by getting enough folic acid in the diet through supplementation, it will prevent homocystine from being produced. So you can see that we are learning our diet is probably responsible for, I would say, seventy-five to eighty-five percent of the problems wc have.

WRIGHT

Dr. Mindell, you have said that low-fat diets have made people fatter than ever. How can that be?

MINDELL

Well, that's a good question. Five or ten years back we were told low-fat is the way to go and all of a sudden people started switching over to these low-fat or no-fat things. They didn't realize that the companies that produced foods would load them up with sugar and processed carbohydrates. So it's pretty evident that no-fat or low-fat is not the way to go.

I think we should decrease the amount of the processed carbohydrates and sugar; we're eating 150 pounds of sugar per person per year. To give you an idea how much sugar you're eating and don't even realize it, if you drink a typical twenty-ounce soft drink, you're getting fourteen teaspoons of sugar in that soft drink!

WRIGHT

Wow! Goodness! The only diet supplement I've ever taken is one of these jumbo jobs every day that is time released. But the way I read your book, you almost have to take vitamins with food, right?

MINDELL

Oh, absolutely. You should be taking a vitamin supplement *with* food. I take a pack in the morning with breakfast and then also with my evening meal. You don't time release your food, so why should you time release the supplements? You should be taking them at least twice a day. Theoretically, you should take them three times a day, but that is very impractical for the average person. If I could get people to take them twice a day, I'd be happy.

WRIGHT

And what they do is they supplement what you're not getting?

MINDELL

They supplement what you're *not* getting and they make sure you're getting enough of what you *should* be getting.

WRIGHT

Let me read a quote from you, "Each year 140,000 Americans die from the adverse effects of prescription drug use and 938,000 Americans are injured due to prescription and dispensing errors. Eleven million people are abusing prescription drugs. Drug companies are forming alliances with HMOs to control the drugs you take, often at the expense of simpler, cheaper, and healthier lifestyle changes." Wow!

MINDELL

Well, actually those statistics are a little bit out of date. It's about 140,000 Americans die from prescription drug use outside of hospitals and another 100,000 in hospitals. If you were to take the amount of people in the United States dying from prescription drugs, it's probably the fourth leading cause of death.

WRIGHT

Wow!

MINDELL

And it's getting worse. Let me tell you something, we are definitely subsidizing the world when it comes to the cost of drugs. We pay more than anywhere else in the world for prescriptions. Patients go to Canada, our neighbor to the north and are getting prescriptions filled there at half the price charged in the United States.

WRIGHT

So how do we reverse this trend?

MINDELL

Well, we start promoting wellness—you know, if you're well, you don't need prescription drugs. What a fantastic idea that is! I mean, we have our politicians running around the country saying we have to cut the price of prescription drugs for the elderly and they go on generic drugs. Well if they were healthy, they wouldn't need prescription drugs.

WRIGHT

Dr. Mindell, it would seem that with all the research about the importance of good health, we are in a revolution. Where do you see the future of the wellness revolution?

MINDELL

I see something that was talked about in the book that said, and I agree, that the wellness business—if you want to call it that—is going to become bigger than the sickness business. It will be a more than one-trillion-dollar business because people are living longer. People want a better quality of life and they want to be in good shape in the last years of their life. I mean, big deal—you live an extra year or two years longer if you're put away in a convalescent hospital or are connected to some machine. That's not what you want. We're much more informed of this whole thing now, and it *is* a wellness revolution. It's too expensive to continue what we've done before—wait until you get sick and try to pay to get well.

WRIGHT

Just off the subject for a second, I was looking at one of the articles you wrote when you were one of the contributors in a magazine. It listed several vitamins starting at A and going through B1, B6, and D and C and all. I just started reading what these do. Vitamin A, for example—if I read correctly here—the benefits are that it is essential to eye health and builds resistance to respiratory infections.

MINDELL

Right.

WRIGHT

It boosts the immune system, promotes strong bones, healthy skin, hair, teeth, and gums.

MINDELL

Right.

WRIGHT

So why in the world—?

MINDELL

Well, you know, you said we're probably contemporaries when it comes to age. I remember when I was a little boy (I grew up in western Canada—a very cold climate) my mother would give us a spoon of fish liver oil in the winter. I think we would run to school faster because it tasted so horrible. Fish liver oil is a good source of vitamin A and D. In a cold climate, you're not outside very much, and you don't get the sun as much, so a vitamin D supplement was important. Vitamin A is an anti-infective vitamin, and yet today people don't know about it. Today we don't give our children fish oil or whatever—we give them antibiotics. So maybe people knew something back then that we have ignored.

WRIGHT

Let's change the subject for just a minute. What do you think of the Surgeon General's report on obesity in the United States?

MINDELL

It's about time! I'm glad that the Surgeon General now calls obesity and overweight a disease. (Actually it was the last Surgeon General.) He has stated that 300,000 Americans die every year from the complications of obesity such as heart disease, diabetes, hardening of the arteries, high blood pressure, strokes, and how about this one: If we could get people's weight back to normal (two out of three Americans are overweight), and if the average American was at an average normal weight, forty percent of the cancers we are afflicted with would not occur. *Forty! Four zero*! It's about time. In fact, some years ago, one of the national newspapers' headlines claimed one-third of Americans born in 2000 would get diabetes. It's pretty frightening to think that we're bringing up a generation where a third of the children are diabetic.

WRIGHT

Goodness! You know, as I looked at all the information about vitamins, I ran across the definition of minerals. Now, do you mix the two or are they mutually exclusive or what? For example, I was interested in this one (I guess it's called selenium). It acts as an anti-oxidant which I really don't understand. It says it slows the aging process.

MINDELL

Well, let me say this. I really should have called my book *The Vitamin/Mineral Bible*, but minerals are the Cinderella of the nutrition world. They don't get the play that vitamins do, but they are as important—if not more important—than vitamins. You cannot make a single mineral in your body so the two, of course, work together.

The main thing to mention about selenium is that not only is it an antioxidant but it also has anti-cancer properties. It's found in things that people don't eat a lot of such as onions, garlic, brown rice, and seafood. It works along with vitamin E and other anti-oxidants to make it even more potent.

Here's the best way to describe what it does: There's the good guys and the bad guys. The good guys are called antioxidants, and the bad guys are called radical oxygen molecules that are increased by stress, by the things in diets that are called the "fat cats"—fat, alcohol, tobacco, sugar, and salt. They keep the radical oxygen molecules from being produced. Anyway, the bad guys speed up the aging process and lead to degenerative diseases such as heart disease, cancer, and stroke, etc. (We're not dying of old age—we're dying of degenerative diseases and I believe eighty or eighty-five percent of them can be prevented.) But you want to have more of the good guys in your body than the bad guys and selenium, vitamin E, the carotenoids, vitamin C, and things such as green tea, grape seed, soy foods, and garlic are a very rich source of antioxidants. All these foods and nutrients help to neutralize the bad guys.

Isn't it pathetic though? You know, here's you are—I'm sure you are a well educated person—but you know so little about these health subjects. I'll bet you know which drug to take if you have a headache though.

WRIGHT

You know it's embarrassing. I've spent half my life in some school or another, but my gosh! It's unbelievable how little I know.

MINDELL

You know, there is such a need to really reeducate people about wellness, and I think it's going to happen only because of the financial situation. Once people start being really hit in their pocketbook—. I mean, anybody who has what I call "sickness insurance" (as opposed to health insurance) knows every year it keeps going up and up and up and there's no end to it. If you haven't had a prescription filled recently, the average prescription now is $65.00 on the way to $100.00. You say, "Oh I have a policy that I pay a co-payment." Well, watch out because that co-payment is going to be close to $25.00 to $50.00 very soon.

WRIGHT

Right, and actually medical insurance in this country is so expensive that we don't take out medical insurance—we just make monthly payments on our medical bill.

MINDELL

Exactly.

WRIGHT

Even though you pay just a small portion of the co-pay, the other is indicated in your premium.

MINDELL

Yeah, and then there's taxes too (you might have heard of those). So if we continue to do this—if we don't start focusing on wellness and prevention—we're going to bankrupt the country.

WRIGHT

You know with our book, *Health Mind, Body, & Soul*, we're trying to encourage our readers to be better, to live better, and be more fulfilled by listening to the examples of our guest authors. Is there anything or anyone in your life who has made a difference for you and who has helped you to become a better person?

MINDELL

Well, absolutely. My mentors are many. I knew Dr. Linus Pauling, an amazing, brilliant scientist who studied the benefits of vitamin C, etc. Jack La Lanne has always been one of my heroes. Still in his upper eighties, he has been exercising forever. He says he still doesn't like to exercise but he does it anyway. I can go back to Robert Cummings, an actor that was into this in the twenties. I had the opportunity to meet the Shute brothers from London, Ontario, who were the first people who did the research on vitamin E. So it goes on and on, but I think the big thing I'd really try to tell people is that we have got to take as good care of ourselves as we do our dogs, cats, automobiles, and rose bushes, because if you really look at it, most people take better care of their cars than they do themselves. You hear these ads all the time: every 3,000 miles take your car in for an oil change, and make sure this is in order. People get their car washed on a regular basis. Well, how about our bodies? Why don't we know how to take care of them? I think when a baby is born we should get a maintenance manual. That probably would be a good idea.

WRIGHT

Robert Cummings—boy, I tell you, that brings back great memories.

MINDELL

He was a wonderful man.

WRIGHT

He was young looking.

MINDELL

He *is* young looking. He was into this back in the twenties and I had an opportunity of knowing him and learning from him. The health field is not new. It was probably started in the twenties. We're doubling our knowledge about nutrition every eighteen months, yet the average person is still in the dark and doesn't hear anything about this, and they really should.

WRIGHT

I remember thirty or thirty-five years ago, I got involved in this company called Nutri-Bio that was some vitamin company, and Cummings was one of the—

MINDELL

He was the spokesperson for that company.

WRIGHT

Yeah, and I'll tell you, he was taking vitamins daily. I mean morning, noon, and night.

MINDELL

Well, guess what? I still am and I'm in my sixties now, and I've been doing this for forty years. I'll tell you I get compliments all the time by people saying, "Yeah, you look fifteen to twenty years younger than you are."

WRIGHT

If you could have a platform, Dr. Mindell, and tell our readers something that you feel would help them or encourage them, what would you say?

MINDELL

I would say that if you want to be healthy, you have got to take responsibility for your health in your own hands. It's as simple as that. If you want to be sick, don't worry about a thing—it's going to happen. They are waiting for you at $3,000.00 a day. They have got a nice hospital bed and they are ready to come with the paramedics in the ambulance to pick you up.

WRIGHT

Today we have been talking with Dr. Earl Mindell who has become a household name in the health and wellness industry. And as we have found out today, he probably knows as much if not more about vitamins and minerals than any man who lives on this planet.

Dr. Mindell, I really appreciate the time you have spent with me today.

MINDELL

Thank you and stay healthy!

WRIGHT

I will.

# About the Author

Earl Mindell immigrated to the United States in 1965 and was naturalized in 1972. On May 16, 1971, Mindell married Gail Andrea Jaffe. They have two children, Alanna Dayan and Evan Louis-Ashley. Mindell received a Bachelor of Science in Pharmacy from North Dakota State University in 1963 or 1964. He earned a Master Herbalist Diploma from Dominion Herbal College in 1995. Mindell's Ph.D. was conferred in 1985 by Pacific Western University, an unaccredited institution at the time. Mindell has been a frequent guest on radio and television programs, such as Oprah and Regis, typically speaking on nutritional topics. He is currently a registered pharmacist in the State of California and Professor Emeritus at Pacific Western University. Mindell is also responsible for the recent promotion of functional foods such as soy and Lycium barbarum (wolfberries).

In February 2007, Mindell was inducted into the California Pharmacy Hall of Fame. In total, Mindell has published over 55 books. His most notable publication, *Earl Mindell's Vitamin Bible*, is a glossary of micronutrients and is a world-renowned guide to the correct use of vitamins, supplements and alternative therapies.


Earl Mindell, RPh, MH, PhD

www.drearlmindell.com

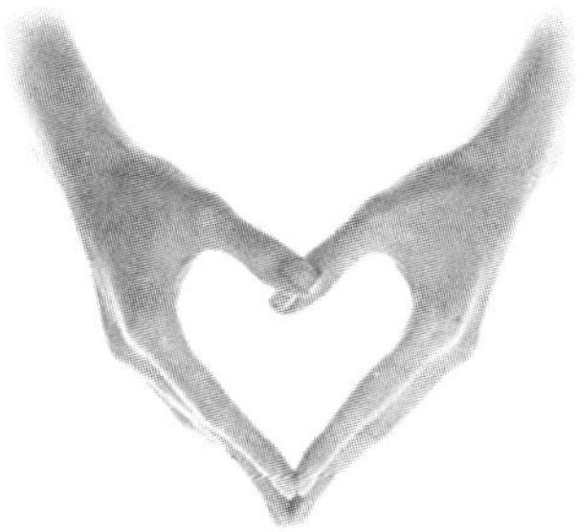

Chapter Nine

# Changing Your Attitude to Transform Your Life

## with Jana Beutler Holland

THE INTERVIEW

---

DAVID WRIGHT (WRIGHT)

Today I'm talking with Jana Beutler Holland. Jana is the Founder of Life in Motion Coaching and is a Certified Personal Fitness Trainer, therapist, and life coach in Tucson, Arizona. Jana has a master's degree in Educational Psychology with an emphasis in Counseling. She is a published author of various topics including "Changing Your Attitude," "Stages of Change," and "Identifying Thoughts that Keep Us Stuck." She is also Founder and Co-owner of SWAT Fitness. SWAT is an acronym that stands for Strength, Wellness, Athletic Training. SWAT is a Tucson, Arizona-based personal training and fitness company specializing in transformational weight loss, wellness, and fitness.

Jana, welcome to *Health: Mind, Body, Soul.*

JANA HOLLAND (HOLLAND)

Thank you so much. I'm glad to be here.

WRIGHT

As a life coach and fitness professional, what do you find are the biggest challenges people have when it comes to making changes in their life?

## HOLLAND

The first challenge most people face is accepting that there is something in their life that needs to change, whether it be unhealthy relationships, unhealthy behaviors, career or work/life, or simply wanting to be a happier person, making the decision to change must come first.

In many people, denial that there is any kind of problem can be very strong and can leave them feeling stuck for long periods of time. Unfortunately, gaining insight about why change is necessary is often gained only through crisis or consequences. Perhaps a serious health scare or threats of divorce or being turned down for a promotion or even just a simple inability to feel joy and happiness can motivate and stimulate change. For many, it's only when some negative consequence or experience takes place when the problem and its solution become a priority. This provides the catalyst and motivation for change.

Other people experience the challenge of having a desire to change but not knowing how or where to start. The process can seem overwhelming, so they don't start at all. Still for others, one of the obstacles to making changes and transforming their life is their desire to be perfect. If one's expectation is that change will happen suddenly or smoothly, then he or she is bound to be disappointed. The likely reaction to this is to say, "To heck with all of this! It's just too hard. I'm doing my part, why aren't things happening for me?"

Transformation is not an event or epiphany or accomplishment. It is a process that can be lengthy and arduous at times. The inability to accept change as an ongoing process rather than as a one-time event has led many to people to relapses, failed weight loss goals, problems in relationships, and feeling like a failure as a human being.

The fact is that change is hard and it takes time and consistency and patience with the process. And that starts with being patient with oneself, and giving up the need to perform, meet expectations, or be perfect in any way.

### WRIGHT

What do you find are the issues that affect women in particular when it comes to making change?

### HOLLAND

What I have noticed in my work with women is that one of the biggest issues they face is how they see themselves. Women often have an inaccurate perception of themselves. Their ideas of how they are perceived by others and see themselves—physically and emotionally—are often skewed negatively.

For women concerned about their bodies or their weight, for example, I often hear women describe themselves as "fat" or "flabby," although they are healthy and appear of normal size and weight. As their own worst critics, women who obsessively cling to ideals of what they should look like, will rarely find peace or self acceptance. It is imperative that women evaluate the truthfulness of their "self-talk," and break the cycle of self-criticism and judgment that keeps them trapped and unhappy with themselves and their bodies. As long as the focus is on what the body *isn't*, women will continue to suffer, be dissatisfied with themselves and others, will likely be resistant to change, and will never really truly know joy and happiness.

There may be a strong professional woman who prides herself on her assertiveness, but is concerned about being perceived as "bitchy" in business, and in personal relationships as well. Women may worry excessively about appearing too needy or overly emotional and then that same excessive worry about how the world perceives her is what motivates a lot of behaviors that are actually inconsistent with her true self. Of course this leads to anxiety and fear and an external focus that blocks her ability to gain insight and tap into her own power to make change. This may lead her to feeling victimized or misunderstood. Some people describe feeling like a fraud if the face that they show to the world contradicts who they truly are.

Another issue that women face is often labeling themselves and negative self-talk. The labels and words we use to describe or talk to ourselves have a lot of power. The words often infiltrate our thoughts and become the reference for how we feel about ourselves. If a woman uses words like "fat" or "bitchy" or "needy" to describe herself, or if she see herself as overly emotional or undeserving of love and success, then what she pays attention to as she lives her life and walks through the world are the things that just serve to reinforce those negative beliefs about herself.

We know that we're evidence-seeking individuals, so once we come up with a theory or belief, our tendency is to only see the things that prove it to be true; then we mistakenly magnify their importance. If you think of yourself as unattractive, then every time you look in the mirror you'll look for examples and evidence that you are unattractive.

We see women who obsess about their weight or the way they look in a certain pair of jeans or the flab on their upper arm or their skin or the size of their nose. It's endless and destructive. Not only that, but it is this constant fault-finding that takes a significant toll over time and affects how they think about or treat themselves. And that is how they then present themselves to the world.

The other challenge that women specifically face is the pressure to be perfect. It is hard to accept that true change and progress come only when we're only willing to admit to ourselves that we have flaws. In fact, all humans have flaws. Wisdom comes when we accept that they are just a small part of us, and not who we actually are as a whole and true person. True personal growth comes when we accept all those flaws and imperfections in ourselves, and can do that without shame. We heal when we can admit them and even display them to the world and to people that we love and walk through the world with. Believe it or not, it *is* possible to recognize physical flaws or character defects without magnifying their importance or taking them on as evidence that we are unworthy, worthless, hopeless, or unattractive.

Then finally, another thing I see as an issue for women, is being so focused on getting things done that they forget they are human beings and cannot do it all—and shouldn't try—if they want to be happy. The important part in the term "human being" is the word "being"—realizing that we are *not* human doings, we're human *beings*.

Many women identify their value as individuals with the roles that they play in the world—mothers, wives, sisters, employees, etc., and they are focused on the external behaviors that give them a mask or façade. And yet it's their ability to be able to look inside and accept their wholeness. Their wholeness includes all their strengths and unique abilities, as well as their faults and flaws. If women find themselves feeling distant or disconnected or if feel as if they are acting a part to the world, then women are prohibited from actually developing strong connections with people in an honest and authentic way and will be trapped by feelings of inadequacy, dissatisfaction, and unhappiness.

### WRIGHT

Would you share with our readers some reasons why people procrastinate or are resistant to change?

### HOLLAND

For most people, procrastination is an issue that keeps them from reaching goals or exploring and discovering their strengths, abilities, and talents. One of the first reasons is a lack of clarity about who we are as individuals and about the reason for desiring or needing change.

For example, you may want to change to make others happy or appear differently to others without buying into the process. Some people make huge changes in their lives without ever identifying if or how it's really important to them as an individual.

Another aspect of that is not really having a sincere desire to change at all, or just not being ready or willing to do the work. We know that change is hard, and if you aren't willing to do the work then nothing is going to change and you'll just get more of what you've already gotten. If this is the case, the pleasure or end result is not appealing enough to motivate you to change or the pain is not great enough to do anything about it.

It's when we're able to look at and examine a cost and benefit analysis, and when the benefits outweigh the costs to us that we're finally ready for change. An example of this would be that you may want to lose weight but you aren't willing to exercise; you may want the promotion but aren't willing to work on performance goals; you may want to quit smoking but aren't willing to experience the discomfort of the craving; or you may want to find a love relationship but aren't willing to put yourself out here or create opportunities where you can interact with others.

Still another reason why people procrastinate is feeling overwhelmed and simply not knowing where to start. In this case, you may need the support and guidance of a professional to help you set small incremental goals that mark the path to getting what you truly want. For many this may include consulting with a life coach, hiring a personal trainer, getting a counselor, or finding a mentor who has already attained what you want. Going it alone rarely provides structure or accountability or support—all elements that are needed to affect long-lasting change. Relying on the expertise and experiences of other people you admire and respect can give you guidelines to follow and a road map to success. Building a team around you provides you with life strategies and tools that can help you along the way to getting what you want.

### WRIGHT

So what stages of change do people go through when transforming their lives and/or their body?

### HOLLAND

There actually is a process of change that we go through, much like the stages of grief, and is well documented in research by colleagues Prochaska, Norcross, and DiClemente. What they found is that there are a number of steps by which people have been successfully treated and taught to manage their problem behaviors.

The first stage is called "precontemplation." In this stage, a person is unaware that he or she really has a problem or is under-aware of the problem. At this stage people don't notice any real problems related to their bodies. They may be in complete denial. At this point, they have expressed no specific desire to make any changes and don't feel any real concern or immediacy for anything to be any different.

The second stage in making long-term and effective change is called "contemplation." In this stage an individual has become aware that there is a problem and has begun considering doing something about it. An overweight person might notice that he or she is out of breath when walking a short flight of stairs, or notices that his or her clothes don't fit the way they used to. People at this stage may realize that their health is in jeopardy, and are beginning to actually wish that things could be different. We hear a lot of "should" in this stage (e.g., we "should" go to the gym, we "should" say no to chocolate super fudge brownies, we "should" take a course, we "should" improve the way we interact with our loved ones). It's a "should" stage—after awareness, but before any action or commitment has taken place.

This leads into the next step, which is called the "commitment" stage. In this stage, people have become more aware than ever that they do have a problem and they are motivated to do something about it. So their health may be at risk or they don't like themselves or they're self-conscious or overcome with feelings of insecurity. Fortunately, it is when they finally get sick and tired of being sick and tired when they go beyond just saying that I "should" do something about it.

They begin seriously saying, *"I will."* As unpleasant as that is, admitting that they are willing to do something about it, is where life starts getting better.

Of course, this is one of the most difficult stages to get to. We enter this stage of committing to change only when the alternative is no longer tolerable. At this point, the thought of not changing is unbearable and we can't stand being out of shape anymore. We're sick of the way we feel about ourselves, we're sick of watching life instead of participating in it, and, in this stage, change and progress really begin.

The next stage is "preparation," where you have made the decision to change and done a lot of research. You've come up with a list of possibilities and start brainstorming strategies and tools that can be used to get to the goal.

And then finally there is the stage of "actions." We've committed and we've prepared, and we're really ready physically, emotionally, and spiritually to embark on the journey to improve our lives. We then go into action and follow our plan.

So the action stage is the "I am" stage where we hear clear messages that reflect our commitment: "I am working out three days a week" or "I am feeling better," "I am watching how I speak and interact with others," "I am proud of myself," "I'm doing," "I'm acting responsibly." This often results in the changes we have prepared for and wanted for so long.

The key to this, I believe, is really enjoying the doing as much as the results of doing. If we are able to take pride in the fact that we are behaving better and that we deserve respect and that we are doing more than most people and that we are way ahead of where we were, then the secret is to keep doing and focus on the actual behaviors that we can do on a daily basis, rather than staying so focused on the end result. For example, if the desired end result is weight loss or a promotion, we risk losing sight of what we can do today. We know that it takes less than a week to form a bad habit but it takes at least thirty consistent abstinent days to break one. So we need to give ourselves time to form good habits and just keep doing.

Then there is the "maintenance" stage, once we're noticing changes and experiencing a positive result and have more self-confidence. The danger of the "maintenance" stage is that we tend to get complacent. We're no longer so uncomfortable that we *must* change, so we're at higher risk for relapse into past unhealthy behaviors. We may find ourselves in old patterns of behaviors, or catch ourselves in ineffective or hurtful interactions with people we love. It must become as much a priority now as it ever was when we were experiencing negative consequences as a result.

WRIGHT

So when you work with individuals on making changes, how do you get to the heart of the matter?

HOLLAND

In my position as a life coach, I work with a lot of people who are in transition from a divorce or between careers or looking for something that really needs to change. What I have found is that what people think they want is really a cover for something else that is more personal and really more important than they may even realize.

For example, for a person who wants to lose weight—their *stated* goal—their *actual* goal may actually be to find love or acceptance. A person who states that they want to be successful financially may actually be seeking security or power. By peeling back the onion and continually asking why it's so important, the real emotion or desired feeling is uncovered.

Then it is our task to gather the tools and resources and have the courage to get to the root of our desires. What I find is that often at the root of the superficial desire or need is something else intangible. Uncovering the *real* goal can be the key to setting an appropriate task for personal growth and change and really transforming one's life.

WRIGHT

What are the traps and pitfalls one can avoid to make change easier?

HOLLAND

The first trap and pitfall to avoid is lack of clarity with who one is, and what one wants, and identifying what the goal is.

I have a client named Sandy who came to see me recently. She was struggling with her daughter who had just left for college. Sandy found herself being very controlling and calling her daughter all the time. Then, when she did get her on the phone, Sandy was very critical and judgmental. She initially presented this and said that the change she wanted to make was to have a closer relationship to her daughter, when really the actual goal was she needed to be needed. We were able to change what her end goal was and she was able to do a lot of things to fulfill the need of being needed that didn't have anything to do with her daughter. As a result, the relationship with her daughter improved.

Then, of course, other things that can be pitfalls and traps to making change are: blaming others, feeling victimized, unspoken resentment, and holding back from asking for what you truly need. Sometimes we do this to protect others, to protect their feelings, or to avoid conflict, but underneath we really feel slighted or disrespected. This can lead us to become passive-aggressive, talk badly about others, become a martyr, have sarcastic or hurtful exchanges, or to even withdraw from people we love the most.

In order to experience change and get a different result than in the past, it is very important to recognize that just because you think something doesn't make it true. It's a difficult concept to understand, but thoughts are just thoughts and feelings are just feelings; our minds are powerful creators of thoughts and feelings that mislead us and get us into trouble and mistake good intentions for bad.

Some of the examples of irrational thinking are thinking that people must like you for you to be valued, having all-or-nothing thinking, thinking that if something falls short then it's a total failure, and making broad generalizations. For example, if someone doesn't like you it becomes, "No one likes me," or "I am unlikable," so using words like "everyone," "nobody," "always" and "never" are a sure sign that our thoughts are running away and telling us things that aren't true. Another irrational belief is the idea that our past determines our future or that the idea that all suffering is a result of other people or acts that are forced upon us and are beyond our control.

WRIGHT

So what is the process that you advise clients to go through if they desire a transformation—a major transformation?

HOLLAND

The first step toward transformation is to identify the problem or challenge and then to accept the responsibility and stop blaming others. Growth and change comes when you take control of the situation, identify the real goal lying underneath what you state the goal is, and find out if there is something deeper there. Make a plan that includes small opportunities to experience success today. Ask yourself, "What can I do today to bring myself closer to my goal?" I recommend that you start each day with an intention for the day and then commit that you will do your best. Then end each day with an inventory of the day, going back and reviewing how well you did and recognizing and acknowledging progress. It's also very important to forgive slips or errors and realize that it's just part of the process, then doing that again every day, adapting and modifying the plan as needed.

### WRIGHT

What is your advice for keeping motivated when challenged or facing obstacles to change?

### HOLLAND

One of the most useful tools I use with clients is what I call "playing the tape." If we play out the scenario all the way to the end, often we'll realize that what we think is really important in the moment is really not that important at all. Picking up that fudge brownie might be satisfactory right now but what are the long-term effects of doing that repeatedly? Does it lead to total abandonment of the diet or giving up or feeling bad about one's self or having to buy bigger clothing?

If you want to quit smoking or drinking for example, what are the effects of having that one cigarette or drink now? It could become a binge that gets out of control, and result in missed work, health problems, and a lack of self-respect. So playing the tape to the end can make the immediate gratification less appealing and make it easier to resume the difficult task of really muddling through. I also ask people to complete a cost/benefit analysis, reconnecting with what the benefits of the changes are and the costs of not doing so. Focus on how getting what you want will really benefit and improve your life and identify how what you have been doing thus far has cost you. And be sure to identify not just financial costs, but costs that are personal, emotional, or spiritual as well.

I also warn people that if they are in a state of plateau to reward themselves and acknowledge small successes. So if you made it through the day without getting into the office vending machine then that deserves a pat on the back. If you walked away from a potentially volatile confrontation with someone, acknowledging that effort and progress is really important.

Then the final thing I suggest to people to get them through is to be patient with themselves. Results and rewards are rarely immediate. So not focusing on the end result and focusing instead on the short-term goal of doing what you can *today* will move them forward at a much more rapid rate. Focusing on behaviors rather than results is key to success. With the example of weight loss, for example, focusing on the exercising and eating right rather than the numbers on the scale is helpful and leads to higher success rates and long-term happiness.

### WRIGHT

In your experience and especially in your work, how do these principles apply in the following applications: career, health and fitness, relationships, and life/work balance?

### HOLLAND

In career, identifying goals and barriers to success in the workplace is a topic that I often work on with people. When we're able to improve our communication with others, have a more positive outlook and attitude, and take pride in our work, we are better able to strategize and develop tools for success and gain the necessary personal skills that will improve work performance and lead to greater work satisfaction.

In terms of health and fitness, making changes to our physical appearance and our physical bodies through weight loss or improved health and fitness can lead to more self-love and acceptance and the ability to overcome plateaus and obstacles.

In relationships, I often see clients make changes and get outstanding results through improved communications, more intimacy and closeness, and better and more satisfying family relationships and friendships.

In terms of life/work balance, which is a huge challenge for most of us, I've seen some great results in people who have been able to make transformational change. They experience more peace of mind, their level of happiness and satisfaction with themselves and others improves, and they are truly able to begin experiencing and sharing joy and tolerance and living a fulfilled and satisfying life. And that is the goal for all of us, I do believe.

WRIGHT

Let's say I apply your principles and everything works out fine and I am successful at changing, is the change permanent?

HOLLAND

Change can be permanent, if the new values and experiences and tools are applied and are actually integrated into your new framework and the paradigm of how you see yourself and how you see the world. In order for change to be long-lasting, it's not just the behavior that has to change, but the attitude behind the behavior. We must adopt new thinking strategies, attitudes, and ways of reacting and then integrate those new ways of thinking into what's already in place.

Once you realize that you can choose to think differently, you can choose to feel differently, and you can choose to react differently, then with daily commitment you can experience results and lifelong changes and complete transformation of life and improved satisfaction in your professional and personal life.

WRIGHT

So how do our readers get in touch with you if they want more information about life coaching and your services?

HOLLAND

The name of my coaching practice is Life in Motion Coaching and the Web address is www.lifeinmotioncoaches.com or just give me a call. My number is 520-444-9188, and I'd be happy to set up a free consultation for anyone interested in coaching services with me.

WRIGHT

Well, this has been an interesting conversation. I really enjoyed it; I've learned a lot about change here today and I'm sure that our readers will. I really appreciate all this time you've taken with me to answer these questions.

HOLLAND

Thank you so much for having me. It's been my pleasure.

WRIGHT

Today I have been talking with Jana Holland. Jana is the Founder of Life in Motion Coaching and is a Certified Personal Fitness Trainer, therapist, and life coach. She is also co-owner of SWAT Fitness, a personal training and fitness company specializing in transformational weight loss and fitness.

Jana, thank you so much for being with us today on *Health: Mind, Body, Soul.*

HOLLAND

Thank you.

# About the Author

Jana Beutler Holland is the Founder of Life in Motion Coaching, and is a Certified Personal Fitness Trainer, therapist, and life coach in Tucson, Arizona. Jana has a master's degree in Educational Psychology with an emphasis in Counseling, and is a published author on various topics including "Changing Your Attitude," "Stages of Change," and "Identifying Thoughts that Keep Us Stuck." She is also co-owner of SWAT Fitness (Strength Wellness Athletic Training), a personal training and fitness company specializing in transformational weight loss, wellness, and fitness in Tucson, Arizona. Jana specializes in Wellness for Women in Mind, Body, and Soul.

Jana Beutler Holland, MEd

6127 N La Cholla Blvd
Tucson, AZ 85741
520-444-9188
www.lifeinmotioncoaches.com

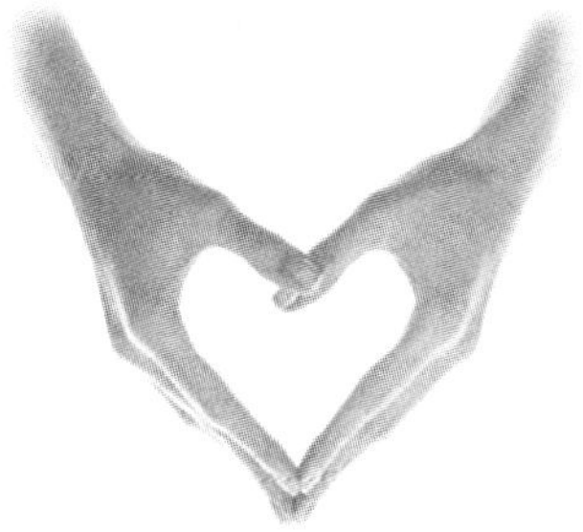

## Chapter Ten

# Health Through Nourishment

### with Kathy Lynch, CHC

THE INTERVIEW

---

David Wright (Wright)

Today I am talking with Kathy Lynch. Kathy is a nutrition consultant, speaker, author, Certified Health Coach, and Founder of Wellskills.com. Kathy's focus is on helping busy adults and families improve their health through better eating and balanced lifestyle.

Kathy speaks to audiences in corporations, educational facilities, health, religious, government, and community organizations, radio and television. Additionally, Kathy offers individual and group coaching programs, cooking classes, and health food store tours. Kathy has done extensive research on nutrition and has written hundreds of articles locally and nationally.

As a mother of two, Kathy feels compelled to share what she has learned about nutrition and health so that other families can benefit, too.

Kathy, welcome to *Health: Body, Mind, Soul.*

Kathy Lynch (Lynch)

Thank you, David!

Wright

Kathy, what got you so interested in the field of nutrition?

## LYNCH

My career took a very interesting detour when several things came together in my life.

First, I was feeling unfulfilled working as a graphic designer. Although I was successful, I felt I could do something more in line with my passion although I wasn't exactly sure what that was yet.

Second, my mother was diagnosed with colon cancer. I wondered why she became ill.

Third, my husband and I started a family later in life. We had our first child when I was thirty-seven years old and our second child when I was forty. Because I was an older mom, I felt a strong desire to be in excellent health so I could be present and well while our children grew up.

Nutrition was the answer on all fronts. I found my passion in studying nutrition and applying what I learned. I discovered that eating differently would have helped my mother. I learned that my mother had irritable bowel syndrome (IBS) for years and the doctors had no idea how to help her. They never discussed diet as a cause or cure for her condition. Eventually, she died of colon cancer.

The more I learned about nutrition, the more questions I had. I knew that eating well was important for good health but I was confused with the many conflicting messages about food that I was hearing and reading about through various media. I decided to look up schools that offered nutrition programs that would further my knowledge.

I thought, "Wouldn't it be nice if I could become more knowledgeable about nutrition, apply what I know for my family, and then make a career out of teaching others so they, too, could benefit from that knowledge?"

I attended the Institute for Integrative Nutrition in New York City for a two-year program, commuting back and forth from Boston to New York City for classes. I love what I learned there and I keep on learning as more and more information becomes available.

WRIGHT

That makes sense. What do you think the public is struggling with in terms of nutrition and health?

LYNCH

Sadly, for a majority of people, health is declining while health care costs are rising. For example, with a dramatic increase of sugar consumption, diabetes, a life-threatening disease, has risen significantly. The Centers for Disease Control predict that about one in three Americans will have diabetes by the year 2050 if the current trends continue. The Kaiser Family Foundation did some research on U.S. Health Care Costs and reported that expenditures in the United States on health care surpassed $2.3 trillion in 2008, more than three times the $714 billion spent in 1990, and more than eight times the $253 billion spent in 1980.

You don't have to look far to see that people are struggling with a vast array of health issues. Obesity, cancer, heart disease, diabetes, arthritis, and many more health issues can be caused or exacerbated by poor nutrition. The old adage, "Let food be thy medicine and medicine be thy food," spoken by Hippocrates around 460 BC, is still true today.

Even if you know that nutrition is essential for good health, it doesn't mean you know how to put that information into practice. For example, there are a lot of people in our culture who do not know how to prepare their own meals or they simply don't prioritize meal planning within their busy schedules. They end up eating fast, processed foods or dining out at restaurants with unhealthy, oftentimes hidden, food ingredients. Preparing your own food from known, healthful ingredients is one of the best ways to take control of your health.

Sadly, many people do not really understand what is and is not healthy. Mainstream advertisements, commercials, and propaganda lead consumers astray. It can be very confusing and frustrating for consumers when new, oftentimes contradictory information is released to the public. It takes real dedication to gain a solid understanding of nutrition and persistence to keep up with new research findings. And, one person's food can be another person's poison—no one diet works for everyone. Each person needs to take into account his or her own health, age, gender, ancestry, geographic location, availability of food, personal preferences, religious, and philosophical beliefs when making food choices.

Unfortunately, most of us live in a culture replete with junk food. Although we eat a lot, we are malnourished because the foods we eat are low in nutrient value. Additionally, many food manufacturers add non-food chemical ingredients to enhance food salability. Texturizers, food dyes, preservatives, artificial flavorings, and more are added to processed foods. One such additive, monosodium glutamate (MSG), has been shown to be neurotoxic. MSG is added to enhance food flavor and, thus, our desire for the food. This may spur consumers to eat more, thereby increasing food manufacturers' profits but, at the same time, worsening consumers' health.

The last struggle I wish to mention here is that of emotional eating. When we have a rough day, feel bored, lonely, or stressed, we may choose to grab something to eat to make us feel better. Too often, we turn to sweet foods for instant gratification and comfort for an emotional problem. The problem is that we are eating not to alleviate physical hunger but, rather, to alleviate an emotional hunger. Eating food in this way can turn into an emotional addiction.

The trick is to get help for negative feelings in a way that does not involve food. For example, when I was in college, I used to procrastinate on some of my big projects. Invariably, I would get very stressed out as the deadline approached. I then found myself fervently munching crackers and candy to help me cope with the stress. I finally became aware of this destructive habit and made an effort to get my projects done earlier so I wouldn't be stressed out at the last minute. I no longer needed food to console myself.

WRIGHT

Are there special concerns with the way children are eating these days?

LYNCH

Absolutely. For one thing, children are eating entirely too much sugar and white-flour processed foods with devastating health consequences. In our educational institutions where children should be learning how to lead better lives, junk food abounds. Schools can and should be a great place for children to learn the importance of eating well and how to do so. But instead, I see that many schools offer junk-food rewards, bake sales, fundraisers, poor-quality snacks and lunches, and celebration foods for birthdays and holidays. When you add up all these instances, you see that "treats" are practically an everyday thing. I have found that I have to provide boxed lunches and snacks for my children so that they eat wholesome, nutrient-rich foods at school. Schools would do well to hire a knowledgeable nutrition specialist to determine what is fed to the children. With food allergies on the rise, this need is becoming more and more apparent.

It is not just the schools that offer children junk food. Friends and family offer junk foods at gatherings and special occasions. Public facilities like banks and hotels place treats in bowls for the taking. Vending machines are stocked with an array of unhealthy choices. I have even seen candy dishes in doctor's offices.

All these unhealthy foods add up to poor health. I found some concerning information on The American Heart Association Web site. Today, about one in three American kids is overweight or obese—nearly triple the rate in 1963. Childhood obesity is now the number one health concern among parents in the United States. Among children today, we are seeing a broad range of health problems that previously weren't seen until adulthood. These include high blood pressure, type 2 diabetes, and elevated blood cholesterol levels. There are also psychological effects. Obese children are more prone to low self-esteem, negative body image, and depression. Excess weight at young ages has been linked to higher and earlier death rates in adulthood.

Not only has eating become increasingly unhealthy, but many children are living sedentary lives. They are spending inordinate amounts of time indoors watching television or playing electronic games. Television has become a big concern because of the promotion of poor quality foods in sitcoms and commercials, not to mention programs endorsing violence, sexism, and commercialism.

Many children do not know what whole foods are because they have not been introduced to them at home. Oftentimes, when I go into schools, I bring a variety of vegetables and fruits and ask the children to name them. Sadly, most of the children have no idea what I am showing them. When parents are present, I find the same thing. In processed foods, it can be very difficult to determine where the food came from just by looking at it. You have to read the label to see what is in the food. When the ingredient list shows a bunch of chemical additives, you know the food has been too highly processed. Children eat too many of these types of foods.

WRIGHT

Do you see yourself as a role model?

LYNCH

I do. I think it's important that I walk the talk—that I practice what I preach. For example, say you go into a doctor's office and the doctor says, "You need to stop smoking. It's bad for your health." But then, when you leave the doctor's office, you notice him taking a smoking break! If someone comes to me to lose weight and eat more healthfully, why would they believe I could help them if I was obese and eating Twinkies and soda for lunch?

I really believe that it's my job to live what I preach. My clients respect that and look up to me as a role model. They are inspired by my actions. It helps me to connect to my clients when I remind them that I used to eat poorly. There were times in my life that I carried excess weight. There were times in my life that were full of stress and I ate large quantities of food to soothe myself. I understand how difficult it is to change eating habits. I live in the same world we all live in and I am continually challenged with making good choices for my family and myself. However, I have worked through many of these challenges. I have worked hard to come up with solutions for my family and my clients. I can offer help to those who are stuck in their current diet routine or want to reach optimal health faster than they could on their own.

WRIGHT

How has eating well helped you and your family?

LYNCH

All of my past health conditions have cleared up by a change in diet. For example, at age twenty, I developed adult acne. As I look back at that time, I realize that the acne came when I increased my intake of sweets and other junk foods at college during stressful times. Although my acne is now largely gone, I still get skin eruptions whenever I stray from eating quality foods. My body speaks to me.

For years, I had recurring vaginal yeast (candida) infections. Not only did I experience vaginal itching and soreness, I also experienced extreme fatigue, emotional irritability, and foggy thinking. It wasn't until I discovered that my diet contributed to the yeast infections, that I improved my diet and chased the yeast infections away—for good.

As for my family, my husband thanks me often for the food I put on the table. With all his business travel, he often eats out, which makes it hard for him to keep his weight down. When he eats my home-cooked meals, he feels better and finds it easier to keep his weight down. My children rarely get sick. Consequently, they have great attendance at school. Their grades are great. They don't cancel play-dates due to illness. I use food as preventive and curative medicine. On the rare occasion they get a cold, I serve them good, old-fashioned chicken soup and oranges for vitamin C. I feel a great sense of satisfaction when I feed my family well.

### Wright

What do you think people need to focus on to eat well?

### Lynch

People who want to eat better need to focus on whole, nutrient-dense foods that are minimally processed or close to their natural state. Humans are omnivores. We can derive nourishment from animal and plant sources. Animal foods include meat, poultry, seafood, eggs, and milk. Some people eat insects, too. Plant foods include vegetables, fruits, herbs, spices, nuts, seeds, beans, legumes, and whole grains. Healthy animal and plant fats are an essential part of a person's diet as well. My favorite dietary fats are found naturally in meats and fish, dairy (butter, ghee, and cheese), and plant sources including olive oil, coconut oil, and fats found in nuts.

The good news is that humans can thrive on differing diets as long as our bodies get the necessary nutrients from a variety of foods. We need to understand our own bodies and what works for each of us. Focusing on how we feel after eating different foods is a good way to gauge what does and does not work for us.

### Wright

What foods should people steer away from?

### Lynch

We really need to work on reducing processed foods, especially sugars and white flour products (e.g., candy, cookies, cakes, doughnuts, sodas, pretzels, white bread, etc.). Even too much fruit sugar (fructose) can pose a problem. A lot of people love sugar because it tastes good and it provides a quick surge of energy. However, what many people do not realize is that what goes up must come down.

After a high rise in blood sugar, comes a crash in blood sugar, leading to irritability, depression, and/or fatigue. We also run the risk of developing major sugar-related illnesses like diabetes, obesity, heart disease, and much more.

Many people struggle with food allergies and sensitivities whether they are aware of them or not. According to the U.S. Food and Drug Administration, more than one hundred sixty foods can cause allergic reactions, but the law identifies milk, eggs, fish (e.g., bass, flounder, cod), crustacean shellfish (e.g. crab, lobster, shrimp), tree nuts (e.g., almonds, walnuts, pecans), peanuts, wheat, and soybeans as the eight most common allergenic foods. These foods account for 90 percent of food allergic reactions, and are the food sources from which many other ingredients are derived.

With the frightening introduction of genetically modified organisms into our food supply, food allergies and other associated health problems have increased. Genetically modified foods are new to our food supply, originating in the 1990s—only about twenty years. Jeffrey Smith, author of *Genetic Roulette: The Documented Health Risks of Genetically Engineered Foods* and *Seeds of Deception: Exposing Industry and Government Lies About the Safety of the Genetically Engineered Foods You're Eating*, has painstakingly documented the many health risks associated with eating genetically modified foods. I urge everyone to boycott genetically modified foods. Currently, the five major genetically engineered crops are: soy, corn, canola, cotton, and sugar beets. These ingredients are in about 75 percent of our processed foods. According to Jeffrey Smith, if just 5 to 6 percent of our population would boycott them, we could create a tipping point that would force them out of our food chain.

Trans fats (hydrogenated or partially hydrogenated oils), are very harmful for health, clogging arteries and making people prone to heart attacks and strokes. The fact that the government allows them on the market, knowing this, confounds me.

Soy is not the health food many people think it is. Unless it is organic (not genetically engineered) and fermented as in miso, tempeh, and natto, it is a dangerous food choice. The Weston A. Price Foundation, a reputable nutrition education foundation, has scrupulously researched the many health risks associated with eating unfermented soy. You can go to the Weston A. Price Foundation Web site at www.westonaprice.org/soy-alert for more details.

The last food issue I want to warn readers about is the production of factory-farmed animal foods. It is very disturbing the way factory farmers raise their animals. The use of growth hormones, antibiotics, ill-suited animal feed, and inhumane living conditions makes this practice deplorable. Raising animals that are bred in unhealthy conditions leads to unhealthy animals not fit for human consumption. Rather, eat animals raised naturally in healthy conditions, seeing the light of day, and eating food that is meant for them. For cows, a mixture of grasses from open pastures is their appropriate food.

WRIGHT

Thanks for the warnings, Kathy. Now, let's get onto the topic of what we *can* eat. Since meal planning is an issue for many of us, can you offer some tips on how to plan meals in advance?

LYNCH

Sure. The day-to-day preparation of healthy foods can be a challenge for many. However, preparing your own food is one of the best ways to take control of your health. I recommend planning ahead. A little bit of forethought can go a long way. For example, think about what you will eat tomorrow night. Will you need to pull some food out of the freezer and let it thaw overnight? Will you need to soak beans or whole grains over night? Will you need to run to the grocery store or farmer's market to get what you need? If you do not think ahead like this, you run the risk of resorting to fast or packaged processed foods.

You might want to write down a schedule of meals for a period of time (e.g., a whole week). Or, if you do not like planning meals in this way, you might shop ahead for a variety of healthy foods to have on hand and then create meals on the fly.

Recipes are easy to come by on the Internet or in recipe books. If you don't want to hunt down a recipe, create one of my favorite standbys—a stir-fry meal. All you do is toss some cut vegetables and a protein source like meat, seafood, eggs, or beans, and stir-fry them in a skillet or wok with a healthy fat like butter, ghee, coconut oil, or olive oil. Serve as is or on top of some brown rice for a great well-rounded meal.

A quick and satisfying main course is eggs. They are nutritious and versatile to work with. For example, you can hard boil them, make them into omelets, scramble them, cook them over easy, poach them, or use them in a quiche or impressive soufflé.

Another tip is to do batch cooking. For example, over the weekend, make a big salad to last the entire week. Make a big bottle of salad dressing from olive oil, apple cider vinegar, and some added herbs and spices. A good staple food to have prepared in batch size is brown rice. During the week, you can use the brown rice in a variety of ways. You can eat it plain as a meal accompaniment. You can make a fried rice dish with diced vegetables and eggs or meat. You can take leftover brown rice and make it into rice pudding with milk, cinnamon, and raisins for dessert. Some people like to create big batch foods and then freeze them in meal-size portions. They pull the frozen meals out of the freezer as needed. By making big batch foods, you save time in the kitchen overall.

### Wright

What are some quick grab-and-go foods that are good for us to eat?

### Lynch

Many of us want grab-and-go snacks or mini-meals that we can quickly bring with us on the run. I'll share some of my favorites. I love fruit as a grab-and-go snack or dessert. Grab an apple, pear, grapes, or banana, for example. Fruits are all ready to go in their own package. For larger fruits, like melon, papaya, or pineapple, cut them into bite-size pieces and place into an air-tight container. There are dozens of fruits available. Have fun trying new ones.

One of my favorite snacks is organic popcorn, air-popped and topped with olive oil, sea salt, and nutritional yeast flakes. Rather than eating microwave popcorn, make it with an air popper or a covered pot with coconut oil at the bottom. Sometimes, I make it a day ahead of time and then place it in small bags for the kids' lunch boxes.

Cut vegetables are great grab-and-go foods. Chop red, yellow, orange, or green peppers. Cut broccoli and cauliflower heads. Slice carrots, radishes, celery, bok choy, cucumbers, kohlrabi, and jicama. Cherry tomatoes are ready to eat as is. Just rinse them and pop them into your mouth. There are dozens more vegetables to try. If you like dip with your vegetables, I recommend guacamole, salsa, yogurt-based dips, and hummus.

Trail mixes are tasty and satisfying. You can make your own concoctions with nuts, seeds, and dried fruits. There are so many nuts and seeds to choose from. Try almonds, pecans, walnuts, macadamia nuts, Brazil nuts, hazel nuts, pistachios, peanuts, pine nuts, pumpkin seeds, and sunflower seeds. You can find dried fruits such as raisins, prunes, apricots, cranberries, blueberries, and cherries.

Then there are whole grain hot meals you can prepare and put in a container to take with you. Oatmeal, brown rice, millet, and quinoa are my favorites. I top them with butter, cinnamon, or dried fruit.

Smoothies make great grab-and-go drinks full of nutrients. When I have a big batch made, I drink some of it and place the remainder into popsicle molds for later enjoyment. I make smoothies with a variety of ingredients including coconut milk, yogurt or kefir, cocoa, nut butters, and fruits. Smoothies are great for sneaking in vegetables and supplements, too.

Dark chocolate is both delicious and nutritious. I like chocolate dipped in nut butter or I melt chocolate into a sauce and dip strawberries into the sauce.

Homemade muffins, breads, and cookies are usually a hit. I use minimal amounts of natural sweeteners like maple syrup, honey, and date sugar, for example. You can make these recipes ahead of time on big batch days and stick them in the freezer until needed.

Raw cheese, nitrate-free deli meats, beef jerky, fruit leather, hardboiled eggs, and brown rice mochi are more great grab-and-go choices.

WRIGHT

What can you offer in terms of encouragement for eating well and living a more healthy and fulfilled life?

LYNCH

Eating well is a process, not a one-time event. It takes time to implement positive change. It takes one step at a time. Each step forward is a step in the right direction. Sometimes, you will take a few steps backward. Setbacks happen but just keep at it. Your efforts will pay off in good health and well-being. If you are stuck, don't be afraid to ask for help.

If you want to move quicker than you currently are, don't be afraid to ask for help. You don't have to go it alone. There are people out there who are further along the path than you are and who can help.

Invest in your health so you reap the benefits. You will live a longer, more energetic life. You will feel better. You will look better. You will perform at your best. You will think more clearly and become more conscious about many aspects of your life. Your self-esteem and life satisfaction will increase. When we change our food, our whole mind, body, and soul awaken. These parts of ourselves function optimally—the way nature intended.

WRIGHT

Well, what a great conversation. I've learned a lot from you today. You have mentioned foods that I didn't even think were good for me. I can go back to eating them now! I really appreciate the time you've taken with me to answer all these questions. I have really enjoyed it. I have taken notes and I am sure our readers are going to get a lot out of this chapter.

LYNCH

Super! Thank you for the interview.

WRIGHT

Today I have been talking with Kathy Lynch. Kathy is a nutrition consultant, speaker, author, Certified Health Coach, and Founder of Wellskills.com. She works with busy adults and families to improve their health with balanced nutrition and lifestyle.

Kathy, thank you so much for being with us today on *Health: Mind, Body, Soul.*

LYNCH

Thank you, David. Good luck to you on your food journey!

# About the Author

Kathy Lynch, Founder of WellSkills, works with busy adults and families to improve their health through better eating and balanced lifestyle. Kathy has educated thousands of individuals through wellness seminars, individual and group programs, cooking classes, and health food store tours. She is a Certified Health Coach and graduate of the Institute for Integrative Nutrition as well as the University of Maryland. Kathy is a co-leader of the Temecula chapter of the Weston A. Price Foundation and the Temecula Valley chapter of Holistic Moms Network. She is a member of Slow Food USA, the Temecula Valley Garden Club, the National Speakers Association, and Toastmasters International earning Distinguished Toastmaster (DTM), the highest honor for a Toastmaster. Kathy has written hundreds of articles locally and nationally and has spoken on a number of television and radio stations.


Kathy Lynch

*WellSkills*

Innovative change agent for optimal nutrition and health

Temecula, CA

978-337-4450

KathyLynch@WellSkills.com

http://www.WellSkills.com

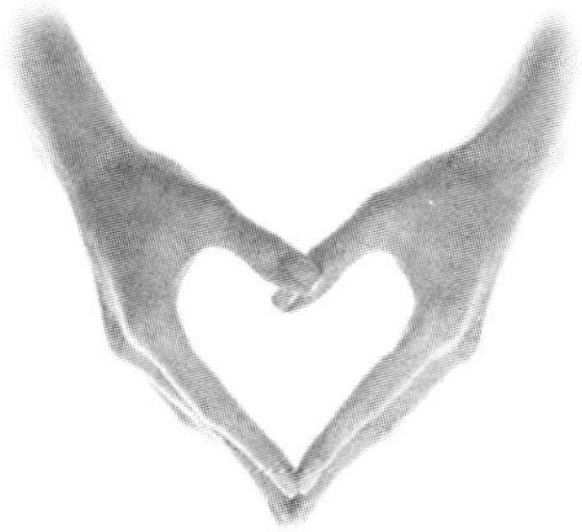

## Chapter Eleven
# Living Without Limits

## with Andy Holder

THE INTERVIEW

**David Wright (Wright)**

Today I'm talking with Andy Holder. At the age of thirty-six, Andy, also known as IRONANDY, was diagnosed with type 1 diabetes. This came with no family history and no warning. Being a husband and father of two young boys, he was determined to overcome the disease and he was not going to let it limit his life. He decided to do something extraordinary in an effort to motivate and inspire other people struggling with diabetes. Despite never having done a triathlon before and not knowing how to swim, Andy decided to accomplish what most consider the ultimate test of mental and physical endurance—the Ironman Triathlon.

Andy Holder, welcome to *Health: Mind, Body, Soul.*

**Andy Holder (Holder)**

Thank you. It's a pleasure to be able to share my story. I hope everyone who reads this can find some inspiration and motivation and apply it to their lives in a positive way.

**Wright**

You became IRONANDY after you were diagnosed with Type 1 diabetes at the age of thirty-six. Tell me a little about your life prior to that.

## HOLDER

Sports played a central role in my life as a child and well into my teens. As far back as I can remember, I dreamed of some day being a professional athlete. That dream never came to fruition and after college I found myself stumbling into a career that I didn't have a passion for. I was envious of people who loved what they did, but for me work was just that—work.

After a few years in the investment business I resigned myself to the fact that my happiness would have to come from somewhere else—from my family and friends. I started to accept the fact that I would not find fulfillment from my job and it was just a means to pay the bills. I wasn't happy that I didn't jump out of bed every day and rush to the office, but I didn't know how to change that. However, I never gave up on the hope that I would find something bigger and more meaningful to do with my life, but to say that I was frustrated, that I didn't know how to go about that would be an understatement.

Then, at the age of thirty-six, type 1 diabetes hit with no warning. I once read a quote that says, "We never realize the most significant moments in our lives while they are happening to us." But in this case I knew—I knew that diabetes was the spark or the catalyst I had been waiting for to live an extraordinary life, the life I had always wanted.

My wife tells a story of when I was driving home from the doctor upon hearing the news that I had type 1 diabetes. I was talking with her on the phone and was so upset that I could hardly get the words out, but I was still able to tell her that I was going to make something good out of this. The few weeks immediately after the diagnosis was a very emotional time for me but deep down, I knew that I would find a way to not only overcome diabetes and show my family that I was not about to let it define me or limit me, but I also knew I could use it as a platform to inspire and motivate other people.

WRIGHT

Type 1 diabetes is also called juvenile diabetes, but you were diagnosed later in life. How did that make you feel upon hearing the news that you had juvenile diabetes at your late stage of life?

HOLDER

I think it might be helpful to talk a little about diabetes, primarily the two major types, type 1 and type 2. Type 1 diabetes is an autoimmune disease in which the body no longer produces insulin. It is usually diagnosed in children and young adults, and was previously called juvenile diabetes. Insulin is a hormone needed to convert sugar, starches, and other foods to energy.

Type 2 diabetes is the most common form of diabetes. In type 2, either the body does not produce enough insulin, or the cells ignore the insulin. Type 2 diabetes is normally managed with medication and lifestyle change. In some cases, rare but highly commendable cases, type 2 can be managed by lifestyle change alone.

So despite feeling confident that I would find a way to overcome this disease, my initial reaction was confusion. Like most people, I thought only children got type 1 diabetes. Whenever someone finds out that I was diagnosed at thirty-six, they assume I have type 2 diabetes.

I was also a little scared. I didn't know if having diabetes meant my life expectancy was just cut short or if it meant I would have complications later in life. But more than anything, I was angry. I was angry because I worked very hard to be healthy. I ate right, I exercised every day—I was doing all the things that are preached to us about how to live a healthy life. But more so, I was also angry because I was a new father. At the time of my diagnosis, my sons were two years old and six months old. I had always imagined how amazing fatherhood would be someday. But now in the face of diabetes, I worried about how this disease might affect how they see me. I wanted my sons to see me as a superhero, not someone who has to test his blood sugar dozens of times a day by pricking blood from my finger tips. Not someone who is connected to an insulin pump just to stay alive. Certainly not someone whose blood sugar gets so low at times that his speech is slurred and his hands tremble. That is not how I imagined fatherhood to be! Diabetes is a very humbling disease, especially when you are, for the most part, a healthy, strong adult. And this angered me.

I will never forget the moment when the reality first hit me that this wasn't a bad dream and I had diabetes. It was the first time I had to give myself an insulin injection, and my oldest son who was two years old at the time was watching me. It was in that moment when I realized this was real—I have diabetes—and there was nothing I could do to make it go away. I also knew there would be a lot about the rest of my life that wasn't always in my control. Despite all the planning, counting carbohydrates, weighing my food, and testing my blood sugar, sometimes things are out of my control.

But I knew there was one thing I had complete control of. The one thing that everyone has complete control of every day of our lives—my attitude! I knew that if I could control my attitude, this disease would not get the best of me and I could use it as a platform to inspire and motivate other people who were struggling.

In short, I turned a diabetes diagnosis into an opportunity to inspire children struggling with this disease and to bring hope and comfort to their parents who worry about them. I have also been able to motivate people to have a positive attitude and overcome life's challenges.

### Wright

In reading your bio, I noticed you did not know how to swim prior to your diagnosis, why did you choose the Ironman Triathlon?

HOLDER

The short answer is, because it was the hardest thing I could think to do, and if it was easy nobody would care and nobody would be inspired.

The longer answer to why would somebody who is thirty-six years old and has never done a triathlon before, doesn't own a bike, isn't a runner and who doesn't know how to swim decides to do an Ironman. An Ironman Triathlon is where you: swim 2.4 miles, bike 112 miles, and then you run a marathon 26.2 miles! The Ironman triathlon is something I had seen on television before; every year the Ironman World Championships from Hawaii is broadcast on television. For obvious reasons, I'd never had any aspirations to do the race myself, but when I had watched it on television in the past, I remembered being in awe of what these athletes put themselves through for eight, sometimes seventeen hours. And it's not only the physical aspect of this race, but also how mentally grueling it is. It was also the fact that in addition to some of the top triathletes in the world, there are also ordinary people competing in this event. Often they are there to complete a bucket list item or to raise money and awareness for a certain cause—an ordinary person doing something extraordinary is a phrase commonly associated with Ironman.

When I put those two words together in my head, ordinary and extraordinary, that's when it hit me—I would become an Ironman in an effort to inspire people with diabetes, to prove to them that this disease doesn't have to limit their lives. I also thought it would be a great way to motivate people who are struggling with life's challenges. Finally, I felt this was how I could find passion in my work and have a profound effect on the lives of others.

WRIGHT

I can't imagine how hard an event like this must be for someone who *doesn't* have diabetes. Tell me about some of the added challenges you have to face to train for an event like this.

### HOLDER

There are a numbers of challenges I face every day just managing diabetes. But if you layer training for an Ironman on top of that, it can get overwhelming. That's not a complaint because I choose to do this. But there is a tremendous amount of planning, preparation, and mental toughness just to get through a typical day.

The biggest challenge is managing my blood sugar so I can get through a particular workout. If you don't have diabetes there isn't as much thought or preparation needed to exercise as I have, you just lace up your shoes and hit the pavement. I can't do that, I need some lead time to get ready for any workout. The reason is that exercise of any kind will bring my blood sugar down, which is a good thing. Exercise makes the muscle cells more receptive to the insulin I am injecting, in turn converting sugar to energy more efficiently. But in addition to not producing insulin naturally and having to inject it manually, having type 1 diabetes also means my body no longer knows how to regulate blood sugar. When I am not exercising, I can feel when my sugar is low and sometimes when I am high, but without testing I have no idea how low or high it is. During exercise I can't feel blood sugar lows or highs. Therefore, I have to prick blood from my finger constantly to check my levels. Also, when I give myself insulin, it is supposed to bring my blood sugar down. But when I give myself insulin *while* exercising, the combination can bring my blood sugar down too low, and there is really no way for me to know how low or how fast it will happen. So just to get through a typical workout means: planning my pre-workout meal down to the gram of carbohydrate. It means trying to perfectly predict the amount of insulin needed and the timing of when the insulin will do its job, with the timing of when the carbohydrates in that meal will hit my blood stream. And, how the exercise will affect the insulin and subsequently my blood sugar, all the while I am testing my blood sugar when I am on the bike and running. For someone who doesn't have diabetes, all those machinations take place without any thought or intervention.

Now imagine all the above is to get through just one workout. Normally Ironman training consists of two workouts a day, six days a week and you also have to factor in work, travel, family obligations, stress—*life!*

I don't want to gloss over the fact that when I decided to become an Ironman, I had never done a triathlon before. I wasn't a cyclist or runner, and didn't know how to swim. When people hear my story they seem to be more amazed with the not knowing how to swim part than they are with all my diabetes-related obstacles. I can understand that, unless you have diabetes or live with someone who has this disease, it's hard to fully understand how relentless and all-consuming it is. Diabetes is just a word to them. But most people can appreciate the leap from not knowing how to swim to swimming 2.4 miles. And it's not just swimming 2.4 miles, it's swimming in open water with two thousand people elbowing you and kicking you. It is one of the most unsettling situations a person can voluntarily put themselves in.

### Wright

Training for Ironman and having diabetes seems pretty difficult. How about the challenges you face on race day?

### Holder

I am now a seven-time Ironman Finisher so it wouldn't be fair to say that I still don't know how to swim, although I am never the first one out of the water. I would have to say my biggest challenge on race day is managing my blood sugar. Even though a race is a lot longer than any one training session, the process for managing my blood sugar is for the most part the same, but the stakes are higher. What I mean when I say the stakes are higher is that I put a lot of time, effort, and energy all year into getting ready for a race. In most years I will compete in only one, sometimes two full

Ironman events. So to train all year for something and have my performance adversely affected or even worse, not be able to finish because I can't get a handle on my blood sugar, makes race day a lot harder for me than for the athletes who don't have diabetes.

It is almost impossible to predict where my blood sugar will be at any time during a race, and the most critical time for me is before the race even starts. An Ironman begins at 7:00 AM, with the swim being the first leg. Swimming 2.4 miles usually takes me anywhere from an hour and ten minutes to an hour and twenty minutes. That's more than an hour where I cannot test my blood sugar! Under normal training circumstances I would never go that long without testing my blood sugar. What I have to do to combat that is get up three to four hours before the swim starts. I do this because I want my blood sugar to be high at 7:00 AM. High because I can't test while I am swimming and the worst thing that could happen to me is a low blood sugar while I am in the water without the ability to know or to do anything about it. I wake up that early so I can have my prerace meal, but my strategy is to give myself only about 30 percent of the insulin that I would normally give myself on a non-race day. On paper what should happen, since I gave myself less insulin than what is normally required, is three to four hours later, when the insulin is finished doing its job, my blood sugar should be high. That is what I want to happen. This doesn't always work as planned when you factor in race day nerves, adrenaline, and water temperature, but it's the best formula I have been able to come up with to get through the swim.

After the swim is a 112-mile bike ride, which usually takes me about six hours. The race day nutrition plan for the bike calls for taking in calories (mostly carbohydrates) every fifteen minutes. Eating every fifteen minutes means testing my blood sugar every fifteen minutes—while biking at twenty miles per hour! The challenge is not just maneuvering a bike while testing my blood sugar, but it's also trying to get my blood sugar in a stable range and keeping it there. Oftentimes during the bike portion of a race,

I will test my blood sugar forty to fifty times, especially if I can't get a handle on where my blood sugar is trending.

After the bike, I run a marathon of 26.2 miles. The blood sugar issues and concerns continue for another four hours or more. Am I too high, too low? If I'm high should I give myself insulin? But that may bring me too low. If I'm low, I have to load up on sports drinks and gels at every aid-station. Try running a marathon with four hours worth of drinks and gels sloshing around in your stomach, it doesn't lend itself to optimal performance.

WRIGHT

How has becoming an Ironman Triathlete helped you with managing your disease and your overall health?

HOLDER

I think there are a lot of parallels between what it takes to manage type 1 diabetes and what it takes to train for and finish an Ironman triathlon. Diabetes is what I call a relentless and mind-numbing disease; there is no off switch and you can never let your guard down—and that's just to get through a typical day. If you look too far into the future and ponder how you can possibly keep this up for a long period of time, it will overwhelm you.

Ironman is exactly the same. Most people consider a marathon to be an amazing feat, but when I have been on my bike for five or six hours I can't think about the fact that I still have to run a marathon. I just tell myself that when I get off the bike I will take one step at a time; I will keep putting one foot in front of the other. If I get caught up in reminding myself that I still have a marathon to run it will crush my spirit.

Diabetes is the same. Every day I'm planning my meals, I'm weighing my food, I'm counting carbohydrates, I'm testing my blood sugar, I'm making adjustments to my insulin pump, and that's not even factoring in the regular stresses of life, work and family; it's relentless. I have to keep reminding myself to take it one step at a time, one day at a time.

WRIGHT

What advice or guidance would you give to others who need to or would like to make lifestyle changes and improve their overall health?

HOLDER

I believe a positive attitude drives everything we do, so I try to encourage people to begin there. A positive attitude makes us more aware and opens us up to see opportunity where others would not. A positive attitude can help us handle adversity. A positive attitude can drive us to be extraordinary, and in the process inspire and motivate others to do the same. I spent some time shortly after my diagnosis reflecting on and questioning where attitude comes from. Is a positive attitude something we are born with? Because we all know people who are positive, upbeat, seem to handle anything that gets thrown at them. But we also know people who are negative, who make excuses and blame other people for their situations. Personally I don't think a positive attitude is something we are either born with or not. I think we can teach ourselves and train ourselves to have a positive attitude, like forming a habit. If you can get into the habit of being positive every day, even about the minor things, when something major gets put in front of you like a diabetes diagnosis, you'll be amazed and how you can overcome it. That is the first and I feel most important piece of advice I can give people—have a positive attitude!

I also try to encourage people who are attempting to make lifestyle changes that you need to make it fun. You need to take exercise and living a healthy lifestyle off the "to-do" list and make it something that is a natural and fun part of your day. Making real and lasting lifestyle change is about action over inaction. Even the smallest, incremental effort everyday will make a big difference.

Statistics show that most people who do make lifestyle changes don't stick to them, and I think that's because they are not enjoying themselves.

I also believe in balance, you need to have balance in life. If you are working hard to eat right, exercise, reduce stress, and doing all the right things throughout the week, it's important that you treat yourself to the things you enjoy. I would go out of my mind if I never had some of my favorite foods or allowed myself a break every once and awhile.

To sum up my advice—have positive attitude, make it fun, and find balance!

### WRIGHT

What's been the most significant change to your life from all of this?

### HOLDER

I think the fact that at thirty-six years old I had never done a triathlon and I didn't know how to swim, yet became a seven-time Ironman finisher is pretty significant.

But what I am more proud of is how I took a diabetes diagnosis and turned it into an opportunity to find greater fulfillment in my life. Before I was IRONANDY and was in a career that I didn't have a passion for, I was unfulfilled. You try to convince yourself that family and friends are enough and it's okay to not love what you do for work. But I had a strong desire to be doing something bigger and more extraordinary with my life and I'm not the kind of person who can settle for ordinary.

Seven years ago, if you gave me a blank sheet of paper and asked me to create the dream career, this is what it would look like: As IRONANDY I get to be an athlete, an inspirational speaker, and a national spokesperson. I get to meet great people all over the country and raise money and awareness for a disease that is becoming an epidemic. I couldn't ask for a better career and it's still amazing to me how far I have come in such a short time. When I walk into a school auditorium and kids are cheering for me or when I am on the set of a morning show, I still have to pinch myself. This is in part what I want people to take away from my message: it's not only about overcoming obstacles but it's also using that obstacle as motivation to do even more—to be extraordinary!

WRIGHT

You have become an inspirational speaker and national spokesperson; what effect have you had on others?

HOLDER

When this all began for me, my initial goal was to show my sons that diabetes or any adversity was not going to get the better of me. Then I wanted to inspire children with diabetes to live without limits.

One story I like to share is about a young boy I met early on, shortly after I completed my first Ironman triathlon. I was in Miami to race in a half Ironman event and the day before the race I had a meet- and-greet set up with a number of children who have diabetes and their family members. There was one boy in particular who I could tell was having a pretty rough time. From what his mother told me, he was embarrassed about this disease, he hid his insulin pump in his pocket, and didn't test his blood sugar as often as possible because he thought the other kids would make fun of him. I was trying my best to get through to him but I wasn't having much success. I encouraged his mother to come to my race the next day and bring her son. I thought maybe if this boy saw me in a real race he would be inspired. I even gave him one of my Team IRONANDY race jerseys as a souvenir. The next day, I was about halfway through the race when I started to feel terrible. My blood sugar was running very high and I felt dehydrated. I made the decision to stop and call it quits for the day. Sitting on the side of the road waiting for a volunteer to drive me back to the finish line, I started to think about this young boy. I thought about the struggles he was going through and how lucky I was that I didn't have to deal with this disease as a child. I also thought about how the day before I encouraged his mother to bring her son to the race, thinking he would be inspired seeing me cross the finish line. And here I was sitting on the side of the road about to be driven to the finish line in a golf cart. How inspiring would that be?

Thinking about this boy and that the only reason I was doing any of this was to inspire children, I decided to get up and finish the race. Five miles later, as I was approaching the finish line, I saw this boy. There he was at the finish line, standing next to my wife and two sons. When he saw me approaching, the smile that lit up his face is an image I have kept with me ever since. Every time I feel like a workout is too hard or I question whether I am in over my head, all I have to do is think about that boy's smile. When my fingertips feel numb from all the pricking I have to do to test my blood sugar, all I have to do is think about the letter this boy's mother sent me shortly after the race, telling me that her son is now a completely different kid. How he is no longer embarrassed about his disease and is now motivated to overcome it.

Another story I like to tell illustrates how my story has also had an effect on the parents of children with diabetes. In the back of my mind, since the day I was diagnosed, was the thought of what if someday my sons are diagnosed with diabetes and that I would want someone to serve as a role model for them.

A few years ago I was in Hawaii doing another race and making some appearances when I met yet another boy with type 1 diabetes. This boy was a little older than the boy from Miami—he was fourteen. I could tell within a few minutes of chatting with him that he didn't need any motivation or inspiration from me. At fourteen he had already completed dozens of triathlons and was a youth ambassador raising money and awareness for diabetes. Thinking I couldn't possibly have an effect on this boy and his family, I was proven wrong the next day when his mother sent me this e-mail: *"Dear Andy, I want to thank you from the bottom of my heart for being such an inspiration to kids like our son. Your warm words made me forget just for a minute that he has diabetes and things will be okay. As parents, we only want our children to grow up and have a fair chance at life. As I am writing this note the tears that I shed are tears that our son* will *be* okay *and it is special people like you who give my family and I hope."* This boy is still racing, and, as a matter of fact, we did a triathlon together last year. He is still raising money and still serving as a role model to other children. What I have to remind myself about this story is that diabetes is a family disease and it affects the parents and the siblings, too. Once again, whenever I feel that what I do is too hard, it's feedback like this that keeps me going and validates what my initial goal was.

A really cool off-shoot benefit that I never thought would happen is that I have also been able to inspire and motivate people who don't have diabetes. I have received positive feedback from hundreds of people who have told me that I have inspired them to make a major change in their life. Whether it was to lose weight, be better at their jobs, or even to become a triathlete. One of my closest friends who hated running or cardio in any form, after watching me compete in an Ironman has since become a triathlete himself. He and I are scheduled to race in a full Ironman together this year.

I have tried to craft my message so it can apply to anyone and transcend diabetes. If anyone who hears or reads my story can stop using the word *can't*, then everything I put myself through is worth it.

WRIGHT

You seem like the type of person who always strives for bigger and better, so what's next for you?

HOLDER

Nothing gives me more pleasure then when a parent tells me his or her child was struggling with diabetes, but after seeing how I am overcoming the disease he or she now thinks having diabetes is cool, or the child says to his or her parent, "I want to do what Andy does when I get older." That kind of feedback is very powerful to me. So I hope I always have a platform to tell my story. I would like to expand my sphere of influence and reach even more people.

I am also putting more effort into expanding the IRONANDY Foundation. I created the Foundation a few years ago with a simple mission – to help children, young adults, and their families dealing with diabetes to have a proactive approach toward managing and fighting this chronic disease. I want to empower people with diabetes, primarily young people, to be extraordinary in the face of this disease and specifically, to embrace physical activity, raise money and awareness, and to be role-models for younger people with diabetes. Most of the funds we raise go toward sending children and teens to diabetes camps and leadership programs. I am also working on a school-based program that encourages fundraising using physical fitness as the platform.

Another new opportunity that excites me has to do with motivating people toward overall wellness. One frustration I have had since becoming IRONANDY is that after I inspire and motivate someone I have never had a next step—a "what's next?" Normally I will speak somewhere and people may approach me afterward with positive feedback, telling me how inspired and motivated they are. Sometimes they will even keep in touch with me via e-mail or telephone, maybe read my blogs or follow me on Twitter. But for the most part, my influence has been limited to when I am standing in front of them. I am now working with a wellness company called Hubbub Health. With them, I will be able to stay engaged with people by creating wellness challenges for them—challenges that span such lifestyle categories as fitness, nutrition, life balance and more. These challenges are done in a fun, yet competitive atmosphere where people are motivated toward action over inaction. Positive feedback keeps people engaged and they are also encouraged to create their own challenges and invite friends and family to join them. I think this platform will fill a void I have felt and allow me to have a real and lasting effect on people. I will also be able to stay with them and keep them on track.

### Wright

What would you like people to think of most of all when they hear the name IRONANDY?

### Holder

When I give my inspirational presentations, I always begin or end with the following quote, "Our lives are not determined by what happens to us but by how we react to what happens; not by what life brings us, but by the attitude we bring to life. A positive attitude causes a chain reaction of positive thoughts, events, and outcomes. It is a catalyst, a spark that creates extraordinary results." (Anonymous). I never imagined that I would have been diagnosed with type 1 diabetes at the age of thirty-six. I didn't do anything to bring this on and I certainly didn't ask for it. But everyone gets something they need to deal with or overcome in life, diabetes just happened to be my something.

What I would like people to think of when the hear the name IRONANDY is that in life there is really only one thing we have complete control of, and that is our attitude. I would like people to stop wasting time and energy on the things they can't control. A positive attitude can be that spark or catalyst people need, and there is no reason why people reading this can't live the extraordinary life they always dreamed of.

# About the Author

Andy Holder, a.k.a. IRONANDY, lives in a suburb of Philadelphia with his wife and two young sons. Andy is a seven-time Ironman triathlon finisher, a nationally known speaker and spokesperson, and the founder of the Iron Andy Foundation. Andy's inspirational message about using a positive attitude to overcome a chronic disease like diabetes and to live an extraordinary life has been heard by thousands across the country. His foundation has helped hundreds of children with diabetes and empowered them to be extraordinary, too. To hear Andy's inspirational message, you may use the contact information below:


Andy Holder

*IRONANDY, llc*

PO Box 179

Skippack, PA 19474

610-999-6312

ironandy@comcast.net

www.ironandyfoundation.org

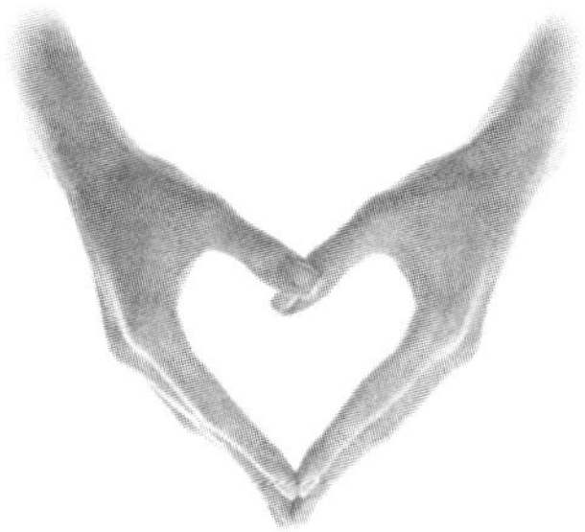

Chapter Twelve

# Navigating the Healthcare System: A Guide for the Overwhelmed

## with Joanna Smith

THE INTERVIEW

DAVID WRIGHT (WRIGHT)

Today I'm talking with Joanna Smith. Joanna is CEO of Healthcare Liaison, a healthcare advocacy practice in Berkeley, California. She founded Healthcare Liaison in 2005 to help people of all ages navigate through complicated medical situations. In 2007, she designed and instituted a credentialing program for medical professionals and consumers who are interested in working as healthcare advocates. In 2009, she founded the National Association of Healthcare Advocacy Consultants, an Association that is dedicated to improving the consumer healthcare experience through professional and public education and participation in developing a consumer-focused healthcare policy.

Joanna, welcome to *Health: Mind Body Soul.*

WRIGHT

As a consumer, my focus is first and foremost on staying healthy; but if I get sick, the healthcare system is very puzzling to me. Can you explain that simply to me?

## JOANNA SMITH (SMITH)

Everybody wants to stay healthy, and prevention is always the first choice, but it is a good idea to have a plan to help you manage if you become ill! I encourage all my clients to do as much advance planning as they can because it will eliminate the more difficult need to try to plan in the middle of a crisis.

There are five different levels of healthcare in our U.S. healthcare system currently:

**Self-care:** This is the first and critically important care. Because many people have high deductible insurance plans or no insurance, self-care is the first approach many people use. It can involve going to the Internet and doing research, talking with friends and neighbors, reading books, and building up your knowledge on a particular condition. Many people try non-prescription drugs or alternative treatments to try to resolve their medical problem.

**Out-Patient Care:** This is the care you receive in a doctor's office. When efforts at solving the problem yourself aren't as successful as you would like them to be, an appointment with a doctor, nurse practitioner, physician's assistant, acupuncturist, chiropractor, or osteopath may be your next step. The practitioner will listen to your concerns, do a physical exam, perhaps order tests, and talk with you about some possible plans (called "treatment plans") to take care of you. Out-patient care continues to become more sophisticated, so more and more healthcare is provided at this level.

**In-Patient Care (Hospital Care):** When out-patient care is not successful, you may need care in a hospital. People who need to be in the hospital (called "acute care") need skilled nursing and physician care constantly and are considered "medically unstable." That means they have conditions that have not yet responded to treatment. They may require surgery or care of a fracture or treatment for cancer or other disease. They could also be receiving rehab care (physical, occupational, or speech therapy) after an accident or stroke. When the condition has been treated as much as it can and the person is considered "medically stable," he or she may be sent to a lower (less intensive) level of care or sent home.

**Post-Acute Care:** If you are ready to leave the hospital but are not ready to return home, you may go to a "Post-Acute Care" facility. It is considered a lower (less intensive) level of care. You could be receiving it at a skilled nursing facility or rehab center. People receiving this type of care still need care delivered by a nurse or physician or a physical, occupational, or speech therapist, but not as frequently as in the hospital. Some care may be delivered by trained aides.

**Home Health**: When you have received all the care that is helpful to you in a twenty-four-hour care facility, you will return home. If you need occasional skilled nursing or therapy services, arrangements will be made for a nurse or therapist to see you at home. These services are generally provided two to three times a week and last weeks to months, depending on your medical needs.

This is the cycle of care in the world of healthcare.

Beyond knowing the levels of care, however, you need to find a "good fit" in the providers who are taking care of you when you're receiving the care. The first step in that process is to decide what style healthcare provider you would feel comfortable with. There are three typical styles of medical care:

**Traditional Style**: You go to a healthcare provider with a problem, and you would like him or her to tell you what to do.

**Radical Style**: you go to a healthcare provider after completing your own research, and you tell the provider what treatment you would like.

**Shared Style**: You see healthcare providers as partners in the process of discovering the best option to select for your care.

In addition, many people today search the Internet and talk with friends about healthcare options. They might use not only Western medicine but also the emerging field of Complementary and Alternative Medicine (CAM). They would seek providers that have specialized service in those particular fields.

Once you know your style and type of provider, it will be easier to find the medical practice that fits your values and your belief system and that will be the "best provider" for you.

The final step is to begin building a strong relationship with your providers so you feel confident, when a medical situation arises, in working with them.

### WRIGHT

I get overwhelmed when I have to go to the doctor, so how do I get my doctor to talk in a language that I understand?

### SMITH

This is a very common question. When consumers see their healthcare providers, they often don't understand what the provider tells them. Frequently people leave their provider's office without comprehending what has been said to them. We do know that when a provider talks, barely 20 percent of what the provider says is absorbed by his or her patient. So visits to the doctor or nurse practitioner can feel overwhelming.

Below are some tips for the doctor's office:

- Bring a friend with you so you will have another person listening to what is said;
- Record what your provider says, either by audio taping or having your friend take notes;
- Ask for definitions of words you don't understand;
- Request written information sheets on conditions or treatments suggested;
- Make sure you have answers to all of your questions before you leave.

WRIGHT

Staying as healthy as I can is really complicated. When there are healthcare decisions to be made, how do I do that?

SMITH

When you are facing a healthcare decision, the question to ask yourself is, "Do I feel that I am an informed decision-maker?" You may have heard about a treatment on the radio or perhaps you saw an ad on television for either a medication or a procedure. Does that mean it is the right choice for you? The way to answer those questions is to become an informed decision-maker. Below are four steps that will help you:

**Step one:** Make sure you understand and are able to describe, in your own words, the diagnosis that a provider is talking about. Can you tell it to a friend in simple words? If you can, and he or she understands you, you have mastered step one.

**Step two:** Can you list the options your provider is considering as possibilities for your treatment? Have you walked through the series of options with your provider, having him or her explain them simply? Again, can you tell these options clearly to a friend?

**Step three:** Do you know the risks and benefits of each option? Every medical treatment has risks and benefits. When you understand them clearly, it will be easier to make an informed decision.

**Step four:** Ask this question of your provider: "What is likely to happen if I do nothing at all?" The answer may be, "I don't know" or "It's not clear." Even those answers, however, give you necessary information to make your informed decision.

When you have answers to all four of these questions, you can begin to make an informed decision.

WRIGHT

Let's go a step further. Often I don't understand *how* my doctor makes decisions about things. Can you explain that to me?

SMITH

We've talked about the styles that consumers have in choosing providers. Now we will look at the different types of "medical thinking" that providers use.

There are two kinds of decision-making approaches that providers in healthcare use to determine what direction to go in. The one that consumers are most familiar with is the approach you experience when you go into the doctor's office. In that situation, you describe a particular condition that is concerning you and the physician or the nurse practitioner or the physician's assistant or other practitioner talks with you so he or she can learn the history of what has happened. Then the practitioner will do a physical exam, perhaps order some lab tests or an x-ray or scan. The provider receives the results and then develops an hypothesis about what your problem is and looks at possible solutions to it. That is the kind of decision-making most consumers are familiar with.

If, on the other hand, you have a true emergency and you need to call 911 or go to an emergency room, you will that see this is a very different kind of thinking. Providers in these situations are looking first at how to help people be "medically stable" and survive so there is time to do other kinds of treatment.

What providers are doing at this point is using a very rapid mode of thinking instead of the more deliberate one described above. They are asking themselves questions like "where have I seen this type of situation before? What was successful in treating it previously? What is the fastest way I can help this person?" They are looking at similar patterns of illness or accident, remembering what has worked effectively before to help stabilize their patients very quickly. What the consumer will see is something that looks more chaotic but is actually a highly functional system where people are trying to do very fast, effective decision-making.

When is this type of thinking used? When time is of the essence and technology may be limited. It could be when the medical team arrives at your home in an emergency; it could be on a battlefield where emergency personnel are treating troops; it could be in a hospital emergency room.

### Wright

I've heard all kinds of stories about what happens inside hospitals. If I have to go into the hospital, how should I prepare for it?

### Smith

The most important planning you can do before you go into the hospital is be an informed decision-maker and do the four steps I mentioned earlier to make sure you understand the risks and the benefits of the surgery or treatment you are going to have.

Next, be sure you have somebody at your side—a friend or family member—who can be your advocate while you're in the hospital. If you do not have someone to be your advocate, you can hire a healthcare advocate to help you. If you're unsure how to find one, consult the National Association of Healthcare Advocacy Consultants at www.nahac.com. NAHAC is the professional association for healthcare and patient advocates. You can do a free search on the site for an advocate near you and read the advocate's qualifications before contacting him or her. You need someone by your side when you're in a hospital setting to ensure that the healthcare team understands your wishes and concerns and is working well together.

Thirdly, make sure you have an advanced healthcare directive filled out with an agent appointed who can make healthcare decisions on your behalf if you become unable to. There are many different forms available on the Internet; be sure to check that the form you choose is accepted in your state. With a healthcare directive, there will be someone the healthcare team can talk with in the event that you are not able to make your own healthcare decisions. Your responsibility is to choose an agent and *talk with him or her ahead of time* about your wishes if you become seriously ill. Would you want surgery? Dialysis? Chemotherapy? If you stop breathing, do you want to be revived? These are topics your agent needs to know in order to carry out your wishes.

### Wright

I have aging parents and young children. How do you suggest I juggle all of this?

### Smith

This is a complex question, particularly for Baby Boomers who are frequently "sandwich generation" caregivers. They are caring for family members older than they are and younger than they are. I suggest that my clients with aging parents encourage their parents to stay active and engaged with other people. We know that people who have strong social connections do better overall—both emotionally and physically—because they connect with other people. Someone who is raising young children and caring for older parents frequently feels the pull to focus more strongly on either the children or the parents.

The best of all possible worlds is to allocate some time and energy in both directions. Your children need your time with them, and your parents may also need help sorting out some extremely complicated medical situations.

Families frequently join support groups to help with this task. There are support groups for Baby Boomers with aging parents, for example. These groups can help them receive support from other families grappling with the same problem.

I also encourage people to involve their children with the process of understanding and seeing what it is like to have aging parents. With this approach, they are not trying to keep the two ages separate from each other. Instead, they are teaching and involving their children—as much as they can understand—in learning how to address aging and help make complicated medical decisions as they age. It becomes an integrated family process rather than an issue that separates families. This will teach your children one of the most valuable lessons—how to care for members of their family.

I also encourage families to set aside some specific times to do activities with their children, even when caring for an aging parent. It can provide a needed break. When there is a young child who is ill, it is important to set aside special time to spend with other children in the family. Frequently the healthy children feel timid about asking for time with a parent because they feel they should defer to their ill sibling. It's important to spread attention and energy throughout the family, rather than concentrating it on only the ill family member.

WRIGHT

I have another question about families with ill children. What about parents who have children who are sick and they're overwhelmed by the medical decisions to be made? What can they do?

SMITH

Healthcare advocates are not just for people with aging parents! While it is true that seniors frequently need help with their healthcare, families with newborns in intensive care units at a hospital or families with a child with a newly diagnosed condition are also overwhelmed by the decisions they need to make. They need help navigating through the complex decision-making that lies ahead.

With a child who is ill, parents have several simultaneous situations. First, they need to understand and figure out "next steps" for their child. Second, they need to understand and be tolerant of behaviors and "slips" that their child makes in development. Third, they need to be aware of other children in the family and how this situation is affecting them.

Let's look at these three tasks one at a time.

**The "next step:"** This is a complex process itself. It means talking with multiple medical professionals and synthesizing what they are saying so a decision can be made. Every parent wants to make the best decision possible for their child. When there are several options to consider—perhaps different chemotherapy options—parents need a solid support system to lean on. That system could be other family and/or friends or other parents who have grappled with these decisions. The richer the support system, the easier this process becomes. It is no accident that parents or grandparents, aunts and uncles, look for social media—on-line support groups or chat rooms—to find "people like us" to provide that critical support.

**The second task**: This step is being tolerant of behavior changes and regressions in development that their child displays and it is equally complex. Children who are ill may show their stress in different ways. A child who goes through a medical procedure with seemingly little difficulty may be the child that is anxious, aggressive, or withdrawn at home or in school later on. Children do not always show stress in the situation that causes the stress; it may appear in another location, either immediately after or weeks in the future. The child may lose skills he or she has had for months—a child with good language skills may revert back to baby talk, a child who was completely toilet trained may start having accidents at home or in school. These are all expressions of stress and are alerts to the parents and family that the stress level is very high. Talking with a trained professional—either a trusted pediatrician or a mental health professional—can assist both parents and child in developing ways to reduce the stress.

**The third task** for parents is to be aware of the other children in the family. When they are concerned with an ill child, it is quite easy to unintentionally overlook the other children in the family. The stress of having an ill sibling is extraordinary. Healthy children may feel guilty that they are well; they may also be frustrated that they have "lost" their parent or parents to their sibling. These feelings can lead to other behaviors—fighting with other children, poor school performance, withdrawing from their friends. It is very important to connect siblings of ill children with other children in the same situation so they have contact with others, and have a "shared experience." These groups can be an enormous support to children.

At the same time, parents need to stay involved with all of the children in their family and try to provide some care and nurturing, especially to the children who are not experiencing a medical illness.

There is one more important point for parents to consider when they have a child with an illness, especially if it is a very serious illness. The emerging standard in work with seriously ill children is to involve the child in ways appropriate to his or her age and understanding in the treatment decisions regarding the child's care. Parents obviously make the healthcare decisions on the child's behalf, but frequently young children have a capacity to understand and grasp many of the complexities of the decisions being made. If they have a part in that decision-making, the experience can be very empowering for the child and the family.

WRIGHT

I have several insurance questions; who can I ask?

SMITH

There are many complicated insurance questions that you may encounter—questions about your bills, the coding on your bills, your deductibles, and co-pays. And, of course, you'll have questions about the insurance itself—what it covers or doesn't cover.

Additionally, finding an insurance policy if you have lost coverage, is especially taxing. People frequently say, "I don't understand why this wasn't covered" or "I don't understand why all of this was put to my deductible; the bill doesn't make sense." Other people ask about denials from their HMO or want to know how to file a grievance or appeal with an insurance company.

A good way to start to resolve these questions is to call your doctor's office and ask to speak with the billing department. Amazingly, many times the questions can be answered simply. Perhaps the procedure you had was coded incorrectly, so when it was sent to the insurer the procedure was denied because of incorrect coding. One of the most frequent reasons that an insurance claim is denied is because the insurer never received the medical records from the clinic or hospital. No records means an automatic denial of payment. You can simply call your insurance company and ask if the medical records were received. If not, you can request that the provider send them again.

Another important detail to know about insurance is that insurance companies have nurse case managers who work for them. If you have a very complicated medical situation, you probably have a nurse case manager assigned to your case. You can call the insurer and ask to talk to the case manager handling your situation. This person can be a troubleshooter for you within the insurance system.

So there are many people available to answer various kinds of insurance questions. Healthcare advocates—a family member or a friend or a neighbor or a paid advocate—can help you sort out in what direction to go with these insurance questions.

### Wright

So there are healthcare advocates. What kind of help can they offer me?

SMITH

Healthcare advocates offer different kinds of services depending on their own skill base. Some people help when you are going to the doctor and want someone to accompany you there and make sure that the right questions are asked. Perhaps you want someone to write down information and record it in the doctor's office so you can listen to it again later. Maybe you want another pair of eyes and ears to ask different questions or clarify information.

There are also advocates who can research treatment options, such as different surgeries or "gold standard" treatments for a particular disease or condition. Some advocates help with researching what the treatment options are and where the centers of excellence in the county are for treatment of that condition. They also can locate the physicians with the highest number of successes in treatment of a particular condition.

Other people will follow you into the hospital to help make sure that the healthcare team is working well together and working with you. Some healthcare advocates work with billing questions, some can help with finding insurance to provide coverage for you if you are uninsured, and some advocates work with grievances and appeals of insurance denials.

Some advocates do all of these services and some advocates only do some of them.

WRIGHT

There seems to be so many kinds of advocates. How do I know what kind I need?

SMITH

The most effective approach would be to determine exactly what you want help with and to find an advocate who has a specialty in that area. If someone is newly diagnosed with leukemia, he or she may want help sorting out treatment options. The person would want to go to an advocate who specializes in research and is familiar with centers of excellence around the county and perhaps some clinical trials that might be helpful.

When you first contact an advocate, the first goal of the advocate should be to sort out whether he or she is the right kind of advocate for you. The advocate should determine if he or she has the right kind skills to help you get your problem resolved. If not, then the first goal would be to refer you to someone with the skill base you need.

A critical question people need to ask themselves as they search for an advocate is, "What is the style of the advocate I can work with most easily?" Advocates have different styles—some are more aggressive in their stance, both with providers and insurers, and some have a different temperament and would approach it from a more collegial perspective. As a consumer, you want to make sure that your advocate reflects your particular style, otherwise it will not be a good working "fit."

Advocates should always have a written service agreement and plan. You should know exactly what services the advocate is offering, what the charges are, what happens in an emergency, and best ways to contact him or her. Lastly, at the end of the first contact or the first meeting, the consumer should have a very clear written plan that says what the advocate is going to do to assist you. When there is a good plan, everybody is headed in the same direction and that will help you get to where you need to go.

### WRIGHT

How does using an advocate help with other kinds of care I might want?

### SMITH

People are sometimes concerned that if they have an advocate, it might affect the kind of care that healthcare providers want to give them. I reassure people that healthcare providers are becoming very familiar with advocates, whether they are other members of the family or paid advocates. The goal of healthcare advocacy is to help consumers understand and use the healthcare they need and to assist providers in providing the best possible care for people. So it is not, by definition, an adversarial position—it's a collegial position and can lead to very effective delivery of your healthcare.

WRIGHT

I see that everyone needs to know about healthcare advocacy, especially in this day and time, and you've really given us some good information. I appreciate all the time you've taken to answer these questions. I've learned a lot and I'm positive our readers will.

Today I have been talking with Joanna Smith. Joanna is CEO of Healthcare Liaison, a healthcare advocacy practice in Berkeley, California. She trains and credentials other medical professionals as well as consumers who are interested in working as healthcare advocates.

Joanna, thank you so much for being with us on *Health: Mind Body Soul.*

SMITH

Thank you, David.

# About the Author

Joanna Smith, LCSW, MPH is the CEO of Healthcare Liaison, Inc., a healthcare advocacy practice in Berkeley, California. She has twenty-five years' experience as a healthcare advocate in both in-patient and out-patient medical settings in the San Francisco Bay Area. In 2007, she developed the first training and credentialing program for medical professionals nationwide who seek to be credentialed as healthcare advocates. This program has been expanded to include training for consumers who want to become certified healthcare advocates. She leads national workshops on healthcare advocacy for consumers and medical professionals.

In 2009, Joanna founded the National Association of Healthcare Advocacy Consultants to bring people in the field of Healthcare Advocacy together to begin to develop best practices and standards for this emerging profession.

Joanna received her master's degree in Social Work from Tulane University in 1978 and her master's degree in Public Health, with a specialization in Maternal and Child Health, from the University of California, Berkeley, in 1985. She is a licensed clinical social worker in the state of California (LCSW #9586) and a member of the National Association of Social Workers. She also holds a credential as a member of the Academy of Certified Social Workers (ACSW) and is a Certified Healthcare Advocate (CHA).

Joanna Smith, LCSW, MPH

*Healthcare Liaison, Inc.*

3030 Ashby Ave., Suite 105

Berkeley, CA 94705

510-704-8476

joanna@healthcareliaison.com

www.healthcareliaison.com

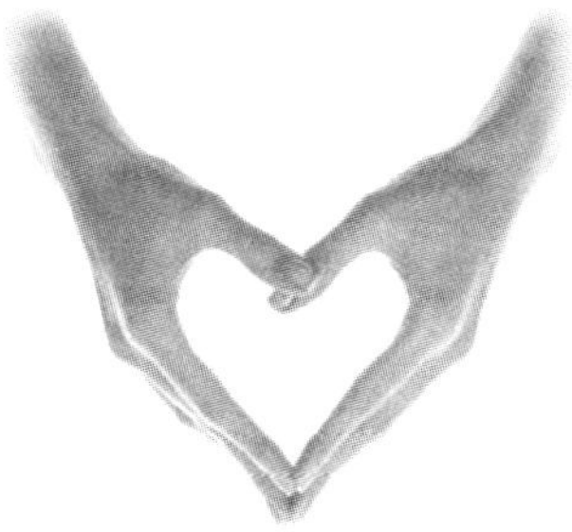

## Chapter Thirteen
# Falling Forward

## with Teej Cummins

THE INTERVIEW

---

DAVID WRIGHT (WRIGHT)

Today we're talking with Teej Cummins. Teej is a Professional Development Coach. She has worked as a successful model, actress, a corporate sales manager, and an entrepreneur. Teej has earned the distinction of Certified Life and Wellness Coach through the International Coach Federation. She is also recognized as the Columbus Life Coach Examiner, writing numerous published articles.

Her experience has spanned diverse organizational cultures including small business, corporate structures, and non-profit organizations. Teej describes herself as a woman who survived and thrived after a life-altering accident. Left isolated and bedridden with multiple injuries, she made the decision to go back to school taking online classes. She graduated, changed career interests, and prepared for what she'd do when she got better. Teej rewrote and redirected her life. She says she "thought her way through." Teej speaks about the power of thought combined with faith. She is a keynote speaker and published author. Teej is the creator of Girlfriends Coach, Adult Daughters of Absent Fathers, and Teejology. Her first book titled, *Short Thoughts to Shift Your Thinking,* is due in 2012. She is a member of the National Career and Development Association, SCORE, ICF, and Global Speakers Federation. She is an example of how even an accident can lead to the "Art of Aspirations turned into Achievements." Teej lives in

Plain City, Ohio, with her husband, Markus, and their dog daughter, Molly Lolly.

Teej, welcome to *Health: Mind, Body, Soul.*

Tell our readers what you do.

### TEEJ CUMMINS (CUMMINS)

I'm a Certified Professional Development Coach, specializing in Career and Entrepreneur Coaching. The International Coaching Federation defines coaching as partnering with clients in a thought-provoking and creative process that inspires them to maximize their personal and professional potential. Coaching is a distinct service and differs greatly from therapy, consulting, mentoring, or training. Individuals who engage in a coaching relationship can expect to experience fresh perspectives on personal challenges and opportunities, enhanced thinking and decision-making skills, enhanced interpersonal effectiveness, and increased confidence in carrying out their chosen work and life roles.

Having the credentials to support my clients offers my practice some real credibility. Statistics show that having the actual training to support your business has proven to be a real benefit to clients.

Consumers worldwide agree that certification/credentials are important for professional coaches and contribute to higher consumer satisfaction with coaching, according to a recent study by the International Coach Federation (ICF). The ICF Global Consumer Awareness Study found that 84 percent of respondents who had been in a coaching relationship considered certification/credentials "important" or "very important." In fact, even for those who had no prior experience with coaching, the importance of credentials remained high at 83 percent

### WRIGHT

Tell me more about your coaching practice.

CUMMINS

I developed a real passion for serving as an anchor to individuals who are moving in the direction of passion and purpose. Partnering with individuals who are transitioning into a new phase, and who are in need of support as they move through the process, is a phenomenal privilege. I also provide Life and Leadership workshops for groups or small business owners. I developed a process that creates a road map to get my clients where they want to go. It includes the following elements: Evaluate, Eliminate, and Escalate. What I find is that if we can uncover the obstacles, we can discover resources to support the vision and a workable plan to get the results they really want.

WRIGHT

How did you become a Professional Development Coach?

CUMMINS

It's a rather interesting story. I like to say, just for laughs, that I somewhat fell into it. That will make sense later.

If you would have told me that this was what I'd be doing as my career, I would have laughed or maybe even cried at the thought and possibility. Growing up, I was certainly more suited to be an artist of some sort—a dancer or actor. It surely would have been something where I spent most of my time barefoot, the use for makeup or pressed clothing didn't exist, more Bohemian than corporate, a life where as long as I had a bicycle, the gift of music, and a dog, I'd consider myself rich. If it felt artsy, it was a fit for me.

In my teens and twenties, that's exactly what I did. I was a model. I worked as a runway and photography model, and I did television commercials as well. I had an agent who saw something in me that I didn't see. Being a bit of a tomboy as a child, this was a real stretch. I didn't pay much attention to the progression of my modeling career. I showed up, did what was required, got paid, and gave it all little thought. I do recall being a bit embarrassed by it all. It was something I did, but then returned to living my life.

One day I was driving along and stopped at a red light, I looked around and saw myself on a billboard; it was the most uncomfortable feeling. I felt completely exposed, even though I was fully dressed. I kept thinking, "What am I doing on the billboard?" I wondered what people were saying about me. What if my ex-boyfriend sees me?" I wondered if people thought that I considered myself better than they were. The truth is, I panicked.

That moment was so much bigger than I was. It was probably the moment when I realized that I could be more than I had even dreamed and from there I could not go backward.

I never was quite comfortable having my picture taken, or on a runway, but I really liked the creative energy and seeing the process of a fashion show or the production of a commercial from start to finish. I was drawn to the environment, and believed that I'd find my place if I would just stick with it.

Some years ago, I was on the set waiting to shoot a commercial and I asked the director a question "why am I wearing a red dress when the script refers to a blue dress?" His reply woke me up. He said, "You're not paid to think, you're paid to be quiet and be beautiful." I started crying and shut my mouth. That was the last time someone ever told me that my thinking had no value. I went on to have what most would think a successful modeling career, but eventually I found my way to an area I was more comfortable.

I transitioned to more of a behind-the-scenes creative area, dressing the models, selecting the garments, doing more radio voice work, and recording PSAs for major companies. I learned I was more comfortable making decisions than having them made for me. I was better at speaking than I was listening. I needed to be where my thoughts had value.

I found my way back to school and discovered business courses. There was a strategy around the thought process that really pulled me in. I was hooked. Media Sales, Business-2-Business Sales,

Sandler Selling Systems, Miller Heimen Strategic Selling—I studied it all and felt more comfortable learning sales dynamics than anything else. I had great friends, volunteer activities I truly loved, and I was in and out of relationships, happy, joyful, fabulous.

My career was launched, I was earning a six-figure income, felt successful—I was off and running. I kept my professional and personal life completely separate, as I had learned the importance of that during my modeling years. However, I was still not happy at the core. Something was off base. As much as my job provided me, I felt no connection to it. I dreaded going to work, but I pretended to enjoy it because it paid well. My boss was absent and going through a transition in his own life that left him unavailable to his staff, and I knew there was nothing more I could gain from staying with that company. I felt out of balance. I made a decision to take a look at myself, instead of what was going on with my career and romantic life. I did what worked in the past, and I started thinking and journaling.

I decided I was worth having exactly what I wanted. I quit my job, stopped dating, stopped spending, and made a commitment not to resurface until I was someone authentic.

There was one question I was most committed to finding the answer to: "What do I tolerate about myself that I would never tolerate in someone else?" Now there's a question that gets you thinking. If you're looking for a way back to center—pure authenticity—ask yourself that question. The details of that journey will remain private, however, when I resurfaced six months later, I knew exactly what I wanted and was even more worthy of having it.

One decision I made was around my career choice; my professional life had to be in alignment with my personal and spiritual beliefs. That process led me to my next Business-2-Business sales position. I was at peace. Eventually I met someone special. Life was in perfect order. There wasn't one thing I would have changed. I was in love, I had a career that was thriving, I took dance classes, I traveled, I had a private life that gave me great value, and I was loved.

On a trip to Germany to meet my new special someone's family, he proposed in front of the Cologne Cathedral. The sabbatical to truth was working.

On the plane home we made plans to meet our closest friends and to celebrate our engagement. Our gathering was on February 6, and all our favorite people were there. We were officially launched as an engaged couple.

The next morning I got up, dressed for work, and drove to my first appointment. It was Feb 7, the day is still as clear as yesterday. The snowy morning, was a left-over from the huge storm the day before. I took special care to put on shoes I could actually walk in, despite the weather—I was known for three-inch stilettos. The details of that day are forever seared in my mind. I walked in the building, greeted Nicki, the receptionist, turned the corner, and headed down the hall to my client's office.

There was a small crowd of people gathered eating breakfast and starting their day. I recall voices and the curly-haired young man who would later come to my side. Suddenly I felt my feet slide out from under me, the floor was wet, I felt like I was moving in slow motion, I could see the wall in front of me so I extended my arm to break the impact. I hit the cement wall and felt immediate pain in my shoulder and hand. I hit it so hard that it threw me backward as my feet slid completely out from under me. I hit the floor head-first, and felt the impact in my neck. The pain in my head and neck was extreme and I could hear yelling coming from others. The curly-haired young man darted from the room and ran to get help. I could see his shoes as he ran away from me. I didn't speak. Finally, I remember the ride to emergency care, then x-rays, MRIs, braces, a cast, pain meds, and the arrival of my special "him" to claim me.

That day changed my life in ways I couldn't have imagined. Unable to sit up for any period of time, unable to dress myself, or even get food for myself, I lay in bed, suffering in pain that was nearly intolerable. The job, career, health, peace, body, and life I loved were all beginning to fade. It's a reality check when you realize who will or will not show up for you in times of need. The accident took me through a process that included physical therapy, multiple exams, and MRIs, spine specialists, and an emotionally draining battle with an insurance company.

Day in and day out, I'd lie in bed, waiting for the next dose of medication to put me back to sleep, and holding on just enough for an update on when I might get more medical attention. Besides all of that, the isolation was far worse. I was left alone with my thoughts. Finally I was at the place where I hated to wake up—consciousness meant I could feel the pain.

So much was happening in the world, and I was so still I could see it all. I remember in April of that same year, the Virginia massacre happened. I had just awakened and turned on my television. The news coverage was showing swarms of police around the school. Young adults were being carried out; their lives had just become a nightmare. I couldn't turn it off. I watched all the coverage I could. I cried for the families and became more angry at my condition, realizing how much worse I could have been, but still the pain was too much.

Six months in, and still waiting to see the spine specialist, I said to my fiancé, "Take the gun out of the house. It's just not good to have it here." I couldn't take much more. Drowsy and dazed from loss and pain medication, I drifted back to sleep.

On one of my worse days, he came home to help me get food, and administer my medications. I'm sure he knew I was depressed and hopeless. Standing over my bed he said, "I met a woman at my morning meeting. She's a Life Coach and she reminded me of you. Here's her card, and when you're ready, I think you should call her." He took the blue card out of his pocket and slid it toward me on the table. The he repeated, "When you're ready."

I opened my eyes and thought, "How in the heck am I going to be a Life Coach? I can't even speak without pain. I can't hold up my head, I can't stand to blink without screaming, and you think I can be a Life Coach. I don't even know what that is." But he left the card on the table and I drifted back to sleep.

A few weeks later, lying in bed in the same position, afraid to move, not wanting to wake up, I heard the phone ringing. I picked it up, keeping my eyes closed to avoid the light. I heard, "Teej, are you there?" it was my long-time girlfriend Mary. I don't know how she heard about my accident but she had. Mary had an accident more than ten years ago and moved to Florida where the heat was better for her fibromyalgia. As soon as I heard her voice I started to sob. She listened while I told her about the pain, the fear, the waiting, and the isolation. Afterward, she said, "I'm going to tell you something that nobody wants to tell you, and I hope you're ready to hear it, so here it goes. "You are never going to feel the same, you're never going to move, or live as you used to. You'll feel better, but that Teej is never coming back." Again, I started to sob.

On my next check-up, I decided I was going to ask the question. After all, I'm waiting to see the spine specialist as though he's the Great and Wonderful OZ. In comes my primary doctor who checks me out, records my statistics, measures my range of motion, and re-writes prescriptions. He, too, is frustrated at the limits the insurance company has placed on me.

At the end of the exam I asked, "Am I ever going to feel better—the way I was before?"

He looked at me and said, "I never discuss that with my patients until they're ready to hear it. It's been more than six months. The body will start to recognize its current state as normal. The answer is no, you're never going to feel the same. But we can get you comfortable."

His words shifted me into action. I was holding on to false hope. I went home and with my working hand I printed, "Stop hoping and start knowing."

I finally realized that waiting for change made no sense anymore. Things had changed and they weren't changing back. I asked for my journal. Since I couldn't write with my right hand, I'd print one or two words with my left hand, just to get something on paper. I wrote: Breathe, God, Time, Sad, Friends. Pretty soon I got better at being a left-handed printer, and I considered it a success.

It's the oddest thing, but I can tell you today, one of the things I really missed was my signature. I had mastered a signature through years of elementary school practice and deciding how "my T" would look different than anyone else's. My signature had become a part of me. Now I thought, "Who am I if I can't even write my name?"

Weeks after the appointment with the doctor, I thought I was ready. I asked my fiancé to bring down my laptop from my upstairs office and help me arrange my bedding so I could have it on my lap. He propped me up in my bed, supported me with pillows, and I started to research Life Coaching. What is a Life Coach? He was right—it defined me. I went from site to site drinking it up: What's needed to get certified? Can I do it online? I reconnected to possibility, and opened a new door.

From there, I started classes and completed an eighteen-month Coaching Certification in six months. I jumped right back in for more, this time focusing on wellness. With my own personal challenges, understanding the dynamics of wellness was really interesting to me. I completed my Wellness Certification and License the very next year.

Time was passing, and instead of hand surgeons, neurosurgeons, spine centers, Industrial Commission hearings, examinations, spinal injections, prescription refills, and isolation, I had something that kept me sane and believing that I could have a new career. Clearly, I was in my element. I fell back in love with learning. I hired my own mentor coach to keep me focused on the possibilities. I created a plan to launch my business, and slowly had a reason to believe I'd be all right. I had created something worth fighting for.

WRIGHT

What did that experience teach you?

CUMMINS

That experience taught me about the power of my thinking. It taught me that even in the midst of something really challenging, I had a center to return to. In the beginning, when I felt completely out of control, I thought that the pain and grief of the life I knew was where I would live. My thoughts began to invite me to consider options that I would have never considered otherwise. I honestly just wanted to just drift off and never wake up. If you've ever lived in pain, or experienced a devastating loss, the magnitude of it all can feel bigger than you. It also taught me about looking beyond the obvious options and to deepen my beliefs about what I'm capable of. The sabbatical from years before had actually prepared me, although I didn't recognize it right away. I didn't connect this accident to a spiritual awakening and it was my most profound. I am amazed at how much more I have become because of how low I went. I feel resurrected for sure.

WRIGHT

Would you talk about the power between health, mind, body, and soul?

CUMMINS

Sure, let's do that. My belief is that it's impossible to connect to the body when you don't include your mind. When we look at our overall heath, it requires us to fully participate. Our decisions, thoughts, and beliefs are all a part of how we participate in our well-being. If we believe that Eastern medicine works, there's a better chance that it will. If we stay true to more traditional practices, and believe that they will work, it's more likely they will. But no matter the choice, our thoughts behind the choice are the motivating factors. At the end of the decision, if we are in sync with the choice, it creates a peace in our soul that remains in appreciation of our action.

I wasn't really sure what would help when I needed medical care. I tried many modalities. Finally when I quit trying and started researching, asking, and choosing, I felt better about the results. Being a mindful participant in the area of your heath is essential. The doctors who were on my team—Kantor, Bennett, and Pacquelet—were more than doctors; they became advocates for me. I allowed them to know me as a person, not just a patient, and they were then allowed to treat me on a personal basis. We established trust levels with one another, and to this day I have personal relationships with one of my doctors. We will always know one another.

### Wright

How does what we think affect our lives?

### Cummins

It affects our lives in every way! My decision to participate in Health: Mind, Body, Soul was not a simple one. Looking at the celebrated doctors who are a part of the project could have certainly intimidated me enough to think I wasn't at their caliber. Well, that's true, I'm not a doctor, but I am an authority on "my" experience, and that's what my chapter is about. My thought process created a space for me to again "think" about the connection between my mind, health, and spirit. Working on my chapter helped me to re-examine my own thinking and to remind myself how far I've come in developing a process that works for me.

I pride myself on being a deep and analytical thinker. I do very little without thinking of the timing, intent, and outcome. This has not always been my process. Before I invited "timing, intent, outcome" into my thought process, I reacted instead of responding. The results are vastly different if I can focus on my response.

As soon as I shift to "response mode," I know that I am more conscious and present and mindful than my reaction usually would be. This practice has poured out into every area of my life; personal, career, and financial. It's a behavior that has proven to serve me well. It's different than a plan. For me, the practice is a behavior.

It can be quite difficult in conversations when the other side is "intent" on reacting. As I position myself in response mode, anchored in intent and outcome, I've come to master timing and can control my thinking which stops my reaction.

Now, as great as this practice is, it does not remove my emotional reaction. I still support my emotions with a core group of friends I trust to share my true feelings. The documenting of my thoughts through journaling is the best way to connect to my spiritual truth. It's also serves as a reference and keeps me honest should I start to veer off the truth path.

WRIGHT

You've created a collection of quotes that are being made into a book; tell me about them.

CUMMINS

The collection is called *Short Thoughts to Shift Your Thinking.* First I'll say that I wasn't always what I'd consider a person who served wisdom as a first course. Daily pain was and is still difficult to live with, so I used the power of my thoughts to shift me. I remember asking God to help me, to speak to me, and then I thought, "Faith not fear. Faith not fear. I'd say it over and over, and it became my mantra. Each day I'd try to think of one additional thought that would shift me from "pain to purpose." My thoughts became deeper and my pain became smaller. Eventually, as I got the use of my hand, I started to write one thought per day.

The compilation of quotes is actually what I wrote in my journal during my transition back to health. They are the thoughts that shifted me back to center—the thoughts that reminded me of my mental strength.

I remember writing, "Transitions are the road you cross to get to the sidewalk; prepare for heavy traffic," after a most difficult request for medical treatment. In preparation for an Industrial Commission, hearing I wrote, "In the midst of a new transition, remind yourself that you have a history of emerging victorious." And after some of the results were not what I was hoping, I'd write, "In the hush moments, you can hear the answers."

Without my thoughts that changed from a destructive weapon to a resource for survival, I would not have made it. The isolation alone was undermining my well-being. I changed the concept of isolation to "alone with my thoughts," and from that I felt tremendous comfort. I've maintained that by spending as much time with myself as possible and remembering the benefits that thinking provides my health, my spirit, and my clients. I used to think that being alone meant lonely or isolated, both nothing a woman wants to be seen as. I've simply come to enjoy my own company. I have found myself to be quite creative when left to explore the vastness of my thoughts. What could be better than to continually learn that you are more than you were, the last time you checked?

### Wright

Clearly you use your thinking process to create, so where did the term "Teejology" come from? What is Teejology?

CUMMINS

Teejology by definition is the Art of Aspirations turned into Achievements. It also just happens to be the name of my company.

Teejology is the belief in the outcome of the journey. It's what I think, it's how I live, it's what I pray—it's me. Each day I wake up, I spread a bit of Teejology out into the world. I share it on Twitter, Facebook, e-mail, my blog, and I text message a bit of it out every day. Teejology for me is the intention to expand the possibilities of people. By doing that, I continue to expand. I simply wake up with a keen search for more good. For instance, this morning I wrote, "After all is said and done, are you saying more or doing more?" Teejology is a thought-provoking service intended to deepen self-awareness and move you closer to your ultimate purpose in life, career, and spirituality.

Specializing in Professional Development Coaching makes perfect sense for me. I enjoy sharing what I know. I've clearly experienced many professional transitions. I've found the right fit in an industry I'm already a part of, using my current position as a launching pad for something better, furthering my education and training to prepare for the next chapter, launching my own business, and making my passion my purpose.

Teejology offers Professional and Personal Inhibitor Assessments that help my clients laser in on what they really want and what may be a better fit. Additionally, I use my original Evaluate, Eliminate, Escalate process.

**Evaluate:** Assess your personal and professional inhibitors. Focus on finding what you really want. Determine a time frame to launch the next step. Evaluate your situation and develop a strategy for success.

**Eliminate:** Road blocks, fear, procrastination, obstacles, wasted efforts.

**Escalate:** Determine your goals and plan a path for achieving them. Discover the courage to move toward your real passion. Enhance your interviewing skills and boost your confidence. Increase your motivation and self-confidence.

WRIGHT

Tell our readers about what type of clients you partner with and the professional coaching industry.

CUMMINS

I'd be glad to. It's unclear exactly what coaching is to some, and the term is used so loosely anymore. Even though coaching has been around for more than twenty years, I hear it used in everyday business. Even in Human Resources I hear them speak of HR Coaches.

My clients are business professionals, individuals who are a part of large corporations or small businesses, and they are also business owners. There are always some commonalities in people who are seeking support from a coach, usually around the transition element of a career or business.

Statistically speaking, individuals and businesses are using coaches more than ever, placing a real value on the industry.

Here are some recent statistics I like sharing on my Web site. It just shows the legitimacy of the industry.

Business coaching is an expanding industry. Fifty-eight percent of organizations say they have increased their use of coaching in the past year.

Coaching utilization is increasing because it is a cost-effective means of achieving phenomenal results for teams and businesses. Organizations are asking, "Can we afford not to use coaches?"

There is increasing evidence that coaching is one of the most powerful ways of developing people and adding to bottom line business performance. A study of Fortune 1000 companies using coaching showed these percentages of executives reported the following benefits from the coaching they received:

- An increase in productivity (by 53 percent)
- Increased customer service (by 39 percent)
- Increased retention of senior people (by 32 percent)
- Reduction in costs (by 23 percent)
- Increased bottom line profitability (by 22 percent)

The same survey reported that the individuals who received coaching saw improvement in:

- Working relationships with their direct reports
- Working relationships with their manager
- Team-building
- Reduction in conflict
- Business Relationships with clients

(Source: Manchester Review, 2001, Vol. 6, 1; and "Executive Coaching: With Returns a CFO Could Love," Fortune magazine, February 19, 2001, Training magazine, February 19, 2001.)

On a daily basis I partner with individuals who are downsized out, aged out, whose current employer is closing, people who haven't updated a resume in a decade, are not sure of their skill sets and how marketable they are, and are unfamiliar with social media as a resource for job hunting. This process can take a toll on one's confidence and emotional well-being. A healthy partnership with an experienced Coach is a real benefit.

WRIGHT

What are the daily practices you use to stay healthy-minded?

CUMMINS

I start the day asking God to speak to me. Right after that, I share that thought on Teejology. I measure the volume of my pain, stretching and using deep breathing techniques. I just started a little dancing. I focus on creating more joy to quiet the pain, and launch my day. I'm conscious of my choices and each day I'm asking myself to focus on "responding, not reacting." As I said earlier, I spend as much time with myself as possible, and gain real value in volunteering or donating coaching to those who just could never afford the benefits of a coach.

I have a gratitude bell in my house; whenever I need to feel more gratitude, or feel an abundance of gratitude, I ring it. It's actually become contagious. When I have a guest visit, he or she tends to catch on to the practice of ringing the bell. On days when I least expect it, I'll get a text message that says "ring your bell for me today." There's always something to feel grateful for. Because I believe in the celebration of all things good, I tend to give bells as gifts.

WRIGHT

You talk about "staying in grace," How does someone begin that practice?

CUMMINS

For me, staying in grace is a lifestyle—humbled, ego in check, financial conscious, gossip-free, judgment free, deserving of loyalty, living in total truths about who and how I live, paying off debts, and especially apologies that I owe. It's another daily practice. Three years ago I implemented something simple into my life. Instead of saying "thank you" I began replying "I'm grateful." To this day, as recent as last week someone said, "I just wanted to stop in your office and say hello."

I replied, "I'm grateful."

"You don't have to be grateful," the other person said.

I wonder what some people think gratitude is? I say "I'm grateful" because it invites me on a continual basis to feel gratitude. It opens the door for me to stay in appreciation of the simplest gestures and aware of the small ones I could have missed.

I also believe I receive more reasons to feel gratitude because I'm wide open to them.

Here's a story from an experience of mine around gratitude. In a business interview in 2009 I was asked, "What are you the most proud of?"

I replied, "I have found more than a hundred things a day to be grateful for."

The interviewer said, "No, I mean a success—a goal reached."

"Feeling more grateful was a goal," I replied.

She then said, "I mean something measurable."

I took out the picture of me lying in my bed in my neck gear, wrist brace, my ankle in a cast, my arm in a sling, and my face swollen from steroids, (I carry it with me daily). I then said, "Gratitude is measurable." She looked at me as though I were odd and replied, "Oh my God, is that you?"

### WRIGHT

You've clearly been on a journey, and just listening to you I can tell you're not even close to being done. You're already working on your next book. What's it about?

### CUMMINS

The title is *The Kindness of My Mind.* It's the true story of the childhood of one of my clients. She has gone on with her life and is a successful businesswoman, wife, mother, and resource for hundreds of women. She's never told her story. As she's gotten older, like all of us, she can see how telling more truths can serve others. It's amazing to me how the emotionally healed can walk among the wounded and appear to have never been injured. We both agree that it's time. She felt I could tell her story while honoring her, as opposed to showing her as a victim. She would say that she is all that she is because of what she's survived. The book is nearly finished. It's a hard read, but her intention is to offer it as a beacon for girls who believe that where they are is where they will remain. She's been reluctant for years to share the story until she was sure she was ready for the questions that will come, the denial from family, and the telling of the details. She's ready!

### WRIGHT

What would you tell people who are going through a difficult time and are having a challenge moving through it?

### CUMMINS

I'd ask them, "besides the current situation, what other challenges have you faced?" I'd ask them about the outcome. I'd dig until they recalled a success—a moment that made them feel they had conquered a situation that seemed unconquerable. I'd invite them to make a list of all the success that seemed too big for them, but in the end, it was a perfect fit for their courage and life skill level.

I'd tell them stories of people just like they are—just like I am. I had a road to cross to get to the sidewalk, and made it through the heavy traffic. I'd of course ask if I could share one of my original quotes:

"You are the recipient of a million miracles. Give thanks that you have the sight to recognize it, the wisdom to appreciate it, the heart to feel it, and the voice to speak it."

Finally, I'd hand them my book of quotes and my business card and invite them for a free appointment. I'm quite sure I would say, "I'm grateful."

# About the Author

Teej Cummins is a Professional Development Coach. She has worked as a successful model, actress, corporate sales manager, and an entrepreneur. Teej has earned the distinction of Certified Life and Wellness Coach through the International Coach Federation. In 2009, she was recognized as a Columbus Life Coach Examiner, writing numerous published articles. Her experience has spanned diverse organizational cultures including small businesses, corporate structures, and non-profit organizations. Teej describes herself as a woman who survived and thrived after a life-altering accident. Teej is the creator of Girlfriends Coach, Adult Daughters of Absent Fathers, and "Teejology." Her book is titled, *Short Thoughts to Shift Your Thinking.* She is a member of the National Career and Development Association, SCORE, ICF, and Global Speakers Federation. Teej lives in Plain City, Ohio, with her husband, Markus, and their dog daughter, Molly Lolly.


Teej Cummins

*Teejology, The Art of Aspirations*
*Turned into Achievements*
www.teejology.com

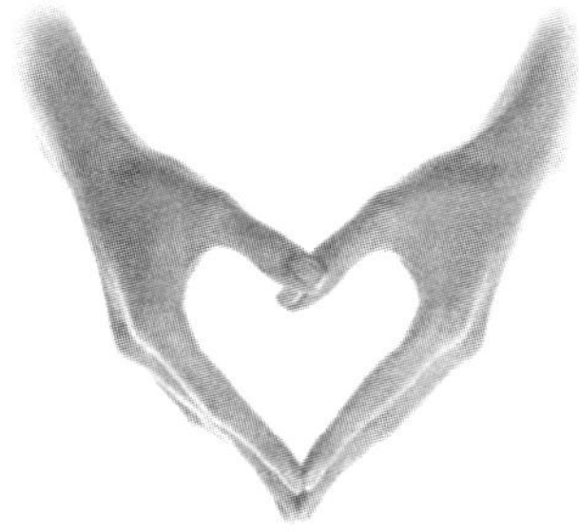

Chapter Fourteen

# Enabling Optimal Performance

with Paul Lewis

THE INTERVIEW

DAVID WRIGHT (WRIGHT)

Paul Lewis is an innovative and accomplished fitness and health professional, specializing in peak performance training. Coaching CEOs, managers, professional businesspeople, and athletes, Paul establishes the path for his clientele to master themselves, physically, physiologically, and mentally. He has been involved in successfully mentoring others for more than twenty years.

Paul, welcome to *Health: Mind, Body, Soul.*

Paul, it is a pleasure to talk with you. What inspired you to embrace this path?

PAUL LEWIS (LEWIS)

Thank you, David; it's a pleasure to share my path and hopefully inspire others. Whether innate or learned, I believe that everyone has the ability to inspire and be inspired. What they do with that inspiration is a matter of choice. I have always been inspired by an array of experiences that continue to affect my path. From a very early age in Sydney, Australia, I dedicated myself to the martial arts, which became a tipping point in my life and path. I was grounded in the philosophy and physical aspects of the martial arts, creating a deeper sense of life, at a young age. This training added to and shifted the ways that I think, process, and perform, and was the first step of many experiences that humbled me and really lit my fire.

David, I'm sure that you're aware of this feeling. If you haven't actually felt it yourself it is an awakening, self-realization, and passion. To whatever degree, most of us just let it slip by. At a young age, many of us have thrilling professional aspirations, only to be uprooted by conformity and/or mediocrity. Whether it is parental influence, spouse, fear, or other external factors, we plod along, not learning to master ourselves.

I possess a strong desire to express myself physically and understand how and why the human body functions. I do this daily, from when I wake through when I sleep and I am forever pursuing, striving for excellence. At times I've tripped over my own feet in an attempt to get there. My mind play involves questions such as: Which neuronal connections create movement? How can performance be enhanced by altering movement? What triggers the body to respond to a threat? This is how I'm programmed. For me, let's just say that this was and remains a never-ending passion. My wife, Sheryl, insists that I'm a workaholic. I laugh quietly every time I hear it! My profession is a *lifestyle* and I feel humbled, knowing that I live my profession and thoroughly enjoy mentoring others to physically and mentally challenge and master themselves.

I embrace the science, discipline, and philosophy of physical and mental performance. For me, gymnastics has created physical and mental flexibility. Martial arts has fomented my internal discipline and control and my physical strength and flexibility. Studies in food technology have deepened my respect for the sciences. Studying under my mentor, Ghim Mun Lam, has taught me humility and patience. My training and experiences have been diverse and my path nontraditional, fulfilling, and ongoing. I have a vested interest in seeing others master themselves, while I personally strive for self-mastery.

I've a great respect for scientists. How can I not? My wife is medical doctor and an epidemiologist at the Centers for Disease Control and Prevention, here in Atlanta. Science is a systematic process that builds and formulates data. It is not perfect and is constantly evolving.

My professional approach is non-traditional. I embrace the science of experiential learning, which makes me, and the clients with whom I choose to work, passionate about what we create together. We are all individuals. We perform differently and have different goals. Because the people I have mentored are so different from one another, I never follow a fixed blueprint. This takes me to my martial arts background. As I began to evolve in my training, I realized that reacting to a physical threat with set responses left gaping holes, leaving me vulnerable. Conditions constantly change and reactions frequently vary according to changing conditions. Learning through my own experience, I gave up on set moves, allowing for more natural responses to changing conditions. The same can be said for my path and my unique approach when I mentor clients—everyone is unique and conditions aren't constant.

### WRIGHT

I understand that you integrate Eastern theory with Western practice. How does this differ from other health and fitness professionals?

### LEWIS

David, power is the measurement of an entity's ability to control its environment, including the behavior of other entities. Your internal power is the ability to harness inherent strengths, and to utilize this power only when necessary. Learning to master oneself is the foundation for achieving excellence, and I empower my clients by challenging them mentally and physically to exceed their goals by conquering weaknesses and capitalizing on strengths.

At age eleven, I became fascinated with martial arts, as many children are to some degree. For me, martial arts represented—and still does—the flow of human movement, and man's living in symbiosis with nature. I remember being in a dojo (martial arts school) and recognizing the ease of movement I had developed, coming from an inner source of strength and balance. The ease of movement was something I couldn't explain.

As time moved on, I was fortunate to study under a teacher, mentor, and friend, Ghim Mun Lam, a doctor in Chinese medicine, and Taoist philosopher. A life lesson I embrace daily is described in the Tao Te Ching, the classical Chinese text: *"Emptiness is the absence of thought, the absence of concern or enthusiasm, it simply . . . is!* It is "being" instead of doing, a mind-set that is too often frowned upon in the in the West and considered laziness. The Eastern explanation is that the act of "being" is freeing the body and mind and being effortless. Translated into Western terms, it is spontaneity, flow, being unhindered.

Practically, I adapt this theory for my clients, so they work toward excellence, physically and mentally. I insist that my clients approach our sessions with an "empty glass" without ego, to be filled with unlimited physical, internal, and mental challenges and results. This is where mental fortitude becomes the foundation for my clients' success! Mental discipline and fortitude I derive from Eastern theory—strengthening internally, physically, and mentally. External strength and fortitude I derive from Western practice. Integrating both creates excellence. This is what I prescribe and teach my clients, and this is how I live my life.

Let me say that I have a tremendous respect for all health and fitness professionals, providing that they are in it for the right reason—to make a difference in the lives and health of others. For me, *making a difference in the lives of others* is the bottom line. I have always been intrinsically motivated and excited by the process, not just the end result. David, by this I mean that my passion is my driving force. I desire to live an extraordinary life; embrace wisdom and knowledge; educate and mentor others in human movement, body mechanics, nutritional excellence, and physiology of human performance; and attain the mental edge under adverse conditions.

Creating change in others is not something that I take lightly. It has taken me more than thirty years to evolve. I say evolve, not perfect. We should always strive to meet perfection, understanding that it will always be just out of our reach. I will only accept a prospective client if he or she is motivated by a desire for excellence. If someone is happy with mediocrity, I'm happy to advise him or her of another avenue, because without drive and passion to succeed, the interaction and process will fail.

Establishing the baseline is the first of many stages of the process. It's comprehensive and revealing, as I create a mutual trust with my client based on respect and privacy. Without mutual trust, the process is flawed. The basis of my clients' success is their accountability, transparency, commitment, and full engagement in the process. What I offer is a path to excellence combining structural alignment, physical challenge, nutrition, and mental discipline. What I do together with my clients enhances their daily function and performance. It takes a determined and self-motivated person to meet these objectives.

My clients will succeed and I guarantee this. I explain that the journey will be outside the norms and, at times, outside their comfort zones and expectations. I use Eastern philosophy and practice to expose their weaknesses and bolster their strengths. Each session requires focus, is comprehensive, physically demanding, mentally challenging, and highly gratifying. By the term "exposing their weaknesses," I am not talking about attempting to lift a thousand-pound weight above your head. I'm talking about weaknesses that expose rigid movement, pre-emptive responses, and lack of mental focus and endurance. We often perform with such rigidity in daily life, in business and at home. Together, the client and I overcome ego, physically and mentally, coming up with a Western equation for excellence that is both mental and physical.

## Wright

Providing an example, will you explain the process your clients undergo to enhance their daily function and performance?

## Lewis

Because the process differs for each client, watching them evolve is most gratifying. Let me give you an example: John (not his real name) had a rigid personality. As a leader, John was all about control, devoted and determined to his own cause. Both at home and work, he walked over others and was thought of as intimidating, though no one would ever say it to his face.

John's mother, alive and energetic at the age of ninety-two, was an afterthought to him, which is the way John treated everyone around him. Devoting 80 percent of his waking hours to work, his life had no balance, similar to his father who had died at the age of sixty-two from a massive heart attack. He was also a workaholic and narcissist.

Eventually, John realized that his successes, as grandiose as they were, had become routine. One morning, he awoke feeling empty and lacking energy. John was seventy pounds overweight, his breath was labored, and his last physical exam showed elevated cholesterol levels and blood pressure, pre-diabetes, and mild arrhythmia. He had been obstinate and refused to see the indicators for his declining health and lifestyle. This time, with a jolt from his physician, he began to recognize the risks: four hours sleep a night, two unhealthy meals a day, high stress levels that caused him blinding headaches and a short temper, three cocktails at night, and no exercise except for a recent weekly round of golf, and the list goes on.

David, it would surprise you how many Johns there are. They are highly motivated time-bombs.

John was referred from another successful client, so I decided to meet with John, screen him, and question his commitment. What I learned from my conversation with him was a willingness to do what it would take to reverse his symptoms. Recognizing his egotism and desire to control, I wrote a contract for John to sign, and I offered him the opportunity to quit within the first week if he wasn't ready to accept the process with a willingness to absorb rather than repel and with an *empty-glass* approach (that is, without ego).

The first week was overwhelming for John, as his focus altered and he became wholly accountable. He held his own, and the layers of stress, anxiety, and narcissism began to fall away, revealing his inner strength. After a few ups and downs, John lost seventy-five pounds and is now lean, muscular, and within his recommended weight range. He is physically and mentally more flexible and is an acceptable 18 percent body fat. He is physically active, works hard, and takes a vacation every three to four months with his wife and, at times, extended family as well. Other symptoms stabilized and, at his last physical exam, his physician of twenty years literally didn't recognize him. He was astonished at John's youthful appearance. This process was John's decision, and I'm proud of his ability to endure unconventional training, which significantly enhanced his performance. He is one example of many!

Learning to master ourselves shouldn't be outside our ability, yet too often we remain complacent and rigid and we neglect our health. We turn away from other responsibilities, such as family, accepting mediocrity in other aspects of our lives. We progress by creating self-worth, promoting physical prowess and musculoskeletal strength, and improving nutritional intake and our capacity to deal with physical and physiological stressors. Whether physically maintaining a five-minute isometric hold, understanding and consuming complete proteins, developing ideal body mechanics, enduring verbal confrontation without becoming agitated, disarming a three-hundred-pound attacker, or empowering yourself to overcome fear, you are challenging self-doubt both physically and mentally, re-training the way you process and function, and challenging yourself to achieve a higher level of performance. What was thought of as unthinkable becomes reality through practice, application, failure, success, and fortitude.

WRIGHT

Paul, it sounds as if you've personally been down this track. Have you?

LEWIS

Absolutely! We all have genes and baggage whether we like the end product or not. As I had mentioned, I have experienced failures and successes and, although I was never a John, stress was an issue for me and this concerned me. I observed a constellation of symptoms in others—fatigue, lack of passion, complacency, physical pain, the list is never ending. I began addressing the root causes of their physical and mental stresses. Observing their issues and symptoms allowed me to recognize my own. With the exposure and grounding I have in Eastern philosophy and Chinese medical theory, I focused on mastering myself. This is an ongoing process, as is reaching for excellence.

WRIGHT

What triggers your clients to recognize a need for change and how do you address their needs?

LEWIS

Triggers vary widely. The more we age and neglect ourselves, the less flexible we become, physically and often mentally. For some the triggers are one of those *wow, this can't be me* moments.

We recognize the need to slow down physically, as the aging process takes over and performance dwindles. For others, it's despondency. They think, "It won't be long before I can't compete any more. I can't sit for so many hours as sitting triggers my sciatic pain. I have to give up golf next year."

I tell clients that we can't reverse the clock and relive our past. What we can do is address all current conditions—internal and external—to improve our physical and mental well-being and ultimately strive or continue to strive for excellence. And this is exactly what we do! I ensure that all my clients are motivated and eager to attack their fundamental issues in order to improve their quality of life. Sitting for eight to ten hours a day without, for example, stopping for a workout or for short breaks to walk around the floor or up and down stairs or without incorporating simple exercises that can be done at the desk is enough to write an open check to your orthopedic surgeon. Your psychiatrist is called in as your stress gains momentum.

I assess clients' needs, bolster their resolve, and focus on faults in structural alignment, conditioning of core stabilizer muscles, weight loss, physical balance and stability, while addressing joint wear and tear. Together we discuss issues that hinder performance and then set measurable objectives. Our one-on-one interaction becomes transparent. Therefore, clients, all of whom are motivated, uncover physical issues they might have forgotten but which are barriers to optimal performance. We address stressors that they might or might not have recognized, so that they can visualize their performance potential and possibilities for excellence. We are all individuals so objectives and specific results might differ. The one result that is universal for all clients is that they exceed their initial objectives. I expose them to additional possibilities that will be met. Now we're talking excellence!

When a potential client strives for excellence, I know that she or he is ready to commit and will respond to both challenge and guidance. For the busy professional, overwhelmed with daily events and stressors such as meeting deadlines, budgets, production, employee productivity, lack of sleep, poor nutrition, and what at times seems to be incurable employee issues, physical and physiological health spiral out of control. Prevention becomes critical, and this is where I step in. Addressing both physical and mental well-being, we work on preventing the undesirables—heart attack, mental overload, hypertension, high blood pressure, diabetes, chronic low back pain. Together, we become proactive by recognizing trends that limit performance and creating a healthier scenario to combat stress.

Together, we become proactive!

### WRIGHT

You describe physical alignment affecting mental and physical performance. Will you clarify what you mean and the methods you adopt when mentoring clients?

### LEWIS

As I mentioned, we are all individuals, though there are common threads in our physical structure that are markers and identifiers. I gain a large amount of information observing someone's gait and pelvic and postural alignment. The process begins by my creating a *picture* of my clients—injuries, pain syndromes, structural imbalances, all of which tend to negatively affect performance.

For example, if you suffer from chronic low back, pelvic, knee, or ankle pain, this, over time, affects your gait, spinal alignment, balance, and stability. For many, poor physical alignment has a snowball effect, often affecting focus and performance. If you have postural faults and related pain syndromes, how do you fare when performance is critical, whether you are an athlete or busy professional who sits ten to twelve hours a day? Your productivity and performance are at risk!

There is definitely a connection between physical pain and mood, which affects performance. We've all spent years abusing our bodies and neglecting injuries and the resultant pain that might have originated from a minor car accident, being tackled by a defensive linesman, or sitting relentless hours. You wake up one morning, say five, ten, or even thirty years down the track and you feel as if a stack of bricks is pinning you down. Your luck has run out, you've beaten yourself into submission, you suffer pain, especially lower back pain, arthritis, and a host of other maladies have kicked in. It's inevitable that your quality of life begins to diminish as you begin overcompensating, and that can cause a pain trail throughout your body.

Let's say, for example, you suffer from debilitating sciatic pain, which affects the way you sit, stand, and stride. Inevitably, the discomfort affects your quality of life, and your overall mood is consumed by pain. The day has come, you're not twenty years old anymore, even though you try and act it, and you respond by gradually backing away from challenges. There is no room for surrender in excellence! The practical methods chosen to enhance performance depend on the clients' issues. Before beginning the performance program, we address spinal and pelvic alignment, gait, and limitations in range of motion.

After a lengthy physical assessment, we modify the client's habits and performance: ergonomics—the way you sit and function throughout the day, sleep patterns (I will talk about that later), level of activity, and internal stresses. This will often require patience, a hands-on approach, and follow-up exercises to readjust the imbalances. Together we stabilize the foundation before constructing the building. If not, the foundation will crumble. Patience, motivation, accountability, and full engagement are key for success. The relationship is a synergy, based on trust, as we share, explore, learn, and condition!

These are the reasons why we begin by addressing structural alignment and pain syndromes, along with other baseline indicators. It's astonishing to be a part of improving clients' physical alignment and progressive pain reduction.

For example, I was recently working with a client whose primary function is corporate presentations. He postponed or cancelled six presentations in a year, a result of chronic pain. Not impressive! His presentations were affected by his health and subsequently, his ability to be "present," yet in the past he blew off sensible recommendations for pain management. Physical structure—gait, pelvic, and shoulder alignment—make a significant difference in the way you appear in front of a large or small audience. Focusing on his structural alignment—especially pelvic, shoulder, and neck alignment—and ergonomics decreased his lower back pain and significantly improved his focus and performance, adding to his already charismatic style.

When you improve poor physical alignment, mental performance improves as you focus on the task at hand rather than persistent, distracting pain. Obviously this is oversimplified. The process does take time and commitment. But so does excellence in any field!

### WRIGHT

You claim that the key to excellence is physical well-being, nutritional health, and stress management. Why these three and, providing an example, how do your clients accept a need for change?

### LEWIS

We create, influence, and positively or negatively affect our health, yet our health is too frequently overlooked or abused. When we subdivide overall health, some traits are predetermined and difficult to influence, such as predisposition to certain conditions such as diabetes or high cholesterol. However, with patience and trial, we can even influence these stubborn diseases by adjusting the way we function.

For most, the formula for improving overall health is relatively straightforward—adjust our habits to combat sedentary lifestyle, make the right nutrition choices in order to maintain a healthy weight, address your reactions and the way you respond, to avoid high stress levels and probable decline in health. Looking at contemporary poor health, lack of physical exercise, poor nutrition, and high stress levels are too often intertwined. There is nothing to blame except our own neglect and lack of action. If we are stressed, we don't make time to eat. If we lack physical exercise, we care little about our nutrition. If we don't consume nutritious foods, our energy levels drop, resulting in lack of desire to exercise and heightened stress levels. This is the vicious cycle and to break the cycle we often need to address the mental stressors and overcome excuses. This, along with planning, exercise, nutrition, and stress become *relatively* easy to manage.

For a client motivated by desire for excellence, the results are always staggering. Self-motivation and accountability are typical of all my clients, as their ability to adapt and take charge sets them apart from Mr. or Ms. Average, who sits on the fence, is partly accountable, and is satisfied with partial health and average quality of life.

Self-awareness is essential when attempting change, and here I'll provide an example of the methods that I use. Jill (not her real name) battled with excess weight for more than thirty years, looking no further than the scales. A senior director in a large company, she was impartial to others and had limited interaction with peers, creating blame, rather than taking responsibility.

Jill has incredible drive, always pushing forward in her career. With all her success, she never took responsibility for her stress, which filtered through her company and created animosity among her peers. Jill is beyond bright and is driven. She was averse to change, especially change in her approach.

As often happens, Jill contacted me through a client with whom I was working at the time. When we met, she was guarded and apprehensive, stubborn and assertive. This was her "presence"! As she walked toward me, I recognized her traits before we met. Her manner was abrupt and impatient when we sat, so I moved my chair, placing it and me behind her, and faced her back.

Jill's response, and now I can laugh was, *"What the hell are you doing?"*

*Shifting myself from your control,"* I responded. I continued, *"When I choose to accept a potential client, he or she needs to arrive without the ego, so together we can fill the empty glass!"*

Returning with my chair I sat opposite her, and her rounded shoulders, protracted head and hardened features began to soften. I accepted Jill as a client. The methods I used with Jill were somewhat similar to our first interaction, as I continued challenging both her body and mind. At times, during the initial stages of the process, she remained defensive and controlling until we began rounding off the edges. Today, nothing stands in Jill's way and she doesn't stand in anyone else's. She has lost thirty-seven pounds, well beyond her weight loss goal of twenty pounds. Her obsessive control has turned to confidence, and she smiles when you approach her. Jill's energy resonates with all, and she now inspires rather than demeans.

## Wright

You prescribe sleep as an essential component of physical and mental stress management. What are you recommending to time-constrained professionals?

## Lewis

We are all part of a generation of sleep deprivation. Effective sleep is fading, and the only spare time we have is allocated to preparing the next task or meeting. As crucial as sleep is, we race against the clock to complete all our responsibilities, rarely considering the effects of sleep deprivation, short- and long-term—decreased performance and fatigue, impaired memory, high blood pressure, heart failure, decreased quality of life, and the list goes on and on, and so do you!

Why do we choose little and ineffective sleep, in light of the adverse effects and overall diminishing returns? We don't know how to compartmentalize and shut down. Recent studies suggest that healthy adults have a basal sleep requirement (sleep for optimal performance) of seven to eight hours nightly. Whether you feel it or not, sleep deprivation accumulates. Studies indicate that mortality increases with four to five hours of nightly sleep. A short nap throughout the day might be appealing, though deep REM (rapid eye movement) and delta sleep is where our body needs to be for healing and recovery. This is the seven to eight hours that the body needs. For the time-constrained professionals, I always emphasize the importance of sleep and the symptoms of sleep deprivation.

For all of you out there, focus on your more important tasks, delegate responsibilities, turn off your mental overdrive an hour before bed, and sleep! Your life, mental state, and performance depend on it and this is reason in itself for averaging seven to eight hours nightly.

### WRIGHT

How do you maintain your life as an example for others and how do you use this to inspire clients?

### LEWIS

In short, with passion! For me, the quest for health and fitness is a lifestyle I embrace every moment of every day. I'm fully aware of the consequences of poor health and fitness, and I lead by design. This is comprised of daily exercise, quality nutrition, and stress reduction. I'm passionate about what I do, and I begin my day the night before with a daily empowerment statement before I sleep. To shape my performance for the next day, I have a self-conversation, creating a powerful and positive mind-set for the upcoming day. This is the lesson of positive affirmation, and it goes a long way! I have my seven hours sleep and wake with a spring in my step, motivated to make a difference in the lives of others and mine. Exercise, healthy eating, breaks during my day, preparation and presentations for my clients, reading, social interaction and stress reduction activities—whether it's classical music, a rigorous workout, Qigong, deep breathing exercises or a topic of interest in which I become absorbed—all provide me with a mental edge. I constantly challenge myself, as I challenge my clients, and this ensures that I pursue the life I prescribe to others—a life of excellence!

I'm as passionate about the health of others as I am passionate about my own health. Like the anticipation of climbing a mountain, the peak begins as a distant speck. As we close in on our objectives, the peak takes form. The higher we climb, the greater the challenge as the air thins and we learn to shift from physical to mental fortitude. You feel elated as you reach the peak, among the clouds. You've achieved your goals. However, this isn't the real peak. As you smile: facing you, above the clouds, is a mountain a thousand feet higher than the peak you're standing on. You drive harder, mentally and physically, reaching beyond your initial objectives. This is the life of excellence, the life of leaders, and the success my clients achieve.

Zeal is passion; it's innate and highly gratifying. It's also not for everyone, as I have witnessed too often in the past. Good intention rarely results in great performance without passion, drive, accountability, knowledge, and wisdom. I extract these from my clients! The methodology is always different, the achievable result is excellence!

### WRIGHT

What principles and process would you have others employ in striving for excellence?

LEWIS

Firstly I always ask potential clients: *"What's your interpretation of excellence?"* And by interpretation, I don't mean literal—I mean a projection of tomorrow, the next day, the next year, the next decade. What, where, and how do they see themselves achieving during this time span? I've met exceptional people who've responded, "I'm currently living excellence and have all that I need in life." I congratulate them and then ask the hard questions, as we take a reality check.

*The first principle:* Excellence has an infinite value. When you think that you have reached it, you realize that it is always moving, just out of your grasp.

*The second principle*: Overcome ego. You know *nothing!* Oh, I hear it, *"Who are you to tell me that I know nothing?"* This is the conventional Western mind. The term "nothing," in Eastern philosophy, equates to emptiness, stillness, the ability to wholly absorb without preconceived ideas. The most successful path toward excellence is the wisdom of the "empty glass." Approach without ego and you will absorb rather than repel.

*The third principle*: Patience. There is no magic pill for mental and physical excellence. What there is, is passion, drive, accountability, knowledge, and wisdom. Muscle doesn't grow by staring at it; mental rigidity doesn't fade by wishing it. Rather, the application of correct technique, persistence, and patience are enabling.

*The fourth principle*: Go back to the first principle, you are not ready for the fourth. Remember, what we do is an individualized process requiring commitment, patience, and fortitude.

*Process for excellence*: You need to address current performance levels, history of injuries, current and projected lifestyle and habits, current and past performance levels, daily function, physical, physiological, and mental performance, and the list continues. What is crucial is drive, self-motivation, and accountability, based on personality type and a yearning to be challenged. A comprehensive baseline assessment discussing physical, physiological, and mental weaknesses follows.

Then the real challenges begin: 1) progressive physical challenges depending on the individual: martial arts and applied self-defense; balance stability, and structural alignment; strength through movement; monitored cardio programs, 2) physiologic challenge—placing the body under progressive physical and mental stresses, which are charted as measurable responses; 3) mental challenge—the ability to overcome adverse changes and conditions. The result is oriented techniques, theory, and practice to overcome daily stressors, creating mental balance.

Each one of us has the ability to strive and excel, whether you believe in innate talent or hard work and discipline to achieve extraordinary results. The term *striving* becomes critical as you embrace opportunity by exposing your inner strengths and facing up to your weaknesses, turning them into strengths.

### WRIGHT

You are certainly passionate about your profession. How does this passion affect other areas of your life?

### LEWIS

My family brings passion to my life. I moved to the States for the love of a woman and married her. Sheryl, my wife, is both intelligent and a phenomenal human being, giving, compassionate, and accomplished. Need I say more! Our twins, Caleb and Brianna, are the ultimate joy in our lives. Being a parent is humbling, rewarding, and challenging and I wouldn't give it up for a second.

The rest of my life is filled with passion to teach, to learn, to constantly be the healthiest I can be, to strive toward excellence. I'm not rattling off a list—I possess an innate and overwhelming desire to give, share, and learn. I wake up in the morning energized, inspired, and passionate about driving myself and others toward excellence and self-mastery.

# About the Author

Paul Lewis is an exceptional health and fitness mentor. Highly inspiring, he brings more than twenty years' experience in health, fitness, and wellness. As a private student of the Singapore-born doctor of oriental medicine, Ghim Mun Lam, Paul integrates body and mind awareness through his inclusion of martial arts theory and practice, studies in food technology (Western University, Australia), Chinese medical massage, therapeutic exercise, and the operation of a pain and injury clinic (Israel). He redefines human performance, challenging individuals and groups to conquer weaknesses and capitalize on strengths. Instructing CEOs, managers, professional businesspeople and athletes, Paul focuses on physical, physiological, and mental performance in achieving excellence. He is the inspiration of the athletics and wellness department of Atlanta's Ravinia Club and Spa.


Paul Lewis

*Driving Force*

404-387-0994

phlewis27@hotmail.com

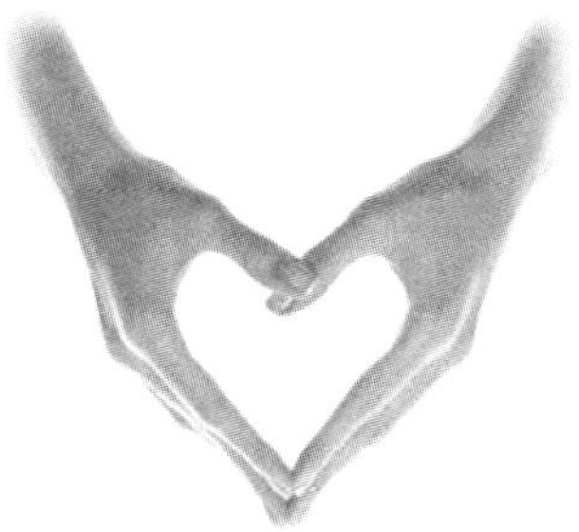

## Chapter Fifteen

# Taking Care of Our Intellectual, Emotional, and Physical Health

### with Dr. Norman Rosenthal

THE INTERVIEW

DAVID WRIGHT (WRIGHT)

Today I'm talking with Norman Rosenthal. Dr. Rosenthal is best known as the psychiatrist and scientist who first described Seasonal Affective Disorder, SAD or winter depression, and pioneered the use of light in its treatment during his long and distinguished career as a National Institute of Mental Health research. For this work he was awarded the prestigious Ana Monica Award, an international prize for research in depression. He has conducted extensive research into disorders of mood, sleep, and biological rhythms that resulted in more than two hundred scholarly publications.

Besides his scholarly writings, Dr. Rosenthal has also written several books for the general public, including *Winter Blues: Seasonal Affective Disorder, What It Is and How to Overcome It,* and *St. John's Wort: The Herbal Way to Feeling Good.* Dr. Rosenthal's latest book is, *The Emotional Revolution: How the New Science of Feelings Can Transform your Life.* Dr. Rosenthal's skill at communicating complex, scientific material in a way that is both readily understandable and engaging has made him a popular television and radio guest. He has appeared on many national shows including *Good Morning America, CBS Sunday, CBS Morning News,* CNN, *Fresh Air, All Things Considered,* ESPN, and *The Today Show,* just to name a few.

Dr. Rosenthal is the Medical Director of Capital Clinical Research Associates and maintains an active private practice in suburban Maryland. He has been listed among the best doctors in America and in The Guide to America's Top Psychiatrists.

Dr. Norman Rosenthal welcome to *Health: Body, Mind, Soul.*

NORMAN ROSENTHAL (ROSENTHAL)

Good to be here again.

WRIGHT

Dr. Rosenthal, seasonal affective disorder is a fascinating subject. How long have you been engaged in the study of SAD and light therapy?

ROSENTHAL

A little more than twenty years ago, the whole concept of seasonal affective disorder came together for me. I had come from South Africa to the United States and here, much further away from the equator, I felt the seasonal changes in my own mind and in my own body. Then, when I saw that other people had similar changes, the pieces of the jigsaw puzzle came together with the help of my colleagues. We described seasonal affective disorder, a condition of regular winter depression.

WRIGHT

Most of my life I have lived with four distinct seasons, and I have always felt differently in each one. I thought it was caused by the memory of events such as swimming in the summer, hiking in the fall, or sledding in the winter. Why did I really feel differently as the seasons changed?

ROSENTHAL

Seasons are so rich and so complex it's hard to pinpoint exactly one thing. I think they provide us with tremendous variety. I have heard people who have lived in these temperate areas where seasons change and then move to the tropics or closer to the equator say they really miss the seasons; they miss the diversity and the richness. I think we cannot exclude memories—the things that we do in different seasons, the colors, the changing colors, the changing feelings, the smells, the sights of the different seasons.

We also need to remember that seasons have a powerful effect on our biology just as they do on many of the animals we know about—the squirrels, the bears, the very seasonal animals that breed at different times of the year. Seasonal changes have an effect on us as humans, too. Although we have thought that we've escaped our environment, we remain very locked and have actual changes in our mood, in our bodies, in our biology, and in our brain chemistry in the different seasons.

WRIGHT

You have said that the pain of depression, anxiety, and other emotional disturbances is as real as physical pain; it deserves to be understood, studied, treated, healed, and reimbursed by insurance just like the pain of any other illness. I know your pioneering work in the field of SAD and light therapy has helped in the identification and treatment of seasonal depression in people, but do the insurance companies recognize these advancements and do they cover them?

ROSENTHAL

This is a sad fact of American life. Of course, firstly there are so very many people who don't have medical insurance at all, but even among those who do there is a double standard whereby physical illnesses get properly reimbursed or reimbursed at higher rates, and mental illnesses get reimbursed at a very low rate. Members of Congress have tried to turn it around but so far have been unsuccessful. To a psychiatrist who sees the pain that conditions like depression or schizophrenia causes in human beings, it seems just plain wrong not to reimburse them at comparable rates to other kinds of illnesses.

WRIGHT

Someone told me in an interview a few months ago that the pharmaceutical industry financed almost everything in the medical community. That shouldn't make any difference, should it? The pharmaceutical companies would come into play with medicine for anxiety and that sort of thing just as much as the paying of ulcers, wouldn't they?

ROSENTHAL

Indeed, the pharmaceutical companies are a huge power in developing new forms of treatment. I think we are quite indebted to them for coming up with many novel medications. Prozac and Zoloft, just to name two, have been huge best-sellers with many others as well. I won't list them all, but these come out of research that is funded by the pharmaceutical companies, so I think that they have a lot to offer. To some degree, the pharmaceutical companies are also very powerful, however, and that should be balanced against government funding of research, which is also very important.

WRIGHT

One of your clients has written, "For years my mood energy dropped with the leaves and I felt ashamed and saddened by inability to control my winter depression. Dr. Rosenthal's book, *Winter Blues,* gave me the tools to effectively treat SAD; now my winters are productive and happy." What tools do you give your readers in your book *Winter Blues?*

ROSENTHAL

The first tool I try to give my readers is just self-awareness to understand how their moods are changing with the changing seasons. I think insight and knowledge is power when it comes to the brain, as in other aspects of life. Once they know what they're suffering from, in the case of winter depression, they can plan, they can prepare, and they can use some of the techniques that have been found helpful like increasing their environmental light, exercise, stress management and dietary control, and, in some people, medications may also be extremely helpful.

WRIGHT

You have been internationally recognized for your work in depression research, and you are listed as one of the Best Doctors in America and in the *Guide to America's Top Psychiatrists*. How prevalent is depression in the United States and how does it negatively affect our lives?

ROSENTHAL

They estimate that about seventeen million people suffer from depression, which is really a huge number.

WRIGHT

Seventeen million!

ROSENTHAL

Yes, it's a huge number and there is also evidence that depression is occurring more and more in younger people, which takes a huge toll on the county in so many ways. They have also estimated that just to try to quantify the cost of depression to society, they reckon it's forty-three billion (that's billion with a B) dollars per year, both in terms of the cost of treatment, but also in terms of lost productivity, absenteeism (or what they call "presenteeism"), which means a person is there at work but is really unable to be properly engaged in productive efforts.

WRIGHT

Is it caused by stress?

ROSENTHAL

Stress can certainly bring it on, loss can bring it on, there is also evidence of a genetic basis and I think a lack of community and a lack of good things in a person's life can do it. So many things can bring on depression. In the case of winter depression, the lack of light can do it, so there are many ways whereby somebody can become depressed.

WRIGHT

Why do you think it's beginning to affect people at a younger age?

ROSENTHAL

They really don't know. One thing that has been raised as a possibility is drug use, certainly drugs can induce depression. People have suggested perhaps that the young people are less connected with their families and communities that are protective influences perhaps in the development of depression.

WRIGHT

I can't remember a time when I was a young boy that I did not eat meals with my family. Now I have a college-age daughter, most of the time we do not eat together.

ROSENTHAL

I think that really does say something, doesn't it?

WRIGHT

It gives me something to think about, I tell you.

Let's talk about light therapy. First of all, what is light therapy and how does light affect us?

ROSENTHAL

We've known for centuries that light is critical for enabling us to see, what's really quite new during the last couple of decades is the idea that light has important biological effects on us, over and above enabling us to see. One of these effects seems to be to maintain our mood and energy level. That is why, when light levels decline in the fall and in the winter months, some people who are sensitive to this lose energy and have a decline in their mood. Light therapy is simply an attempt to replace the missing light. This is done by means of special light fixtures—boxes with fluorescent tubes filtered by a plastic diffusing screen—that have been shown in research studies to be highly effective in reversing the symptoms of winter depression.

WRIGHT

Are the same bulbs used as the fluorescent that we can go down to our friendly Wal-Mart store and pick up, or is it special light?

ROSENTHAL

The tubes themselves can be regular off-the-shelf tubes. The trick, however, is to have a lot of light packed into one place because it seems that the amount of light is very important. Also the timing of light can be very important. Light treatment in the morning seems to be the most effective type of treatment for most people.

WRIGHT

I found a few places on the Internet that sell light boxes? I didn't know what they were. They also called them "dawn simulation." Are these the tools you recommend and do they work for everyone suffering from SAD?

ROSENTHAL

Yes indeed, there are some companies that put out light boxes. I have listed them on my Web site, in case readers would like to know about this, go to www.normanrosenthal.com. I have listed a link to the light box companies that have been around for many years and whose products follow certain guidelines; they stand behind their work. For people with SAD, they can be extremely helpful. But nothing works for everybody and that's why it's always good to have some tricks up your sleeve.

So for some people, the lights may be somewhat helpful but they don't the entire job. Those people may require medications as well as light therapy. For other people, they may be a nuisance to have to use and for those people, it's also a comfort to know that other treatments are available.

WRIGHT

Would it also help to be out of doors more often early in the morning when there is light rather than staying in the house?

ROSENTHAL

Definitely I recommend people go for morning walks. I follow my own advice and I feel that it's a very good thing to combine aerobic exercise with exposure to light. Walking around the neighborhood, if it is a safe neighborhood, is another way of linking yourself to the community and having that combination of social contact with light and exercise, combining all these healthy and pleasurable influences together.

WRIGHT

Many people around the world became acquainted with you because of your study of the herb St. Johns Wort and its effect on emotional health. For those of us who don't know much about this herbal remedy, will you tell us a little bit about your findings?

ROSENTHAL

It's intriguing to think that the extract of a plant can actually improve our mood but, in fact, St. Johns Wort is really the oldest documented antidepressant around. There is an Italian chemist named Angelo Sala who, 350 years ago, carefully documented how he would give the extract of St. Johns Wort to melancholic people—people who suffered from depression; it seemed to be specifically helpful to depressed people. Then in Germany, in the early part of the twentieth century, a lot of research was done in St. Johns Wort. Now there are many, many studies that show an effect of St. Johns Wort. It is an active antidepressant and should be considered one of many options for people suffering from depression.

### WRIGHT

When it comes to herbal remedies and treatments there seem to be two camps—some people are completely open-minded about the positive effects of natural treatments and give credible personal testimony, others seem to be completely closed-minded. Is there a correlation in the scientific community to a person's predisposition about the effectiveness of herbal medicine and the actual clinical effectiveness?

### ROSENTHAL

Remember that the idea of medications coming from herbs is nothing new. Digitalis came from Fox Glove, and an anti-cancer drug came from the little Periwinkle. So the idea that plants are sources of potent medications is not a new thing. There was an act passed by which herbs and dietary supplements are not regulated like medications. What that really means is it's hard to know what you're getting when you get herbal extracts because they are not standardized. They don't conform to the usual standards, they don't always have as much herb in them as claimed and, because they are not easily patentable, there isn't the commercial incentive to study them as rigorously.

Those are the problems in terms of knowing exactly what's what with herbs. They probably have tremendous value in some instances. As I said, St. Johns Wort is helpful with mood. Kava Kava is an herb that is helpful for anxiety, although recently there have been some reports of liver damage, which justifiably scares people away from it. If it was a pharmaceutical product, the company would swoop in and figure out how to prevent any damage and would produce a safe product. Since it's not a regulated, there is a "halo" of discomfort that surrounds it. Valerian is good for sleep. So many herbs can affect the mind in positive ways; it's just that you are not quite sure what you are getting with the preparation.

WRIGHT

I take Saw Palmetto.

ROSENTHAL

It's an herb for prostate.

WRIGHT

I take that religiously, at least twice a day. I read an article just a few days ago about another thing that helps an enlarged prostate—pumpkin seeds. The article said to go to your health store to find them. I went to the health store and of course they didn't have it. I don't know about any empirical evidence but the anecdotal evidence was fantastic. The real problem is that you have to get up to go the bathroom several times a night; Saw Palmetto helped considerably. If anything else would help I would certainly be open to take it.

ROSENTHAL

There certainly is data in relation to Saw Palmetto; I don't know about the pumpkin seeds.

WRIGHT

In the last decade I've noticed more and more breakthroughs in medical research that contradicts long-standing beliefs about health and medicine. I'm certain that you have been part of some of this research. How can an average person with limited understanding of these things know what is real and what is "snake oil"?

ROSENTHAL

I still believe that science is a critical method for separating the real from the illusory. I think we should go with things that are scientifically backed. That having been said, sometimes the science just isn't there, and we still may need to go with our own experience or the experience of those we respect in deciding how best to lead our lives.

WRIGHT

Dr. Rosenthal, do you have an overriding personal philosophy of health that you could share with our readers?

ROSENTHAL

Yes, I believe that we need to keep in line our intellectual mind, our emotional mind, and our body. These are the three domains we need to take care of. If we take care of all those, we'll have the best chance of not only of leading long lives, but of leading good and healthy ones as well.

WRIGHT

Before we close, would you tell us what is on the horizon for Dr. Normal Rosenthal?

ROSENTHAL

I would follow up on what I think leads to a healthy life by outlining how I personally am going to try to pursue that, in terms of physical health. I exercise regularly, and I have started yoga. Yoga is wonderful; it's so different from a Western way of thinking. It emphasizes relaxation and stretching and moment-to-moment consciousness of being. I think these are tremendously valuable. So I am careful with exercise, with yoga, with diets, and of course with regular checkups with my own physician—all the ordinary things that Western medicine can give us now. For example, we have now learned that lowering cholesterol is very valuable and the drugs that do it, the—statins—can have all sorts of unexpected payoff.

So that's the physical piece, the emotional piece I feel it's very important to identify the meaningful people in one's life and keep in touch with them and have a constructive to and fro dialog. If there are people who are important to you whom you really care about, but there has been a falling out, I think if you can mend your fences it is good thing. I think it's so unhealthy to carry anger and negative feelings with you if you don't have to. To divest yourself of that is good and enables you to dwell in a positive zone.

These are things I personally try and follow. I think they are not only good for our bodies; they're good for our soul. But for myself I love adventure, and writing those books has been a huge adventure to me. Now I have embarked upon an adventure that is both new and old, I am back to doing research—basically testing new medications in various psychiatric illnesses. I am also eager to continue to study the effects of our physical environment on our brains and our bodies. It's an intriguing thing to me. I had left research for three or four years and now that I am back in it again I feel like a Labrador that has been let loose in the water and it's so much fun and I am eager to both discover and contribute at the same time. These are some of the things that I hope to have in store for me.

### Wright

Well that's good news for those of us who will be recipients of that work, I can assure you.

I certainly appreciate all the time you have taken with me today Dr. Rosenthal. It's always a pleasure to talk with you. Before the interview started, I told my wife I had an interview to do. She said "Who are you going to speak with?" and I said Dr. Norman Rosenthal, she says, "Uh-oh, he is one of your favorites. You respect him as much as anybody," and she is right about that.

ROSENTHAL

Well, I think you and I have a mutual admiration society because I remember after our last conversation feeling quite elated for hours afterward because you are so enlivening and so positive; one ends up feeling so good having spoken with you. Are you sure you weren't a therapist in a previous incarnation?

WRIGHT

That could be.

ROSENTHAL

Anytime. I look forward to continued conversations over the years.

WRIGHT

Thank you so much for being with me, Dr. Rosenthal. Today I have been talking with Dr. Norman Rosenthal who is best known as a psychiatrist. He is also known as the scientist who first described the SAD or Seasonal Affective Disorder or winter depression and, as we have learned today, he is quite knowledgeable on that and other topics as well. Thank you so much Dr. Rosenthal.

ROSENTHAL

Have a good day.

# About the Author

Dr. Norman Rosenthal was born in Johannesburg, South Africa, and attended the University of the Witwatersrand, where he obtained his medical degree with high honors. He moved to the United States and was resident and chief resident at Columbia Presbyterian Hospital and the New York Psychiatric Institute. He conducted research at the National Institute of Mental Health for over 20 years. It was there that he led the team that described Seasonal Affective Disorder and pioneered the use of light therapy to treat it.

Dr. Rosenthal has maintained a private practiced in the Washington, DC Metropolitan area for over thirty years, where he treats a wide variety of psychiatric problems using many forms of therapy. Dr. Rosenthal was awarded the prestigious Anna Monika Foundation Research prize for his contribution to research in treating depression. He has been listed as one of the Best Doctors in America and as one of this country's top psychiatrists.

He is the author or co-author of over 200 professional articles and five popular books, including Transcendence: Healing and Transformation Through Transcendental Meditation, Winter Blues, The Emotional Revolution, St. John's Wort and How to Beat Jet Lag.

Dr. Rosenthal currently serves as medical director and CEO of Capital Clinical Research Associates in Rockville, Maryland, where he directs clinical trials in both pharmaceuticals and complementary and alternative medicine.

Dr. Rosenthal and his work have been widely covered in the popular media and he has appeared on The Today Show, Good Morning America, National Public Radio and many other forums.

Norman E. Rosenthal, MD

normanrosenthal.com

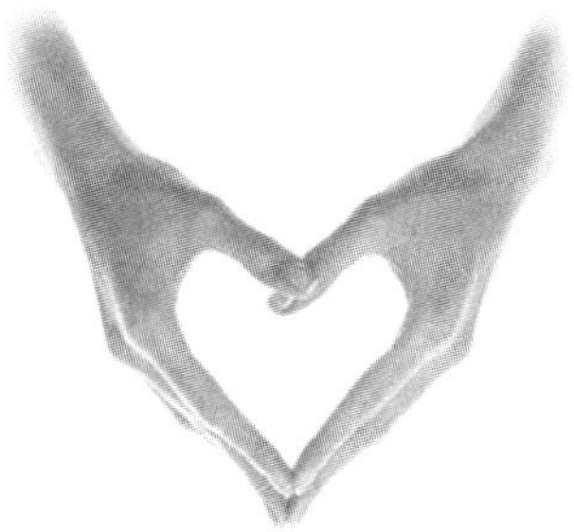

## Chapter Sixteen

# Life is All About Choices!

### with Dr. Tim Weir

THE INTERVIEW

DAVID WRIGHT (WRIGHT)

Today I'm talking with Dr. Tim Weir. Dr. Weir has been in chiropractic practice for thirty years. He has excelled in patient care, but then has branched out from there. He wrote the book, *You're Not Crazy: An Overcomer's Guide to Fibromyalgia,* and from that came up with the "Relax Formula" to help these patients sleep and relax. He is the host of the national television show, *The First Choice Life Show,* that airs on the Sky Angel Network. He is known for his humor and his ability to break down the complicated into bite-sized pieces. He is a sought-after speaker to both healthcare and spiritual audiences. He currently practices in Raleigh, North Carolina, at Weir Wellness and Neurologic Relief Center.

Dr. Weir, welcome to *Health: Mind, Body, Soul.*

Dr. Weir, there are many definitions of health, healing, and wholeness. What is your definition?

DR. TIM WEIR (WEIR)

Health is when your body is working 100 percent of the way God created it to work! Health is not the absence of pain or symptoms! If your child gets a fever, is he or she sick or healthy? If you go out to eat and you get food poisoning, with its symptoms of diarrhea and vomiting, are you sick or healthy? The answer is healthy. Your body is getting rid of the toxins and poisons that will make you sick. The fact is, in Western medicine, we have compartmentalized people so much that it is scary. We have become "the gall bladder in room 2017" or "Mrs. Jones, the Fibromyalgia patient."

No! We must move beyond pain and symptoms and get to the real issues of health. There has been so much talk about healthcare reform and it actually makes me mad. Until we "reform our health," we are going to keep spending money on healthcare like it is water. People have the idea that they can just take a pill or drink a potion and they will be fine. It really doesn't work that way. We have more cancer, heart disease, and other conditions that are out of control. We have to stop! We are incredible beings who are comprised of a spirit, soul, and body and if we treat just one, we lose sight of the wholeness of man. I love the quote, "You are not a body having a spiritual experience, you are a spiritual being having a body experience." You are an eternal being that happens to be in a temporary tent.

### Wright

What do you mean, "You are a spiritual being having a body experience?

### Weir

The fact is, we tend to look at everything around us through our fleshy body, which is so temporary, living 105 years at best. But the truth is, you are an incredibly powerful being who will live forever. We tend to judge our day on how our body is doing! Are you having aches or pains, well, maybe then you can't do such and such. Balderdash. You need to discover the truth of the real you—the spirit who lives in a body and uses a mind to maneuver through life. What would your goals in life be if you had a real epiphany on that! It would no longer be a highlight of your day to go to Walmart. You would realize that the sky is the limit. You would stop allowing this temporary dwelling to dictate to you how your days are going to be. You would allow the spirit side of you to help steer in the directions where you need to be.

### WRIGHT

What is the biggest challenge we have in today's society about being healthy?

### WEIR

We don't live in the same time as Grandpa and Grandma did on the farm. They ate fresh veggies out of the garden and they milked Bessie and drank it right away. They took some of that cream from the milk and made their own butter. Fresh meat? Are you kidding me? The chicken you fed this morning is feeding you this evening at dinner. Stress? Stress was when Bessie broke through the fence and got into Mrs. Johnson's garden.

My Lord, if Grandpa and Grandma had to go through one day with you, they would drop dead in about five minutes. You eat veggies that were picked months ago and sprayed to keep them from spoiling. The meat you eat has so many antibiotics and hormones in it that you could open up your own pharmacy. Milk? It has been so homogenized, pasteurized, and other-ized so many times that what good was in it ain't there no more! Stress? You wake up to an alarm clock that sounds like a tornado warning alarm. You turn on the news and listen to the same mess you did yesterday, just different names and dates. You sit down to a breakfast of over-processed grains, you have toast with chemicals in a product made to look like butter but it's not and then cover it with tons of sugar in the form of jelly. You then drink the over-processed milk and enough orange juice to put an elephant into a diabetic coma. Then you get in your car, drive sixty-five miles per hour surrounded by other people in these dietary comas and they are late getting to a job they hate. You spend eight to ten hours performing duties you can't stand. You spend all day bad-mouthing your boss, company, and your mother-in-law.

For lunch you have eaten some cheap bread made with, guess what? Over-processed wheat filled with luncheon meat made from God only knows what parts of some animal. You work some more, rush home to eat mac and cheese, washed down with five cups of coffee. You watch thirteen people get killed, two rapes, and three natural disasters all in thirty minutes of news and then lay down and try to sleep—and nothing happens. You toss and turn and recount everything that happened during the day. Why not turn on the television in bed and watch some more violence? You get up and take some sleeping aid and finally, at four o'clock in the morning, you fall asleep and hear the tornado siren again at six!

WRIGHT

Why are so many people not in tune more with their own body?

WEIR

We are on so many medications and pills it's not funny. We watch the television and listen for a drug company to tell us which pill to take for which symptom. Sometimes they don't even tell you what you're taking the pill for! Just go to your doctor and ask him if the little pink pill will work for you.

I don't know if you have noticed, but drug commercials are videos of some pretty people fly fishing or lying in a tub by the side of a lake, while a person with a smooth voice is telling you everything that could go wrong if you take this pill.

My fourteen-year-old asked me, "Dad, did you hear that if you take that pill, you could die?" Oh, that the adults were listening as intently. I think I would rather have sinus problems than have impotence, hives, muscle spasms, headaches, nausea, vomiting, dry mouth, cardiac arrest, asthma, or possible death.

The answer is this—we are so "numb" to our body's own signals that we are lost. Our nervous systems have been anesthetized with pain-killers, mood-elevators, sleep medications, and a handful of others. I have had people come in for consultations and their medications have to be listed on an Excel spreadsheet. They take pills to go to sleep and then more pills in the morning to wake up. The fact is, your body turns on the fire alarm in the form of pain, and rather than get to the cause, it is so much easier to cover it up. Wow. We have to get back to the premise of what chiropractic was built on—"The power that made the body is the power that heals the body." It's not the drugs, surgery, massage, or even chiropractic adjustments that heal you—it is the power of life within!

### WRIGHT

What inspired you to be a chiropractor?

### WEIR

In 1956, my father was in a wheelchair. My mother took him to the Mayo Clinic in Rochester, Minnesota. Their diagnosis was severe—with six months to live. Their advice was to take him home and make him comfortable. She decided to go against tradition—she took him to a chiropractor. That chiropractor treated my dad three to four times a day! Within days, he noticed a change and within six months he was out of the wheelchair and back to work! He lived another thirty-two years of a full life.

We were raised with chiropractic care. When I got the measles, it was the chiropractor who was called! Not only did those days inspire me, but my two brothers as well. My oldest brother, Dr. Mike Weir, has been my mentor for thirty years of practice. Our middle brother, Dr. Kevin Weir, was a great friend. He passed away about six years ago. He loved practicing, and there are times when I miss being able to pick up the phone and call him. His son, Dr. Michael Weir, practices in Bellevue, Washington. We all have the understanding that there is more to living then taking pills to survive.

WRIGHT

In the past thirty years, have you noted a change in the health of patients?

WEIR

It is amazing to watch how things have changed. Back in 1981, you never heard of "Fibromyalgia." These patients grew on me, and so in the late 1990s, I wrote my book on it. Now, every day, I have patients contact me with a new diagnosis of fibromyalgia, and they want answers other than some new drug. Cardiac disease used to be what your fat, old uncle died from. Now, it is one of the leading causes of death in women. There is no one reading this book who does not now or in the near past, have someone they know with cancer. In the 1950s and 1960s, it was so rare, that no one gave it a second thought. Pain is such a common symptom. Walk into any drug store and find multiple counters filled with pain meds. Sinus pain medication, arthritis pain medication and the list goes on. One of the biggest problems is people cannot sleep. They go months without any nights of real sleep.

WRIGHT

Why do you think that there are so many people in pain?

WEIR

I believe it is a three-strand cord—poor nutrition, heavy stress, and lack of sleep. If you look at the average American diet, it is filled with wheat and sugar. We have been conditioned to have bread or pasta at every meal. If we don't have a sandwich, then by all means, at least have a biscuit. Never in our history has there also been as much gluten sensitivity and celiac disease.

A study was done on children in Italy, and they are finding that about 70 percent of those children are sensitive to gluten and wheat. In my book, *You're Not Crazy,* one of the first things I recommend eliminating from the diet is wheat. I often tell this to patients and they come back, still on wheat. I ask them why they didn't stop eating it. What I will typically hear is something like, "My doctor did a test, and I am not allergic to wheat and he told me to continue to eat it." I don't care if the Pope told you to eat it, you will have problems. Most all of the grains are extremely inflammatory in the muscles, joints, and cardiovascular system. See why fibro patients need to get off it fast?

The average American consumes more than 160 pounds of sugar per person, per year. That does not include high fructose corn syrup, which weighs in at sixty-five pounds per year. It is in everything you eat that has been processed! Read labels! Then we feed it to our kids like it is manna from heaven. One of those little cute yogurt drinks for kids with nice fruit has eight teaspoons of sugar! It is no wonder they can't sit still in school, and they are getting diabetes in record numbers.

Stress—it is with us as never before. We are surrounded by stress-causing conditions and some of it we bring on ourselves. Who cares if the neighbors have a new car every year? They also have marital stress. Do you want that to go along with your new car?

This also leads to number three, the inability to sleep. This, I believe, is the main underlying problem with fibromyalgia. Since your body does all of its healing during the phase four sleep, when you don't get that you will have problems. It was this problem in treating fibromyalgia patients that lead me to formulate my "Relax Formula." It is a powdered drink mix that you make and consume right before bed. It has some magnesium, MSM, potassium, and a couple of other vitamins and minerals.

People tell me it sounds like I am anti-medicine. There are some patients who absolutely need medications. Thank God for them. The fact is, patients have often been treated with a "cookbook method" and given medications hand over fist.

WRIGHT

You wrote the book, *You're Not Crazy: an Overcomer's Guide to Fibromyalgia,* have you seen an increase in this disease?

WEIR

It used to the disease of women, but I am seeing more and more of it in men. It is often characterized by painful muscles, trouble sleeping, short-term memory loss, fatigue, IBS, and a plethora of other symptoms. Yes, there is a tremendous increase in these cases. Here is the sad thing—a lot of these people have tried the drugs, etc. and they have given up. Many of them have applied for disability and they continue their downhill spiral. We have to wake up and find the cause of diseases like this and not just treat symptoms.

WRIGHT

What have been the greatest tools in your toolbox that have gotten you success in treating these people?

WEIR

I have gotten great results with these patients with a two-fold attack: 1) *Nutrition.* Get off all wheat and sugar. Hard, yes. Necessary, yes. I put all of these patients on my Relax Formula. I use a lot of nutritional testing with these folks and often times I find the adrenal glands depleted. If you wake up at 9 AM, and you have to take a nap at 10 AM, then you have a problem that needs to be addressed nutritionally. 2) *Chiropractic care.* This is a nervous system disorder, and there is no other type of therapy that helps it more than a low-force chiropractic technique. I had good results with lots of people, but I was still not satisfied. I then got turned on to the Neurologic Relief Center Technique. With this technique, I have seen literal miracles in the lives of patients with these types of problems.

WRIGHT

You mention the NRC Technique, is this different than traditional chiropractic?

WEIR

Yes. It is so different. It is based on the meningeal covering of the brain and nervous system. For whatever reason, there can be a compression in this covering. When this occurs, there is a backup of cerebral spinal fluid. The really cool thing is there is a test that is performed to see if this compression is present in the meninges. The patient lies down on his or her back, and then certain pressures are placed on the meninges at the base of the skull. If meningeal compression is the problem, the patient will know, and so will I within eight minutes. Patients who come in with ten out of ten pain levels, tremors, migraine headaches, and joint pain will sit up after eight minutes with a tremendous relief in that pain level. By tremendous relief, I mean usually down to zero! Can you imagine suffering with that kind of pain for twenty years and in eight minutes it is completely gone? I have seen more miracles in three months than in thirty years of practice. It is unbelievable. To me, it is a gift from God to severe pain patients.

WRIGHT

Out of having a very successful chiropractic practice, you became the host of the national television show, *The First Choice Life*. What is your motto for the show?

WEIR

"Life is about choices! The choices you make today determine your future tomorrow." It is just that simple. That is usually too simple. If you don't like your life today, it is because of some choices you made a couple of years ago. Here is the good news: if you want a good future, change your choices that you are making *today!*

WRIGHT

What choices does a sick person have to make to get well?

WEIR

A lot! Are you going to make the choice to give up wheat? How about sugar? The main choice is this: do you want to be healthy?

One of my favorite stories in the Bible was when Jesus went down to the municipal pool. It didn't have a water slide, but it was known for this: an angel would come and "stir the water," and when that happened, the first one in would get a miracle. So, as you can imagine, there were a lot of crippled people there. Jesus saw a man who had been there for years, and yet still crippled because no one was there to help him get into the water when the angel dangled his toes in the water.

Jesus turned to him and asked, "Do you want to be made whole?"

For years I read that and thought, "For being the Son of God, you are mighty 'slow'." My God, this man has been "trying" to get healed; he just hasn't made it yet. Then I got into practice and realized that not everyone wants to be made whole. There may be different issues at play. Someone may have a disability case he or she doesn't want to give up or there may be some emotional issues that have the person tied to the disease. So, step number one is: Make the Choice.

WRIGHT

You have been quoted as saying, "In order for your life to change, you have to change how you see your life." What does that mean?

WEIR

How do you see your life? Do you see yourself in a wheelchair, crippled? Then you need to change that vision. Do you see yourself always broke, never able to pay your bills? You need to get a new picture in your mind.

Another favorite verse is this: "As a man thinketh in his heart, so is he" (Proverbs 23:7). Interesting that it is not "As a man thinketh in his head, so is he"—it is a heart issue. Most people who are dealing with these issues are crippled. Not in their bodies, but in their hearts. You have to change what you see. I am amazed that people are so willing to give up a fabulous life for a mediocre life. Most people around you are hurting and suffering through life. They need a mental enema. We carry around so much baggage and crap in our minds, that it is no wonder we have trouble making it from day to day. Einstein said that the definition of insanity was doing the same things over and over, but expecting different results. Imagine pouring water into the gas tank of your car and expecting it to run. It doesn't, and so you pour more water into the gas tank. You keep that up for months, getting more and more frustrated. Change! Decide that you are going to change what you are doing. You are going to put gasoline into the car, and suddenly, it works.

### Wright

What is your motto for life?

### Weir

You have to have fun. If you are not having fun doing what you do, then you have some big problems. If you "live for the weekends," then 70 percent of your life is crappy and only 30 percent is spent enjoying life. It should be 100 percent of your life is spent enjoying life. How do you do that? Make a choice to change how you are thinking. When is the last time that you gave thanks for your job? When is the last time that you told your husband that you love him and appreciate all he does for you and your family? Have you told your wife how good she looks and that you appreciate her keeping your home in one piece?

Through the years I have heard people say that when "such and such" happens, they will be happy. "When they get out of college, they will be happy" or "When they get married, they will be happy." If you are tying your happiness to a certain condition to take place, then you will never be happy. Happiness is not a condition, but a choice. If you decide to be happy just to be happy, then it doesn't matter where you work, or if your spouse looks like Shrek, you will be happy. A way overused cliché is "success is a journey, not a destination," and I'm going to be a part of the cliché over-use club. Pardon my Christian friends who are so stuck on going to Heaven, that they are useless on Earth. They have tied their happiness to a place where there is "no sorrow, no tears, no death," that they can't enjoy what they have here. Decide that you are going to enjoy the ride. You are going to have the time of your life.

WRIGHT

Why is laughter so important to getting well?

WEIR

Serious people scare me. I'm serious! It isn't that laughter is so important, it is the state of mind you are in that calls for laughter. There are changes in the endorphin levels in your body when you laugh and even when you watch someone else laugh. It is a light-hearted state that causes changes in people around you, circumstances you are in, and life outcomes. Rhonda Byrne in *The Power* writes this: "When you are feeling happy, and you keep feeling happy, then only happy people, circumstances, and events can come into your life."

When I was a kid, my parents owned a store. Every January, we had "inventory." We closed the store and all of us would walk around the store counting every single piece of merchandise in the store. We counted how many nails were in a box of nails. Man, I used to hate January for that. But guess what? It showed us what we did and did not have in the store.

Maybe it is time for you to "close the store" for a while and have "inventory." Close the store. If you have a lot of commitments to do a bunch of stuff that you really don't like doing, close the store. Tell who ever you have made commitments to that you need to take some time off. This does not include your job or your marriage! (*Nice try!*) Then find some time to be alone every day for a couple of weeks.

Get a pad of paper and begin to ask the questions, "What in my life makes me happy" and "What am I doing that doesn't make me happy?" You may list some things that are as simple as counting a box of nails; put them down. Often times it is the simple things that we do that bring us the most joy.

Let your mind go free in its quest to do this inventory. As you do this, your mind may go back to a time when you were ten and building model airplanes. Maybe you dreamed of being in a kitchen baking. Write all of these thoughts down on your inventory sheet. Then look carefully at them. Some of them are keys to regaining your happiness in life. Maybe you need to pick up a model airplane kit again and start building. Maybe you have the desire to get in the kitchen and bake a cake. Who cares if the first three look like burnt sacrifices? The key is to start. The second thing about laughter is this: When is the last time you laughed? I'm not talking about a little chuckle. I'm talking about being over at your cousin's house when you were twelve, and someone passed gas at the dining table and you laughed so hard milk came out your nose? When is the last time you laughed so hard that the next day your belly hurt?

I love a good movie—ones that make me laugh. One of the best movies I have seen for this is *Bridesmaids*. It is crude humor that the pastor warned against, but I loved it. I belly laughed. Find some things to do that will help you regain some of those belly laugh muscles. This exercise will really do you good!

WRIGHT

What can people do in the spiritual aspect of life to change their health?

WEIR

Let's take this back again full circle. Remember that you are a three-part being. You are a spirit that lives in a body for a span of about seventy to a hundred years and you have a mind that reasons and thinks and holds memories. It is this spirit force that keeps you alive. This is the breath of life that the ancients talked about. You must feed this spirit. You have to take time to nourish the real you—the inner spirit. Much like a computer, this inner spirit thrives on what you present to it. If you fill it with trash, then you will end up with trash. If you feed it good, then good will come from it.

How many hours do you spend alone in your car traveling every day? I spend about two hours every day going to and from work. For a long time, I just turned on the local radio station and listened to the local disc jockeys and radio hosts talk and play music. They were good, but it really didn't feed that inner man.

I decided to fill my mind with things that would cause me to grow. It started with cassette tapes. I bought some of the greatest motivation tapes there were and I listened to them in the car. Then I tried CDs. I bought CDs from Bob Proctor and Mark Victor Hansen and listened to them. Then came the iPhone with the iPod build into it. Wow, I am able to download these incredible speakers and teachers from around the world giving me daily doses of incredible life changing words.

My friend Betsy Barnett has a plaque in her downstairs bathroom that I saw several years ago while visiting her in her home. It simply says, "Whatever you focus on grows." If you want lack, then focus on lack. Focus your mind on how it feels to not have enough money at the end of the month. Focus in on how other people seem to have golden opportunities and you get the "crust from the bread." Or, you can focus on what you want to grow. Listen to people on your iPod who know how to be successful. Listen to people talk about the goodness of life and how you can be, do, and have anything in the world that you want. If you want to be sick and in bed, then focus in on sickness and disease. Watch television shows that foster this mentality. Somehow get it into your mind that you deserve to be on disability or you can focus in on health and healing. Find ways to eat better, drink better water, etc. Whatever you feed is what is going to grow in your life. Listen to the words that come into your mind. Are you constantly thinking of ways that something won't work? Do pains in your body immediately make you think of some dreaded disease and you just know you're suffering from it? When you think of going to a nice place for vacation, does your mind instantly fill up with all of the bills you owe, or the money you don't have? Then you need one of those mental enemas. It is quite simple. You are full of mental feces.

The only way to get those impacted thoughts and beliefs out is to fill your mind up with good, positive thoughts of success and health. It is called the "law of displacement." There is not room for both. It is impossible to think of something negative when you have thoughts of positive things filling your mind. When a negative thought enters your mind, simply stop right where you are and mentally change the channel. If your thought is, "I don't have enough money," then in your mind say, "I am rich. I am a magnet that draws money to me. I am full of abundance." You just had a mental enema. The fact is, many of you will have to wear an enema bag around your head for several months before you notice the change taking place!

### Wright

You have a national television show; do you like to talk in front of people about this?

WEIR

I have to tell you the truth, I don't "like" to, I "LOVE" to! I get excited when I stand up before an audience and start sharing some of these great concepts. I'm very comfortable standing in front of a video camera talking about these life-changing ideas. I love sitting with guests and asking them how they made choices that changed their life. It actually produces a lot of energy in me to expound upon the power you have inside of you. Can you imagine helping people break free of limiting beliefs that have them tied up in a little corner of their life?

I really believe that when people pass from this life, they exit their bodies and they realize that they are an incredible powerful spirit and that they have been all along. When they realize this they say "crap." You will realize that from day one in this earth suit, you had the power to do anything you wanted. You are hooked into the source of all energy and power, the source of love. The good news? You are still here, with a body that is at least existing. Make the decision to change right now. Make the choice that from now on, you are going to not just exist, but you are going to reign over life. You will be healthier than you have ever been and that you will live a long, healthy productive life.

WRIGHT

You say on your show that you are not a fitness guru with six-pack abs—you are just a normal guy. Why is that important?

WEIR

Look in the mirror. It is a small percentage of people who, when they take off their shirts their abs look like a washboard! Most of us take off our shirts and the dog runs in the other room and hides and little children run for their mothers. I don't know about you, but I do not have two hours to go to a gym every day. I don't have a personal trainer to be with me several hours every week to hold my hand and get me crunching in just the right way.

My personal chef is a George Foreman Grill. Phillipe does not come to my house to cook me fresh salmon caught the night before in Canada! I work eight to ten hours a day and come home ready to fall into a chair just like you. What sets my television show apart is this same fact—I'm not a Hollywood star doctor. We don't have scripts we go by, we are very off-the-cuff. Sometimes that doesn't work, and that's okay. More good news: if I can make some different choices, so can you.

### Wright

Is there hope for people to once again be healed, healthy, and whole? "

### Weir

Life is all about choices. The choices you make today determine your future tomorrow." Is there hope? Absolutely. You have heard the ancient Chinese proverb, "When the student is ready, the teacher will appear." It is exactly just like that. When you are ready to make changes and when you are tired of being sick and crippled in life, and you make a choice to be different, the sources of your miracles will appear. You will open up a piece of mail and find the name of a doctor who can help you get to where you need to go. You may get a call from a friend who discovered a way to eat that has changed his or her life. When you decide that God is not against you, but really is on your side, your outlook on life will magically change. You will begin to see opportunities for your good and you will quit seeing everything from a negative standpoint. You will see the windows cracking open and a fresh breath of life blowing you way. It's in your hand!

# About the Author

Dr. Tim Weir has been in chiropractic practice for thirty years. He has excelled in patient care, but then has branched out from there. He wrote the book, *You're Not Crazy, an Overcomer's Guide to Fibromyalgia,* and from that came up with the "Relax Formula" to help these patients sleep and relax. He is the host of the national television show, *The First Choice Life Show* that airs on the Sky Angel Network. He is known for his humor and his ability to break down the complicated into bite-sized pieces. He is a sought-after speaker to both healthcare and spiritual audiences. He currently practices in Ralcigh, North Carolina, at Weir Wellness and Neurologic Relief Center.

Timothy Weir, DC

4109 Wake Forest Rd.
Raleigh, NC 27609
919-279-5309
www.DrTimWeir.com

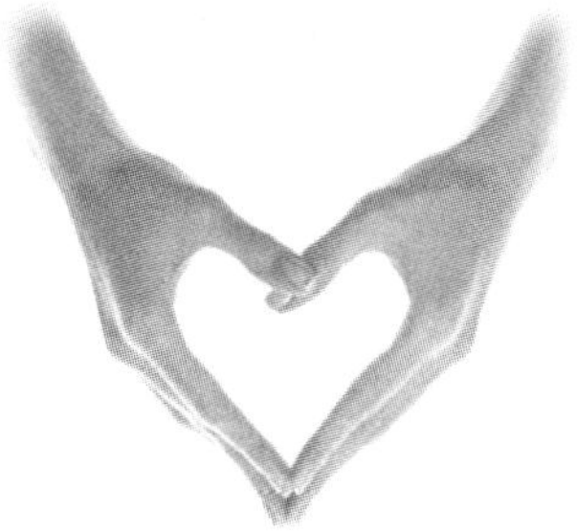

## Chapter Seventeen
# Building Wellness

## with Mark Middlesworth

THE INTERVIEW

### DAVID WRIGHT (WRIGHT)

Today I'm talking with Mark Middlesworth, athletic trainer, workplace ergonomics and wellness specialist, author, and speaker.

Mark, welcome to *Health: Body, Mind, Soul.*

I noticed you have published a new book this year titled Building Wellness from the Inside Out. Will you explain the title?

### MARK MIDDLESWORTH (MIDDLESWORTH)

Wellness is something we need to intentionally build into our lives. Our health is vitally important to us, right? So, we need to make it a priority to establish and execute a plan that will at least maintain, or better yet, enhance our health and quality of life.

I love the quote attributed to Robert Collier: "Visualize this thing that you want, see it, feel it, believe in it. Make your mental blueprint, and begin to build." I think this applies to the way we should be thinking about our health. We first need to think about what we want, then we begin to build.

Here's an analogy to consider: Building a physical structure like a home requires a vision and a plan. The builder needs the plan and blueprints to direct the daily activities and tasks that in the end will produce the desired result. A builder wouldn't dream of beginning to build a house without the blueprints, right? How do you think it would turn out if they didn't have a plan?

In the same way, I believe that it's very important to develop a plan for our personal wellness with blueprints—goals—that will direct our choices and activities. Investing the necessary time to properly plan for wellness is essential. If you grab the cart in the grocery store without a healthy meal plan in mind, you will be tempted to just grab whatever looks good to you even if it is not the healthiest choice. Likewise, if you don't have an exercise plan, it's very easy to let it slide. It's not very smart to wait until you're sick to think about a wellness plan. We need to be proactive and intentional about building wellness into our lives. Considering where we are and where we want to be is an important initial step that we must not overlook.

WRIGHT

Got it—we need to have a plan for our health and wellness. What about the "inside out" part of the title?

MIDDLESWORTH

It's very easy to point the finger of blame on "outside" factors when it comes to our health and wellness. At least that's the way it was for me; I was good at making excuses. We might have thoughts like, "I just don't have the time. I work hard all day so the last thing I want to do is exercise when I get off work. It's my job that is causing my body to fall apart. Standing on this concrete floor is why my feet hurt. I can't afford to buy healthier foods. It's easier to stop and grab some fast food. I'm too old and set in my ways to start being healthy now. Heart disease runs in my family; it's in my genes, outside of my control."

Taking an "inside-out" approach to my personal health means that I need to start first with myself, to take responsibility and remove the excuse list that serves as a barrier to my improved health and wellness. After the "excuse" and "blame" factors are identified and eliminated, I can now go to work on building a better plan for my health.

WRIGHT

You say in your book that the U.S. health care system is upside-down, how so?

MIDDLESWORTH

What if we were to start a full-contact tackle football program for the youth in our community without giving the kids a helmet and shoulder pads to protect them from injury? We tell the parents, "We realize that the risk of traumatic head and shoulder injuries will be significantly higher without the proper protective equipment. But don't worry, we plan to have several ambulances on standby near the field and we will also be sure to alert the surgical trauma team at the hospital so they will be ready to deal with the serious head injuries." How do you think the parents would respond to this reactive plan? Do you think this is the best philosophy and to care for the health of the kids?

Unfortunately, the vast majority of so-called "healthcare" in the United States is reactive. This approach is upside-down. We wait until we get sick, don't feel quite right, or something is not working the way it should. We go see the doctor. The office is packed with sick people. We wait an hour and are lucky if we get ten minutes with the doctor. We get a diagnosis and usually a prescription for drugs. We pick up the pills at the drugstore. We go home and take the pills. We wait and see if the pills make us feel any better. This approach is foolish. In this country, we seem to be addicted to the quick-fix of prescription drugs and passive treatment modalities. Unfortunately, it's our appetite for a magic bullet that drives medical providers and pharmaceutical companies to give us what we want.

The reactive treatment philosophy employed by medical treatment providers for the management of chronic lifestyle diseases is (dare I say it?) a failed philosophy. I don't want to sound like I'm bashing doctors. Doctors are smart, they care about their patients, and are good people doing what they have been trained to do and what they get paid to do. However, in my view, they are using a failed model for the management of many lifestyle-related disorders. The United States medical system, as currently set up, rewards reactive medical providers at a much greater rate than it does programs for avoiding weight gain, improving fitness levels, controlling blood pressure, and combating inflammation with a better nutrition plan. Although medical advances in this country are nothing short of amazing, these treatments are not the best answer for the problem of widespread lifestyle-related diseases in our society. I'm not saying that these treatments are not necessary if the disease process has already diminished or destroyed proper function. Obviously, treatment is needed at that late date, and I'm thankful that such treatments exist to prolong life. But we still need to ask the most important question: What are the causes of the disease? Modern science is beginning to show us that many risk factors are related to lifestyle. So, I submit to you that employing healthy lifestyle habits to prevent disease is a much better answer than drugs or surgery. And by all means, let's give the kids a helmet and shoulder pads!

WRIGHT

What approach should we employ to more effectively manage lifestyle diseases in this country?

MIDDLESWORTH

A very long time ago, Thomas Edison said, "The doctor of the future will give no medicine, but will interest his patients in the care of the human frame, in diet, and in the cause and prevention of disease." I agree with this approach, and we shouldn't wait any longer.

WRIGHT

What are the primary causes of lifestyle-related disorders?

MIDDLESWORTH

In the book, I talk about risk factors such as dehydration, inflammation, malnutrition, fatigue, low physical fitness levels, and other poor health choices and habits.

WRIGHT

Why are proper levels of hydration so important to our health?

MIDDLESWORTH

Our bodies cannot thrive without an adequate supply of water. Water is the single most important nutrient for our bodies. Water plays a vital role in all cellular activities, transporting essential vitamins and minerals at the cell level throughout the body. If your body becomes dehydrated, the capability of your transport system is compromised and you will lose strength and energy. Lack of water can cause metabolic waste and by-products like lactic acid, uric acid, ammonia, and other toxins to accumulate in our soft tissues. Drinking adequate amounts of water throughout the day will ensure that all this junk is properly flushed out.

WRIGHT

How much water does our body need?

MIDDLESWORTH

Many recommend eight to ten glasses of water per day is a good measure. But all people are not created equal and our lifestyle habits differ greatly, so we should probably do a little better than that. Dr. Don Colbert, in his book *The Seven Pillars of Health,* states that to determine how much water your body needs, you can take your body weight and divide that number by two. That's how many ounces of water you need every day. For example, if you weigh one hundred and sixty pounds, you need to take in at least eighty ounces of water per day. I like this simple formula because it gives us a measureable goal to consider. However, you don't necessarily need to consume this entire amount of water in liquid form. You can get up to one third of the water you need by eating five to seven servings of fruit and vegetables each day. So, you can give yourself some water credits for eating fresh fruit and vegetables. Fruits and veggies contain a bunch of water, fiber, and are an excellent source of vitamins.

I'm frequently asked, "Does cola or soda drinks count toward the total needed? It's liquid and mostly water, right?" My answer: Your body yearns for clean and pure water. I recommend that you stay away from liquid junk. "What about coffee and tea?" If a couple of cups of coffee or tea are part of your morning routine, recent research suggests no adverse health effects from this habit. In fact, studies show that there are several potential health benefits associated with lower amounts of coffee and green tea, as long as you don't load it with sugar and you don't exceed three eight-ounce cups per day.

WRIGHT

How can our diet contribute to chronic inflammatory diseases?

MIDDLESWORTH

Inflammation is a primary cause of most lifestyle-related disorders, including heart disease and musculoskeletal disorders. Inflammation is invisible and subtle; it's on the inside, and you don't necessarily feel it. You may not recognize that it's there, but it's a fire within your body that is burning up your soft tissues from the inside-out. Your entire body can be in an inflamed condition. Inflammation looks for small cracks or vulnerabilities in your body, and then attacks those weaknesses. Taking anti-inflammatory drugs might seem like an easy fix to cool down inflammation, but this doesn't address the cause. The biggest cause of this fire within our bodies is inflammatory sugars and fats within our diet. Other contributing factors are stress, lack of exercise, and sometimes food allergies.

WRIGHT

Most people probably wouldn't identify malnutrition as a primary cause of disease in this country that has such an abundant food supply. Obviously, you think malnutrition is a problem. Why?

MIDDLESWORTH

We tend to eat too many calories, and not enough nutrients. We tend to overeat, yet we are undernourished. We don't live in a third world country, yet many of us are malnourished simply because we choose to eat too many bad foods and do not eat enough good foods.

The American diet has changed dramatically over the years. We eat more "dead" foods and fewer "living" foods now than we did just fifty years ago. These poor dietary habits cause chronic diseases such as inflammation disorders, diabetes, arthritis, chronic fatigue, cardiovascular disease, obesity, and more. A healthy diet is one of the most important weapons we have to fight against chronic illnesses. The quality of our living is dramatically affected by the foods we choose to eat. In the short-term, what we eat affects our mindset, mood, and energy levels, as well as our mental and physical performance. Over time, the foods we choose to eat determine what our bodies look like on the outside, how well our body functions on the inside, and ultimately, how long and how well we live.

If we want to live well and live long, we need to be intentional about "setting the table" and making better choices when selecting the foods we're going to eat. The basic formula for healthy eating is really simple. We need to eat fewer "empty" calories from dead foods, and we need to eat more calories from living foods. Living foods include fruit, vegetables, nuts, and seeds. Living foods are harvested. Dead foods are the opposite. They contain man-made ingredients like glucose, fructose, dextrose, preservatives, and additives. Dead foods are not harvested, they're processed.

WRIGHT

Do you recommend vitamin and mineral supplements as a part of a healthy diet?

MIDDLESWORTH

I agree 100 percent with Dr. Mindell's viewpoint regarding supplements. I had a professor in college who was not supportive of taking essential vitamins and minerals in the form of pills. So, for many years I didn't take any supplements. In my professor's perfect world, she thought and taught that I should get all the vitamins and nutrients I need from my diet. That's probably true, but the reality is that I don't live in a perfect world when it comes to my diet. My opinion on this has since changed, in part because I find that I feel so much better since I began taking supplements to fill in the gaps that my diet does not take care of. I take three daily supplements: a high quality multivitamin and mineral supplement, a Vitamin D supplement with calcium and magnesium, and an omega-3 fatty acid supplement. Notice that I didn't say vitamin "replacements." Supplements are not a substitute for healthy eating; they just fill in the gaps. As Dr. Mindell points out, even the *American Medical Association* has had a major paradigm shift on this subject recently; they now recommend the consumption of a daily multivitamin for all adults.

WRIGHT

What about physical fitness?

MIDDLESWORTH

I believe that we should incorporate three types of exercise into our wellness plan: aerobic or cardiovascular exercise, strength training, and stretching or flexibility exercise.

It's widely recognized that there's a direct correlation between poor levels of physical fitness and increased risk of chronic diseases. I think that by now most everyone knows that a sedentary lifestyle is bad for your health and that regular exercise is good for your health. Multiple studies have proven that regular exercise is effective in reducing heart disease risk, lowering blood pressure, reducing pain, improving sleep, enhancing energy, losing or maintaining healthy body weight, and much more.

The fact remains, however, that millions of Americans suffer from all kinds of chronic illnesses that can be prevented through improved diet and regular physical activity. Why is the percentage so low given the benefits? Probably because it's easier to not exercise. Illness doesn't fall upon us on the day that we don't exercise, so the lazy nature in us tells us that another day of neglect won't hurt. Day by day, our lazy nature wins out. But sooner or later, those who think they don't have the time for exercise will be forced to find time for taking care of chronic disease. So, we need to take inventory of the many reasons that we should incorporate exercise into our activities of daily living. Perhaps the biggest obstacle I hear is that we're too busy and just don't have time to exercise. Well, sorry, but I'm not buying it. We need to face the fact that we really *do* have the time. We may not have boundaries or discipline or a plan, but we *do* have time.

### Wright

How would you advise someone who is interested in building a better plan for his or her health and wellness? What steps should the person take?

### Middlesworth

When I enter a destination point address into my GPS, it first calculates my current location before it gives me the directions and road map. That's a smart approach. Considering where we are and where we want to be is an important initial step that we should not overlook. Sometimes it's hard to get moving in another direction because of past failure. I understand that feeling—been there and done that. But we can do absolutely nothing about the past. It's over. Done. So I suggest that you bury your past. Do it, and this will allow you to take control of your future. You can make changes that will stick. You can make changes in your life and lifestyle.

I would also encourage you to take some time to identify some powerful reasons to make changes in your lifestyle. When we identify reasons that are important enough, we will be better equipped to handle the inner battles that will inevitably take place as we seek to form new habits.

Next, it's important for people to make a clear and definite decision that they're determined to take charge and build a better wellness plan. Back in my days as a professional football athletic trainer, our coach was Marv Levy who later led the Buffalo Bills to four Super Bowls. I'll never forget what Coach Levy frequently told our team. He said, "It's not enough to have a desire to win. Everyone has the desire to win, but not everyone is willing to do what it takes to win. Are you willing to do what it takes? That means doing the simple things—the daily disciplines needed to become a winner." A desire to be healthy is not enough. Desire alone is not what gets you there. The question we all need to ask ourselves is: am I willing to do what it takes? It's easy to do something when you feel like it. Based on the strong reasons you've identified and the decision you've made, you'll force yourself to do it even when you don't feel like it. This attitude can change the entire direction of your life and your health.

I would encourage people to become students of health and wellness. That's very important. If you have a desire to be healthy, then you need to study health. Commit to take at least a few minutes each day to build your wellness knowledge base. This will help you stay on track and keep you motivated. Study with discernment and consider the source, then use all the information you've gathered to build a wellness plan that will work best for you.

Setting clear goals is vital. Perhaps the biggest reason that most people fail to change lifestyle habits is that they don't clearly define any goals. Success comes from knowing exactly where you are going, how you are going to get there, what you plan to do along the way, and who will be coming along for the ride. We need to have very specific, written goals and objectives when it comes to building a better plan for our wellness. Work on setting specific goals today. Begin with the end in mind. What exactly do you want? Write it down. Then, set a deadline date for accomplishing your goals. When the deadline date arrives, you'll either wish you had or be glad that you did.

I also highly recommend keeping a journal. Journaling is a great way to keep track of what you eat and how much you exercise. Do you know that people who keep a journal are more likely to lose weight and keep it off? A constant battle is going on inside of us that determines the choices that we make. Which will we choose: a donut or apple, the couch or exercise, Mountain Dew or water, ease or discipline? The path of immediate gratification and least resistance pulls hard on us. Each day we encounter choices that will lead us toward good health, or alternatively toward disease. We know deep down that we need to fight our tendency to take the easy road, and become disciplined instead. The simple action of comparing your goals verses the actual choices that you make each day will really help you stay on top of your goals. It's a vehicle for daily self-accountability. At the end of the day, you will know the score.

Last but not least, the process of changing our health begins and ends with action. Some people say that it's the thought that counts. Not true. Action is the ignition switch. Action is the spark that will bring to us inspiration, accomplishment, and improved health. Our goals determine our actions, and our actions ensure the desired result.

# About the Author

Mark Middlesworth is the founder and president of Ergonomics Plus, leading a unique team of workplace injury prevention and wellness specialists dedicated to helping client companies and their employees achieve enhanced health and high levels of human performance. Ergonomics Plus has had a successful track record with numerous firms throughout the United States since 1989, helping client companies reduce costs associated with workplace injury and illness. Mark and his team at Ergonomics Plus advocate the "Workplace Athletic Trainer" model for employee wellness and injury prevention.

Mark is the author of *Building Wellness from the Inside Out*, a book written to educate and motivate "workplace athletes" toward enhanced health and wellness each and every day.

Mark is a certified member of the National Athletic Trainers Association. He is a member of the National Speakers Association and is a frequent public speaker addressing a variety of workplace wellness and injury prevention topics. Mark is also founder of Indianapolis-based Bright Apple Wellness Network, partnering with outstanding health and wellness providers to promote products and services that make it easier for families to build wellness into their lives.

Mark Middlesworth
PO Box 436
Sweetser, IN 46987
765-384-4499
mmiddle@ergo-plus.com
www.ergo-plus.com

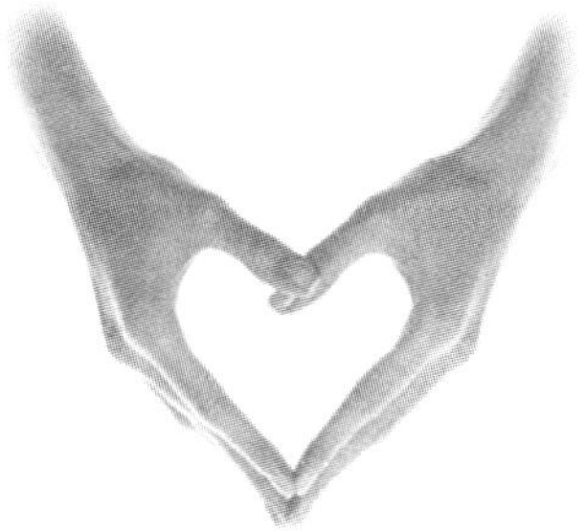

# Chapter Eighteen
# The Rise of Holistic Healthcare

## with Dr. Thomas Johnson

THE INTERVIEW

---

### DAVID WRIGHT (WRIGHT)

Today I'm talking with Dr. Thomas Johnson. Dr. Johnson is a licensed chiropractor who specializes in nutrition, weight loss, and holistic medicine. He owns a very successful holistic healthcare practice that is integrated with medical providers that share his same philosophy in Conyers, Georgia, and helps thousands of patients get well through natural methods.

Dr. Johnson, how did you get into this profession?

### DR. THOMAS JOHNSON (JOHNSON)

When I was twenty-two years old, I decided to become a body builder. I worked out in the gym every day and learned a lot about nutrition. After a couple of years of working out and competing, I developed a severe problem with my back. My back pain was so severe that it would not allow me to work out and do the things I wanted to do. I saw many healthcare providers to try to help my back, I saw my family doctor, did physical therapy, sports medicine, I even saw an orthopedic doctor and I just couldn't get any relief.

As a last resort, I saw a chiropractor who took some x-rays. He showed me something he saw in the x-rays that made a lot of sense to me and I started treatment. It completely took care of the problem. I was able to go back to the gym, I felt better than ever, felt stronger than ever, and I felt more energetic than ever. It was at that point right there when I decided that this was a pretty amazing thing; I wanted to become a chiropractor and do for other people what he did for me. Now I have been practicing for about fifteen years and my practice has evolved from straight chiropractic to a full-scale holistic health care practice that includes nutrition, weight loss, and holistic medicine.

WRIGHT

What exactly is holistic medicine?

JOHNSON

Holistic medicine is about treating the whole body and not just focusing on the patient's symptoms. Our goal is finding the cause of the person's health concerns and using natural methods to help the body "heal" itself. We have patients come in every day who are tired of taking a pill for every symptom or ailment they have and never really feeling that it's getting to the bottom of their problem. They come to us searching for other solutions and want a more natural approach. I have spent many years learning nutrition and holistic healthcare through advanced training seminars, studying, and just trial and error. I feel that I can now offer our patients so much more than just chiropractic. As wonderful as chiropractic is, being able to help the whole body is much more satisfying for me and the patient. More and more people are looking toward holistic medicine and nutrition these days and they are truly taking charge of their own health.

WRIGHT

What is the difference between holistic and traditional healthcare?

JOHNSON

Both types of healthcare attempt to help the patient, but traditional healthcare has a very rigid, strategic way of assessing someone, how to analyze what's wrong, what kinds of tests to perform, and what kind of treatment to do. This is called the standard of care. If you present to your doctor with certain symptoms and a certain history, there is a standard way of testing and standard medicines that are used in an effort to help you. In holistic healthcare, we also get a history and do our testing, but we look at things that most medical doctors don't.

For example, a patient can present with chronic headaches, in traditional medicine a common test might be an MRI to determine if there is a problem within the head or brain. Most often the MRI is normal and the patient is given medication to just suppress the symptoms. In holistic medicine we look at the whole body, there could be a problem somewhere else in the body or an outside influence affecting the body that is causing the headaches. Patients presenting with chronic headaches may be breathing in chemicals or other toxic substances all day at work. Maybe they have food allergies or sensitivities that are causing the headaches, maybe they have a pinched nerve in their neck, or maybe they do have a clot in a blood vessel which is obstructing blood flow to the head or a tumor causing pressure. By looking at all of the possible causes, and looking at the "whole" body, we have helped patients get better very quickly targeting the right cause instead of just medicating their symptoms because their MRI was normal.

WRIGHT

What types of holistic medicines do you use?

JOHNSON

We use a combination of organic whole food supplements, herbs, glandulars, medical food, detoxification products, and bio-identical hormones. We call them "nutraceuticals." Nutraceuticals are very high grade nutritional supplements that can only be ordered by a doctor and are sold only through healthcare providers. These products cannot be bought on the Internet or at your local health food store. A doctor who knows and truly understands these products would prescribe the appropriate nutraceuticals for your specific needs. These products are not intended to replace patients' prescribed medications from their medical doctor, they simply give the body what it needs to begin to work better and help restore their health. Many patients report back to their medical doctor that they are doing so much better after being on these nutraceuticals that their doctor often reduces or eliminates their prescribed medication altogether and asks them, "What are you doing? Well, whatever it is, keep doing it!"

WRIGHT

You see many patients with metabolic syndrome. What exactly does that mean?

JOHNSON

Metabolic syndrome is a condition that is sweeping the country faster than any I have ever seen. Metabolic syndrome is simply a part of a person's metabolism that is not functioning correctly and it manifests itself in several ways; it's often called Syndrome X. With Syndrome X and metabolic syndrome, there are four components. The first component is a problem with blood sugar regulation. The second is a problem with the lipids in the body, which could be a problem with cholesterol or triglycerides. The third is central weight gain, which is mainly belly fat. The fourth component is when the blood pressure starts to rise.

So typically, if you have two of any of those four components then you could be diagnosed with metabolic syndrome. Most people who come to our practice have metabolic syndrome whether or not they have been diagnosed. They have those symptoms and it's interesting because these conditions are well known to be risk factors for things like heart disease, cancer, stroke, and diabetes. These are common conditions we see in our country and seem to be getting worse, not better. The key is to address metabolic syndrome before it turns into more serious health problems.

### WRIGHT

What is your opinion of the current healthcare system in America?

### JOHNSON

The current healthcare system in America is something I talk to my patients about a lot. When I was going through school, from what I was taught, and what everyone hears is that we have the best healthcare system on the planet. We certainly have more doctors, more hospitals, and more medications available than anywhere on the planet, yet when you look at the incidence of many conditions like cancer, strokes, heart disease, obesity, high blood pressure, high cholesterol, ADD, ADHD, autism, asthma, just to name a few, it just seems like we have more of these health problems than all the other countries in the world.

So the question obviously becomes, Why? Now the current healthcare system is great for what I call "crisis care." If someone did have a heart attack or had a stroke, he or she is definitely in the best country in the world. If somebody had an accident and his or her leg was broken, that person is in the best country in the world to receive treatment. But we are poor in preventing health problems that can often be avoided. I once heard an analogy that said wouldn't it be better to build a fence around the edge of a cliff than to have the latest and greatest ambulances at the bottom of a cliff? Sure we need ambulances, but why don't we do something to our healthcare system where we don't need as many?

So I think that prevention of our health problems and having the knowledge and tools a patient needs about how to avoid these conditions is key. Yes, it's great to have medications and surgeries available for health crises, but if we avoid the factors that are well known and well documented to either cause, or at the very least, aggravate, these health problems, then we are on our way to a healthier society. We must empower ourselves with what it takes so that we don't have to rely on so much potentially dangerous medication and surgeries. So in summary, healthcare in our country is great for crisis care but poor for prevention.

### Wright

What makes your system for weight loss more successful than the other weight loss programs out there?

### Johnson

Many of the weight loss programs out there are very "cookie cutter" type systems. They are usually not very healthy and most importantly do not address the person's unique health issues or hormonal make up. Some people can lose weight on just about any weight loss program, but can they do it without jeopardizing their health, or can they keep the weight off long term? I've talked with patients who have literally tried every diet that is out there, and have exercised themselves into exhaustion and still don't lose a pound. My experience has shown me that everyone's body is unique and reacts differently to any one program. One key to weight loss that we have been teaching for years is that you must have a properly working hormonal system, or the weight can be almost impossible to lose.

All healthcare practitioners are taught a very simple concept in regards to weight loss: "you must burn more calories than you eat." We've all heard that, right? And it makes perfect sense except that it just flat out does not work in all cases.

Let me give you an example. Everybody knows people who can eat whatever they want, whenever they want and yet they don't gain any weight. Others can think of a cheeseburger and they gain two pounds! So how does that happen? Or a better question is: *what is the difference between these two people? Why can one eat anything and not gain, and the other doesn't eat a lot but gains?* The answer is metabolism! And what controls metabolism? The answer is the endocrine system—or your glands and your hormones.

Your body produces all kinds of hormones. There are hormones that help you get pregnant, raise blood sugar, lower blood sugar, and raise blood pressure just to name a few. Now there are also hormones that cause you to store fat, and there are hormones that cause you to burn fat.

Now let's look at exercise for example. I have stated to patients that exercise does not actually burn fat. Now you might think I'm crazy but let me explain. Let's say I took you to a health club and we ran a really fancy body fat test on you. Then I put you through a two-hour super intense workout that nearly kills you. Then after the workout we retest your body fat. Guess what it would be? The answer is it would be the same.

Now exercise, if properly done, causes the body to release the hormones that burn fat. But the fat-burning doesn't occur until hours later—especially during deep sleep. So exercise itself causes the release of the fat burning hormones, and these hormones cause the fat-burning. So, what if the hormone system isn't working properly? You exercise, but you don't burn any fat.

This is where the art of "functional medicine" or "holistic medicine" becomes so valuable. You have to become a detective and look for clues as to what is causing the problems. If you don't discover what is off in the hormonal system, you can have great difficulties with stubborn weight.

We make sure that we address these issues with a thorough history and examination including comprehensive laboratory testing. This will help determine the exact cause of a patient's weight issue and where the breakdown is with his or her hormonal system. With this information we can make the proper nutritional adjustments and use the correct holistic medicines needed to switch their body to fat-burning. Most of our patients start losing weight right away on our program and they feel better than they have in years. We feel the body must be healthy first before people can successfully lose weight and keep it off; and it must be a customized program for each individual and that it addresses their specific needs.

WRIGHT

That leads me to my next question. What types of lab tests do you do that help you determine what might be wrong in the hormonal system?

JOHNSON

There are many that we consider. Not all tests are needed on all patients but let me give you a great example. Since the birth of the information age, all patients have access to so much information about their bodies and information that used to only be available only in medical textbooks. So many patients are on the Internet looking at their symptoms and often think they found out what may be wrong.

Let me give you an example. Most women who come in their doctor's office think something is wrong with their thyroid gland. They go on to say how they were doing some research and they notice they had all the symptoms of a poor performing thyroid gland, such as weight gain, fatigue, hair loss, dry skin, loss of libido, cravings for sugar and more. They had this amazing revelation and immediately made an appointment with their doctor. They went in and told their doctor about what they found and ask the doctor to test their thyroid. So the doctor orders up some blood work and the patient waits anxiously to hear the news about their thyroid. The doctor reviews the test and says "Your thyroid is normal." The patient is in disbelief.

From a functional medicine perspective, that doesn't mean we stop looking. There are other thyroid tests that can be performed that most doctors don't do. Also, what very few patients, and most doctors, don't know is that the thyroid may be affected by something else.

I'll give you an example of something we see almost daily in our clinic. There is a pair of glands that rests on top of your kidneys called the adrenal glands. The adrenal glands are your "stress glands" so they release hormones in response to stress. Now, as the adrenal glands are getting the message to increase the output of hormones, such as cortisol, there is a message sent to the thyroid gland that says "slow down." So when the adrenal hormones are high, the thyroid gland is suppressed. Simply by testing the thyroid gland only, you may not get the complete picture. If the thyroid was suppressed because of the adrenal hormones, a person could be diagnosed with hypothyroidism—but they may not actually have a problem with their thyroid gland at all. The thyroid was simply slowing down because that is exactly what it is supposed to do at that moment. So in this situation, we often test the adrenal glands. Sadly, most doctors don't even test the adrenal gland function and a lot of patients have burned out and stressed adrenals that cause numerous problems. This is the holistic medicine approach—find out what is the cause.

WRIGHT

Will you give us an example of how you use a holistic approach to a common health problem such as high blood pressure?

JOHNSON

Here is how I approach this: It always starts with education and an explanation. Hypertension, of course, is high blood pressure. I simply tell the patient that if you look at the word "hypertension," the prefix, "hyper" means up or high. Then, I ask them what causes tension. They'll look at me and say "stress." I say exactly. So hypertension really just means elevated stress. Now, stress can be the thoughts you are thinking about, the things you are worried about. It can be emotional, it can be physical, or it can be chemical as well, so there are many things that can stress the body. If people have high blood pressure, it simply means that their body is overloaded with issues it considers to be stressful or harmful. Now stress can be different to everyone. I jokingly say that if a flyer comes in the mail from Macy's Department Store and it says that there is a one-day sale, my wife is stressed that she is going to miss it and I'm stressed that she is going to go.

Basically, many things can cause stress, so if stress is elevated, it can cause high blood pressure. Now if you have high blood pressure, it can be very dangerous. High blood pressure can cause a stroke, it can cause kidney damage, and all kinds of problems. Doctors have to give medication to try to force the pressure down. Very simply stated, if a person has high blood pressure something must be raising it. So the medication prescribed tends to work well and bring the pressure down. Now when asked how long the person will need to take the high blood pressure medication, the answer is typically "for life."

What if a patient is concerned about the side effects of medications or just decides they don't want to take it anymore, what happens? The pressure goes right back up in the air! Now the reason for that is the medication isn't designed to fix what is raising the pressure—it's just trying to hold it down. The holistic approach would be to figure out what is causing the pressure to rise, and let's work on those causes while continuing the medication. We never have patients just stop their medication because that can be very dangerous. But as their body gets healthier and as they're able to lose weight, the pressure can come down naturally and doctors will happily reduce or remove the medication from that person's lifestyle. We've seen this more times than I can recall.

### WRIGHT

You say that many conditions or many health conditions are actually symptoms of deeper problem. Will you elaborate?

JOHNSON

Absolutely, a lot of the conditions I think that people have are given a name. That's one of the things we do in the world of healthcare is to name conditions. But, with many health problems you have to look deeper. So the question, again, is what is causing this condition? There are causes and there are effects.

Let's go back to the high blood pressure we were just talking about, as this would be good example. If you have high blood pressure, it's not a cause, it's an effect. It's an effect of something else—something else is raising it up. So even though it has the term "hypertension" and it's a condition in and of itself, something else is causing the pressure to rise. So that's the whole point. We have to look at what is the cause. I always say that in terms of medication, some people are told by the doctors that they need to take this medicine for the rest of their life, and I tell them their doctor is right—they will need to take the medicine for life unless we find the cause. Now there is a chance they may not need to take medication forever, if we find the cause.

One of the easy ways I try to explain this is saying if I step on a dog's tail, the mouth will start to bark. The problem is I'm standing on the dog's tail but the mouth is what is communicating, "Hey, there is a problem here." We could tape the dog's mouth shut and the dog wouldn't bark as much. If someone said, "Wow, that tape seems to work really good. How long do we need to leave the tape on the dog's mouth?" The answer would be for the rest of the dog's life *if* we continue to stand on his tail. But if we take our foot off the tail we can take the tape off and the problem is solved.

WRIGHT

You have a saying that you use regarding the Food and Drug Administration. What exactly is that?

JOHNSON

Well, of course everyone knows that the FDA is called the Food and Drug Administration. I like to say that, in my opinion, there is a reason why they call it the Food and Drug Administration. It's because if you eat our food, you're going to probably need our drugs. The Food and Drug Administration governs both of those because the quality of the food over our lifetime has certainly gotten a whole lot worse. The food that my parents grew up on was actually all organic food; they just didn't call it organic back then. The food I remember as a young boy was seasonal. You couldn't get certain things in the wintertime because it didn't grow. Today it seems as though they have found a way to produce food all the time, all year around. Food is being manufactured differently; it's actually genetically modified now. Food is very different. It's not real, by definition, food. If you look up the definition of the word "food," it says something along the lines of *that which is eaten to sustain life and provide nourishment.* So we need to look at what we are consuming and ask ourselves "is this more like a food, or more like a drug?"

Here is an example I use a lot when new patients come into our office. Let's say a man is an alcoholic. He has a problem with drinking and it is affecting his entire life in a negative way. He recognizes it and decides to stop drinking. Now, how will he feel when he first stops drinking? Everyone knows the answer is *horrible*. He will feel worse when he first stops drinking. That is because alcohol is a drug. His body is going through withdraw of the drug.

Now let's look at the other side of this. If a person really loves broccoli, but decides to stop eating it for a month he or she may miss it, but won't feel horrible; the person doesn't withdraw. That is because broccoli is a *food*.

So when patients try to eat less sugar, less sodas, less white processed and refined carbohydrates, and most things that people crave, they often feel worse! This is why I saw these things are more like drugs than food. It can cause a lot of problems in the body and that's a cause of so many health conditions that ultimately require medications. I always like to say that if you keep eating the food that is available—the cheap food, the tasty food, the convenient food—you're probably going to need drugs.

WRIGHT

I'm convinced that the way we are packaging and processing our food supplies now versus when I was a younger child is having an adverse effect on our health. Would you agree with that?

JOHNSON

Absolutely. The quality of food consumed by the average American now is so completely different than that of the generation before us. Basically, food is altered, modified, and changed to look better, taste better, and stay on the shelves longer. The food industry is a huge business. In my opinion, the alteration of our food is the primary problem that affects our health in a negative way. As a general rule of thumb, I tell our patients they should "eat like a caveman." By that I mean, if a caveman could walk out of his cave and find a food to eat, then that is the food you should be eating as well. Could a caveman find doughnuts, ice cream, cookies, chips, or smoothies? Of course not, could a caveman find fruits, vegetables, and meats? He sure could, and that is what you should base your diet on.

You want to eat the foods that are as close to nature as possible. Eat foods that come from the earth; it's what God put on this planet for us to use. The processing, the packaging, the preservatives, the taste enhancers, the hormones, and antibiotics added to the food supplies are not meant to be consumed. These days I tell my patients to try to eat as close as you can to an all organic diet, but I know it can be expensive and is hard to do. In my family, we try to at least eat organic eggs, milk, butter, and chicken. Some people believe that red meats are bad for you, but

I'm not a "don't eat meat" person at all. I am a person who believes that you "don't eat meat that has been fed an unnatural diet, been given hormones, and raised on antibiotics to prevent disease."

WRIGHT

That reminds me, I can't remember the movie, but I believe it was Burt Reynolds who stuck a Twinkie on the rail of a boat and said if I stick this here it will be here for eternity. So the packaging and processing of our foods have certainly changed in my lifetime.

We hear a lot about a diet that is new in America called the HCG Diet. I've heard it was called a cure for obesity, can you explain how this works?

JOHNSON

Sure. Actually this diet was created by a physician named Dr. Simeons who practiced in Italy in the 1950s. Dr. Simeons did some research on people who were overweight. In the 1950s there weren't as many people who were overweight or obese as they are now, but he was intrigued about why he would see some people eating the same foods, living the same lifestyle, and some would be thin and some overweight. So he did some research with a substance called HCG. Now HCG is basically considered a "pro-hormone," it's a substance that is normally in the body in very, very trace amounts. HCG is the hormone that elevates when a female becomes pregnant. If a girl takes a pregnancy test, that's what the test is looking for. If HCG is present it indicates you are pregnant.

The way I like to describe what happens with HGC to a patient is this: When you become pregnant, HCG levels elevate. When HCG elevates it's actually preparing the body to handle the pregnancy. The amount of HCG taken is not a whole lot; it's only if a woman was just a couple of weeks pregnant. It stimulates the part of the brain called the hypothalamus. The hypothalamus is the part of the brain that is actually responsible for everything to do with your endocrine system (your glands and hormones), metabolism, whether you feel hungry or not, whether you are thirsty or not, and whether your body will burn or store calories.

Now to really understand the effectiveness of the diet that Dr. Simeons created, I like to tell a story. Modern females track their menstrual cycle. They keep pretty close tabs on when it is due. If a female become pregnant, they know within in a few days. She changes her diet, she starts taking vitamins, she does yoga, and she's preparing for a healthy pregnancy. But when God designed our body ages ago we didn't have grocery stores, we didn't have pregnancy tests, we didn't have physicians to see, so it's very possible a girl could be pregnant for weeks if not months and not even realize she was pregnant. They didn't change their diets very much. In fact, they didn't eat five small meals per day—they ate food whenever they found it. So let's say it happened to be the wintertime, and there is a foot of snow on the ground. What did they eat? Now remember, they didn't have any canned food, bagged food, or grocery stores. They didn't have prenatal vitamins to take or healthy pregnancy diets to follow. So they ate whatever they could. And the majority of the food in the winter would be meat.

So the point is, females could be pregnant and actually go days at a time without even having any food, and there would still be enough available nutrition for mom and baby.

So it is the responsibility of the hypothalamus to make sure that there is enough nutrition for mom and enough nutrition for baby so they can both survive and be healthy. If our pregnant female is consuming plenty of calories, the hypothalamus really doesn't do anything because there are enough calories being consumed to provide mom and baby with a healthy pregnancy.

On the other hand, if our pregnant female is not getting enough calories, then the hypothalamus gets concerned because it says there's not enough nutrition coming in. And if we don't get more nutrition the baby's not going to survive. So what happens with the presence of HCG in the bloodstream and the presence of low calories? With the two things combined, the hypothalamus dials up your metabolism and starts breaking down stored fat. The fat is where your body stores the majority of your nutrients. So by metabolizing, or breaking down the fat, the nutrients are released into your bloodstream and the body would actually survive from those calories. This is how HCG works in helping a person lose stored body fat.

If you start to take HCG, it will cause your body on average to break down about twenty-five hundred calories of stored fat per day. You will eat a very low calorie diet of five hundred calories per day. Ordinarily I would tell a person never, ever eat a diet of just five hundred calories per day, it's not enough for your body. It can actually break down muscle and break down organ tissue. With HCG you can call it off for the following reason, if you are taking the HCG hormone because it is causing your body to metabolize about twenty-five hundred calories a day, plus the fact that you are eating the five hundred calories, your body feels like it is receiving three thousand calories and technically it is. We have found most patients lose about three quarters of a pound on average per day.

Now what Dr. Simeons found through his research is once you go through a twenty-one to thirty-day cycle of HCG, you will need to move to step two or a phase two, or even "the rest period" portion of the diet. At that time, you can actually have as much food as you'd like as long as it's food that is acceptable. After twenty-one to thirty days of the rest period, Dr. Simeons had found, that the body will be "locked in" at that new weight. So say a person lost twenty pounds over twenty-one to 30 days. He or she would then follow through to phase two. The person would do the rest period and at the end of those twenty-one to thirty days that twenty-pound weight loss is now permanent, provided the person doesn't try very hard to go back to where he or she was. Now that becomes his or her new weight. This is the reason HCG was called a "cure" for obesity.

WRIGHT

Are you seeing that there is a great acceptance of holistic practices in personal healthcare?

JOHNSON

Oh. there is no question. I think the viewpoint of the average patient in this day and age has greatly changed. The number of people who come in my office who say I have this condition, I am on this medication and I want to get off, it's amazing how many of them have a different viewpoint of taking medication. I think even as early as fifteen years ago, when I first started practice, it was clearly obvious that patients actually thought the medication was quite good for them, now the majority of the patients we see know they need the medication currently, but want to make the necessary changes to reduce or, in some cases, eliminate the need for the medication long term." They are always asking: "What do I have to do so I can reduce this high blood pressure medication?" "What do I have to do so I don't have to take this diabetes medication anymore?"

I think that clearly it's changing in a big way. It's usually seen just by looking at our practice, which is growing by leaps and bounds and the word is going out to people who are seeing the success of our patients. For example, many people have tried everything to lose weight, then they come to us for help and they finally start losing the weight. Their friends and families notice right away and immediately want to know what they are doing and how they can do the same thing. We have many patients returning and saying, "I just saw my doctor. I had some blood work done and I was taken off my medication!" It's incredible how many people are realizing the importance of going back to the foundations—the basics—of a better diet, a better lifestyle, and not letting stress affect them so much.

I would say that the answer to your question is that people are starting to take their health in their own hands and are searching for answers other than just taking prescription medication.

WRIGHT

Today I have been talking with Dr. Thomas Johnson, a veteran of fifteen years in the chiropractic and natural health care industry.

Dr. Johnson, thank you for being with us today on *Health: Mind, Body, Soul.*

Disclaimer: The preceding statements have not been evaluated by The Food and Drug Administration. This information is not intended to diagnose, treat, cure, or prevent any disease.

# About the Author

Thomas Johnson, DC, has been licensed by the State of Georgia as a Doctor of Chiropractic since 1996. Dr. Johnson specializes in nutritional and holistic healthcare, and routinely attends post-graduate courses to enrich his knowledge to consistently provide the best possible healthcare to his patients. He is certified in many holistic techniques, Physiological Therapeutics, and several chiropractic techniques. Dr. Johnson has given talks to public groups since 1996 including Georgia Power, Home Depot, General Mills, Sweetheart Cup Company, City of Conyers, Rockdale County, U.S. Post Office, and many more. Dr. Johnson has lectured to more than ten thousand people.

Dr. Johnson took an interest in nutrition and hormones after he decided he wanted to become a professional bodybuilder when he was twenty-two years old. After dedicating a full year of his life to weight training six days a week, he saw very little results. This led him on his search to find out more about how the body works and the role that nutrition and the hormones play in muscle development and fat loss. After realizing the missing pieces to the puzzle, Dr. Johnson competed several times in bodybuilding competitions and was in a Gatorade commercial when he was twenty-five.

After developing severe lower back pain from his intense training, Dr. Johnson thought his bodybuilding career was over. He tried several traditional treatments (pain killers, muscle relaxers, physical therapy, sports medicine) and had no relief. He then decided to try chiropractic care. After a few weeks of chiropractic care and chiropractic-specific spinal rehab, he was pain free and had more energy and strength than ever. After his amazing experience with chiropractic care, he enrolled in college to complete his degree. In September 1992, Dr. Johnson enrolled in Life College. He graduated in 1996 with a Doctor of Chiropractic degree.

Multi-Care Holistic Health Center (formerly Honey Creek Chiropractic) was established in 1996. After experiencing rapid practice growth, Multi-Care has expanded into its fourth location in fifteen years. Dr. Johnson continues to research techniques and procedures (some old and some new) to get better and faster results with his patients. Dr. Johnson integrates holistic techniques with clinical nutrition, along with dietary and lifestyle changes. These treatment techniques are monitored and re-monitored to determine the effectiveness and improvements in his patients.


Thomas Johnson, DC

*Multi-Care Holistic Health Center*
1650-F Honey Creek Commons
Conyers, GA 30013
770-922-2556
drj@multi-carehealth.com
www.multi-carehealth.com